ADVANCE PRAISE FOR

The Stranger's Voice

"*The Stranger's Voice* introduces the relatively unexplored thought of Julia Kristeva to pastoral theologians and caregivers. With theological depth and clinical perception, Schweitzer reflects on the plight of women with depression in Christian communities. Kristevan metaphors such as the abject, the stranger, the voyager, and rebirth, with actions such as for-giving and a maternal discourse challenge the poverty of language that surrounds depression. If metaphors become models to live by, Kristeva's metaphors elucidated by Schweitzer promise new possibilities of counseling and pathways of well-being. To forgive is to offer someone a gift. The gift of this book is a sacramental understanding of depression and the rebirth that flows forth from loving and caring relationships. *The Stranger's Voice* is a liberating and insightful offering to all who know depression in the church or the clinic."

Jaco J. Hamman, Professor of Pastoral Care and Counseling, Western Theological Seminary

The Stranger's Voice

practical theology

Iain Torrance, Richard Osmer, Gordon S. Mikoski

Vol. 1

PETER LANG
New York • Washington, D.C./Baltimore • Bern
Frankfurt • Berlin • Brussels • Vienna • Oxford

Carol L. Schnabl Schweitzer

The Stranger's Voice

Julia Kristeva's Relevance for a Pastoral Theology for Women Struggling with Depression

PETER LANG
New York • Washington, D.C./Baltimore • Bern
Frankfurt • Berlin • Brussels • Vienna • Oxford

Library of Congress Cataloging-in-Publication Data

Schweitzer, Carol L. Schnabl.
The stranger's voice: Julia Kristeva's relevance for a pastoral theology for women struggling with depression / Carol L. Schnabl Schweitzer.
p. cm. — (Practical theology, ISSN 1947-6248; v. 1)
Includes bibliographical references and index.
1. Women—Pastoral counseling of. 2. Church work with women.
3. Depression, Mental—Religious aspects—Christianity. 4. Kristeva, Julia, 1941– 5. Feminist theology. I. Title.
BV4445.S39 259'.425—dc22 2010013259
ISBN 978-1-4331-0884-6
ISSN 1947-6248

Bibliographic information published by **Die Deutsche Nationalbibliothek.**
Die Deutsche Nationalbibliothek lists this publication in the "Deutsche Nationalbibliografie"; detailed bibliographic data is available on the Internet at http://dnb.d-nb.de/.

The paper in this book meets the guidelines for permanence and durability of the Committee on Production Guidelines for Book Longevity of the Council of Library Resources.

29 Broadway, 18th floor, New York, NY 10006
www.peterlang.com

Printed in Germany

To John, for whose patience, encouragement, and love I am grateful.

TABLE OF CONTENTS

PREFACE

If one accepts the presupposition, as I do, that theory needs to be continually reshaped and reformed in light of experience, then this project—the study of the stranger's voice—is for me a life-time project. I begin with this statement to emphasize the reality that I have raised more questions for myself in this study than I have answers for. In any case, the particular strangers of interest in this study have been women who struggle with depression in a Christian context and the voice of one such stranger or foreigner who offers a remedy—Julia Kristeva. Her own place as a stranger, a Bulgarian teaching and residing in France, gives her voice an added note of authority and authenticity. She knows firsthand of what she writes. It is my thesis that Kristeva's critique of Christian religious discourse and the manner in which it frequently situates women in a place of abjection as well as her proposal for a "psychology of motherhood" and a maternal discourse will offer new insights that assist those who want to offer care to these women. It is also my thesis that the very language we have relied on traditionally in the church has become for many a source of oppression. Though my primary focus has been on women who seek pastoral care for their struggle with depression, the correctives offered in what follows may be applied to other situations of pastoral care ministry.

In what ways has Kristeva's critique been instructive for my own vocation as professor, pastor and therapist? At the end of a decade of parish ministry I felt more often than not like one of Job's friends when these strangely silent women whose eyes were distant and filled with tears came to me with their voices quaking seeking help. I now realize that the look I saw in their eyes was that "impossible elsewhere" described by Kristeva and portrayed by Bellini's Madonnas. Many of these women were referred to me by other clergy and the manner in which their plights were described by their pastors troubled me because the women were often denigrated. At the time I lacked the language to refute the pastors' ill-chosen words. In other words, after ten years I still felt inadequate to the task before me and though I reasoned that I should be able to find the resources within my theological tradition to help, I often felt that the "answers" I had learned in seminary were more like pious platitudes or clichés. I could have, in many instances, recounted the orthodox theological responses I had learned but they seemed disconnected from the lives of the women who sought my counsel. At times like these, I was the one who felt silenced and frustrated by my seeming inability to help despite all the years of formal education and clinical training I had acquired. These women taught me the art of listening with tact as Kristeva describes it: "to hear true into speech along with forgiveness."[1] Only now do I possess the language and the theory to describe what takes place in a counseling relationship. The true student of analysis knows that it never really ends and so by analogy, the manner in which my listening and speaking continue to be reshaped and reformed by those with whom I enter into a relationship of care-giving will also never end. What then have I learned from the many hours I've spent in conversation with Kristeva and her interpreters as well as other theorists?

I have learned again and again that all models for a truly interdisciplinary approach to pastoral theology are partial and provisional. Bearing that in mind, I have borrowed a proposal from Donald Capps for my method of study in this work.[2] The method used for relating psychology and theology in this study is one of juxtaposition in which the two disciplines exist on parallel paths and neither is assigned priority. It is, in my experience, a rush to theological judgment in pastoral practice which often exacerbates the self-estrangement that women struggling with depression experience. I have, therefore, chosen one psychoanalytic theorist as the focus of my study and juxtaposed her writing with that of many other theorists in order to discern what new insights might be arrived at through the use of juxtaposition. The purpose of this project was not to improve upon Kristeva but rather to expand the possibilities of my own discourse by listening to her critiques of religious discourse in conversation with the work of other theologians.

Kristeva associates the feminine as well as the maternal with the abject—that which Kelly Oliver has described as "something repulsive that both attracts and repels."[3] The abject in Christianity becomes an experience of threatening otherness and so the abject mother, the feminine becomes located within a discourse about sin. She is a fury to be feared and separated from, but at the same time we are drawn toward her. Insofar as all women are potential mothers, the feminine as well as the maternal is associated with that which threatens the self. Tillich describes sin as estrangement which "describes the disruption of an essential unity and consequently a destructive situation."[4] The abject mother, the feminine, is then a threatening otherness or that which at least has the potential to disrupt an essential unity. Kristeva's association of the feminine with the abject and the subsequent location of the feminine within a Christian discourse about sin helps me to understand why women may be more susceptible to depression. Mothers represent a negative boundary against which all subjects-in-process develop and women cannot have a mother substitute as an object of desire in the same way that men are able to. The women who sought my help and continue to seek my help struggle so frequently to find their voices and be heard because the very language that they are told offers healing and hope often locates them in a negative space. They are not recognized as struggling with *a* problem, rather they are viewed as *the* problem.

How are women to find their way out of this negative space called the abject? By claiming their difference and honoring their place of strangeness or foreignness. Abjection is, according to Kristeva, a feminine experience; the experience of being the foreigner or the stranger is universal. The foreigner, the stranger, the alien or the exile is related to the abject in that one tends to depersonalize the foreigner (we've probably all witnessed extreme examples of the depersonalization of Arabs and Muslims in a post-"9-11" world). And by doing so, the foreigner is abjected as other. An identity is formed, even if negatively, against the boundary of the other. In this instance, the other is not viewed as friend but rather as enemy and thus, potential victim of violence. Though Kristeva uses the terms stranger, foreigner, alien and exile interchangeably to represent the feminine, the "stranger within" is a metaphorical representation of the unconscious. Violence occurs when the other or "stranger within" remains unrecognized and the enemy is externalized in the person of the stranger or foreigner. But I've just made the claim that the place of the foreigner is the *solution* to feminine abjection and yet it seems to be more of the same. The blessing of the stranger is this: when those who are marginalized by culture speak from their place of difference, culture is enriched and a possibility of bringing foreignness to an end for all is offered. That is to say, when I recognize that *I* am the stranger, the enemy is no longer externalized and I am able to honor the "other" who is a fellow pilgrim or voyager.

Not only are women aliens or strangers but the very language which is requisite for healing is alien to them. Kristeva writes in *Black Sun* that "the speech of the depressed is to them like an alien skin; melancholy persons are foreigners in their maternal tongue."[5] The difficulty with language for women struggling with depression is more pronounced because the language which fails them belongs to a paternal order which does not take account of their difference. Silence then becomes a form of resistance and in many instances a sign of strength. Typically, however, resistance is viewed as the antithesis to healing in a therapeutic encounter. Feminine identity is linked to alterity, difference and silence as well as the abject and the stranger.

Kristeva's proposal for a maternal discourse is a controversial one that is rejected by many feminists because it "stabilizes a familiar category—motherhood—to which women have been confined."[6] Yet destabilizing motherhood as a category of the feminine means that a woman is encouraged to continue rejecting that part of herself that identifies with her mother and this runs the risk of deepening the depression instead of ameliorating it. Artists render in images what Kristeva attempts to portray with words: the unconscious truth, the impossible elsewhere, the maternal facet or attitude toward the maternal body which is the place of the first splitting or separation. What has this to do with women who struggle with depression?

Women who struggle with depression need to "touch the mother" or reach the threshold of repression. Kristeva's analysis of Bellini's Madonnas shows us the place that women occupy in a Western Christian culture: the woman-mother looks backward to an impossible elsewhere that reflects on maternal jouissance or forward to an impossible elsewhere filled with grief. The alternatives are confining.

What a woman struggling with depression needs from her counselor is someone who is willing to be a functional mother that helps her befriend, at the very least, her internalized images of her own mother. The role of the counselor is to be a loving, "for-giving other"—someone who listens with tact or a delicate perception of another's affect. To listen with a for-giving attitude means that I give a gift of understanding to another. I must deprive myself of my own understanding and judgment even though I continue to ask questions. A woman struggling with depression comes in want of love and yearns for someone to finally "give for her." Forgiveness does not mean that she needs to refuse power or conspire with her degradation. Forgiveness is the possibility of a new encounter, a reconciliation of an estranged self. The hallmark of the therapeutic task understood from this perspective is "an other who does not judge but hears my truth in the availability of love, and for that very reason allows me to be reborn."[7] It is in and through the gift of self in language that the rebirth occurs. Finally, it is my contention that the gift the pastor/counselor needs to be able to give to the woman struggling with depression is a willingness to use maternal language and images to describe her religious experience insofar as these will assist her in the process of befriending what she never agreed to give up—her mother. The journey toward healing is not a search for truth but rather a search for the unconditional love that is acclaimed in pulpits. What occurs in the context of a therapeutic relationship is only a human approximation of the gospel proclamation but an important one that nevertheless expands possibilities for restored human-to-human relationships as well as a deeper and enriched experience of the divine.

Notes

1. Julia Kristeva, *Black Sun: Depression and Melancholia,* trans. Leon S. Roudiez (New York: Columbia University Press, 1989) 189.
2. Donald Capps, "The Lessons of Art Theory for Pastoral Theology," *Pastoral Psychology* 47:5 (1999): 321–346.
3. Kelly Oliver, *Reading Kristeva: Unraveling the Double Bind* (Indianapolis: Indiana University Press, 1993), 55.
4. Paul Tillich, "Estrangement and Reconciliation in Modern Thought," *The Meaning of Health,* ed. Perry LeFevre (Chicago: Exploration Press, 1984), 2.
5. Kristeva, *Black Sun,* 53.
6. Janice Doane and Devon Hodges, *From Klein to Kristeva: Psychoanalytic Feminism and the Search for the "Good Enough" Mother* (Ann Arbor: University of Michigan Press, 1992), 78f.
7. Kristeva, *Black Sun,* 205.

Acknowledgments

I wish to thank Peter Lang Press and Heidi Burns, Ph.D. for permission to use portions of Chapter Six in a forthcoming article of *Pastoral Pscyhology* – "'For-giving' and Forgiving: Process and Practice in Pastoral Care."

References to Internet Web sites were accurate at the time of writing.

Introduction

Why a Project Focused on Kristeva and Women?

One of Julia Kristeva's interpreters, Martha J. Reineke,[1] begins her book with a note that no other feminist author spoke to her about the lives of women like Kristeva did. I feel the same way. I will not at this early point take up the debate about whether or not Kristeva is a feminist; I will simply say that her analysis of religious discourse and a woman's place within it helped me to understand better the lives of the many women who have sought my assistance during my years as a parish pastor, a counselor, and now as a seminary professor—as nothing else has. This is not to suggest that her texts cannot just as easily be applied to the lives and situations of men—indeed many of the cases she discusses concern men. It is to suggest that my interest in Kristeva grew out of my work with women who live at the borders of society as victims of abuse and who consequently struggle to have their voices heard and their stories recognized as truth. My thesis is that Kristeva's insights will: (1) provide a better understanding of why many women—particularly victims of abuse—struggle with depression; (2) describe the situation which is unique to women who are Christian (i.e., traditional theological metaphors locate women in a place which frequently silences their voices); (3) suggest possible solutions (especially with regard to the choice of new metaphors) for pastoral care givers when ministering to them; and (4) help those who provide counsel to these women to reframe the process as one of "for-giving" in which love outweighs the pursuit of "truth."

In a review of recent literature related to gender issues in pastoral theology, Nancy J. Gorsuch has observed:

> Gender alone is not the most important category of experience or source of knowledge in pastoral theology, but pastoral theologians persist in efforts to specify the complexity of gender difference and its consequences, and to avoid stabilizing dichotomous opposition based on gender. In my view, we do this for the sake of enhancing just and compassionate relations.[2]

The women who are always in the background of my mind as I write are women who have not had the privilege of just and compassionate relations. My hope is that this work will contribute in some way to their voices being heard as well as to an experience of joy in compassionate relationships between ministers and those who seek their wise counsel.

Moreover, as Gorsuch continues in her reflections on the importance of gender issues in pastoral theology:

> Gender analysis serves a crucial role in revising theology and theory, in influencing interpersonal relations, and in helping to change the harmful systemic and structured effect of gender in our culture. Attention to the particularity of experience is the special purview of pastoral theologians.[3]

Revising theology and theory are beyond the scope of this work but having some positive influence on interpersonal relations—if only a keener attentiveness to the details and particularity of women's lives—is not. I appeal to the insights which arise from Kristeva's texts, especially the ones focused on psychoanalysis of religious discourse and/or theological themes, to assist in this task. While Kristeva's own voice is more well-known in the United States in university departments of religion, English, or philosophy than in seminary programs in pastoral theology, feminist theologians have entered into conversation with her writings.[4] I undertake this project in the interest of helping to make her thought accessible to a different reading public.

About Kristeva

Julia Kristeva was born June 24, 1941, in Silven, Bulgaria. She grew up in a middle-class family which was ardently Roman Catholic; her parents did not belong to the Communist Party, and this reality limited the schools where Kristeva could study. The "better" schools were reserved for children of the party-faithful, which led to Kristeva's early education in a French-speaking Catholic school. She did, however, participate in Communist Party children's groups as well as youth organizations. Her first job was as a journalist while she pursued literary studies at the university. Being the recipient of a doctoral fellowship brought her to Paris in December 1965 and she began her studies in January 1966.[5]

She met her husband, Philippe Sollers, novelist and critic, soon after arriving in Paris. At the time, he was editor of the avant-garde literary journal, *Tel Quel*, in which many of her essays were first published. Since they celebrated their thirtieth anniversary in 1996 one might conclude that they married shortly after they met. David Crownfield, however, seems to indicate that they were married in 1976 when their son—and only child—was born.[6] Their relationship has been characterized as a "freely unfaithful and respectfully independent union."[7]

In May of 1968, French workers and students spontaneously revolted. Kristeva maintains that this change in the social climate both affected her work and made it more difficult for her as a foreigner in France since French tolerance of foreigners waned at this time.[8] In 1973, she was awarded her Ph.D. at which time she became a professor of linguistics at the University of Paris VII. The following year her dissertation, *Revolution in Poetic Language*, was published, and she visited China. Her trip to China inspired her book *Des Chinoises* (*About Chinese Women*). Leon Roudiez comments about her return to France saying, "For her, I believe [Marxism] was more a conceptual tool towards social truth, and now it was blunted. As with the French Communist Party a few years earlier, a sort of honeymoon with socialism was over."[9]

In an interview, Kristeva acknowledges that she did not come to Paris intending to stay, but the combination of the stimulating intellectual environment and her acquaintance with Philippe Sollers convinced her to remain.[10] If it was a difficult decision for her, Kristeva only hints at it, saying: "I felt quite vulnerable during my years with *Tel Quel* because I found myself caught between all those angry men. I had a hard time of it."[11] Her novel, *The Samurai*, a somewhat autobiographical account of this period, alludes to her homesickness.[12]

From 1976 to 1979, Kristeva studied psychoanalysis with Jacques Lacan. Her son was born during this period. Her interpreters herald this time as the beginning of a change in her writing style, evident with the French publication of *Powers of Horror* in 1980.[13] Her early works are deemed more theoretical—and therefore, less readable—bringing together perspectives from Marxism, psychoanalysis (i.e., Freud and Lacan), Bakhtin and Barthes.[14] Her later works appear "more relaxed, more readable, more concrete, more plural—some would say, more human—than the more theoretical works of the late 1960s and the 1970s."[15] *Powers of Horror* and subsequent texts begin to focus on the maternal and the feminine in culture.[16] I will focus primarily on the psychoanalytic texts written during the 1980s and 1990s with one major exception—Kristeva's recently published, *This Incredible Need to Believe.*[17]

During the 1980s and 1990s, Kristeva's writings continued to reflect her interest in psychoanalytic discourse (e.g., *Tales of Love* in 1987, *Black Sun: Depression and Melancholia* in 1989, and *New Maladies of the Soul* in 1995). Currently, she continues to write, teach and practice as a psychoanalyst in Paris. She has also served as a visiting professor at Columbia University (1972) and the University of Toronto (1992). Her more recent works continue to demonstrate the shift in the focus of her writing from literary criticism to psychoanalysis; *La révolte intime: Pouvoirs et limites de la psychanalyse II* (*The Intimate Revolt: The Powers and Limits of Psychoanalysis*, vol. 2) published in French in 1997 is one such example. Throughout the course of her later works she maintains a conversation with Freud, Lacan and Christian faith as is most clearly illustrated by *This Incredible Need to Believe.* During the 1990s Kristeva additionally published three novels that she acknowledges are somewhat autobiographical accounts of various periods during her life.[18] She returned to this form of writing again in the first decade of the twenty-first century.[19]

Kristeva: Selected Writings

The first major period in Kristeva's writing might be described as that which pertains to the "semiotic," beginning with *Desire in Language: A Semiotic Approach to Literature and Art* (1980).[20] It concludes with *About Chinese Women* (1977), first published in French as *Des Chinoises* in 1974. I would suggest that this work already points to Kristeva's growing interest in psychoanalysis and begins to depart from her earlier works.[21]

In the introduction to *Powers of Horror* Kristeva acknowledges a change in her style of writing which continues into the present. This work and those which follow it focus on religion and the feminine highlighting the themes of abjection, melancholia and love.[22] Her present psychoanalytic style of writing was interrupted somewhat by the publication of her novels which could be said to represent a third phase in her writing.[23]

The texts which will be of most interest for this project are the ones which address the sacred and the feminine in relation to abjection, melancholia and love. They include but are not limited to: *Desire in Language, About Chinese Women, Powers of Horror, Strangers to Ourselves, Black Sun, Tales of Love, In the Beginning Was Love,* and *New Maladies of the Soul.*

About the Work that Follows

While I will be concentrating mainly on Kristeva's writings, it would be virtually impossible to separate her own personal experience (or "sense of self") from her texts. As one of Kristeva's commentators, Anna Smith, has noted: "As Kristeva tells us, to write on melancholy, one has to be a melancholic; to write on exile, one must be one."[24] Given my own interest in Kristeva's relevance for pastoral theology, her own feelings and attitudes toward her religious upbringing are of special note. The importance of the church in the family of her childhood is evident in the following excerpt of an interview in which she maintains that Sofia, the city of her childhood, is able to be reduced to the cathedral she attended with her father:

> a faithful man whose beautiful voice added to the Saint Nedelia church choir, would bring me to the cathedral before dawn so that I could take communion without being spotted. I eventually rebelled, not because I was bothered by the dissidence of the act but because of universal reason, which is, I still find, harder to understand and to embody than faith is.[25]

Kristeva's concluding statement above is illustrative of a conflict that can be observed throughout her writings. On the one hand, she maintains that she is an atheist;[26] on the other, she continues to concern herself with religious and/or theological discourse and its importance for restoring psychic health in those who do believe.[27] By her own admission, "reason" appears to have caused her to doubt the faith of her childhood; yet she still finds this faith easier to embody and understand than "reason." Does she embody faith or intend to? This is not a question I am prepared to answer—perhaps, it is a question which Kristeva herself only answers indirectly through her writing. Kristeva made the remark about faith being easier to embody than reason in an interview she gave during 1992, suggesting that, after nearly thirty years of teaching and practicing as an analyst, the Catholicism of her youth still informs the questions she raises with regard to psychoanalysis and faith. Indeed in the concluding words of *This Incredible Need to Believe*, Kristeva acknowledges that her current vision for how European culture (or life in general) ought to be lived grows out of the Christianity of her youth. Thus she exclaims enthusiastically that we need not fear Christianity but may instead fear religious fundamentalism of all persuasions.[28]

The primary questions that I raise in this study include:

- How does Kristeva expand religious, particularly Christian discourse to include the experience of women?
- What, for Kristeva, are the points of intersection between

psychoanalytic and Christian discourse?
- How are Kristeva's insights relevant to gender issues in pastoral theology?
- How might Kristeva's choice of metaphors be embraced by those engaged in pastoral care and counseling in order to facilitate healing with women struggling with depression?
- In what ways does Kristeva's understanding of "for-giving" help pastoral theologians address forgiveness in the context of pastoral care?

In Chapter One, I examine what has been described by Sallie McFague as a crisis in Christian discourse. I understand religious discourse, specifically Christian discourse, as language which describes the God-human relationship, relations between persons and an individual's self-relations (i.e., between one's true and false selves). Some have criticized traditional Christian discourse as being both idolatrous and irrelevant in a contemporary culture that Sallie McFague has described as pluralistic, privatized, and secularized.[29] Kristeva herself has cited a crisis in religion which she relates to the current crisis of identity. Since I will be exploring points of intersection between psychoanalytic and Christian discourse, a discussion of metaphorical language is important. That is, both psychoanalytic and Christian discourses recognize the fundamental importance of metaphor for acquiring insights and communicating meaning. This discussion of metaphor will: (1) entail a brief discussion of scientific and religious models; and (2) provide the necessary philosophical foundation for the chapters which follow. I will argue that Kristeva's own metaphors suggest helpful revisions of current, more exclusively religious models for pastoral theologians.

The second chapter focuses on the metaphors Kristeva employs in *Powers of Horror* and *Strangers to Ourselves* (e.g., abject, subject-in-process or subject-on-trial, and stranger). I discuss there the themes of the feminine as abject and the stranger as foreigner, exile, and alien as they relate to Christian discourse on the nature of sin. Kristeva situates the place of the feminine within the abject and moves to suggest that this poses difficulties for women since their place in discourse is identified with what is loathed and frequently identified in theology as sinful.

The third chapter will focus on Kristeva's description of the "melancholic-depressive composite"[30] in women or their "struggle against the sun."[31] I will begin with a brief examination of her study of feminine identity in Western Christianity from *About Chinese Women* and move to her discussion of the time and place that women occupy in religious discourse. Here, too, my primary text will be *About Chinese Women,* supplemented by her essay, "Women's Time." I will conclude with Kristeva's study of feminine depression and melancholia in *Black Sun* noting the difficulty women encounter with religious discourse which allows few options for overcoming self-loathing when solely patriarchal metaphors are employed to describe God and religious experience. Not only do women suffer from melancholia, but they suffer with it in unique ways. This will lead to a discussion of the importance of recovering a maternal discourse in both Western Christianity and psychoanalytic discourse.

The fourth chapter will focus on Kristeva's concern with maternal discourse (i.e., woman as mother) and, more precisely, the absence of an adequate maternal discourse in both psychoanalytic theory and religion. Kristeva notes that her "thoughts on love in *Tales of Love* are based primarily on maternal love, which I believe is at the heart of all loving relationships."[32] She chooses this focus because she believes that "maternal love is also at the base of the nuclear relationship of dependency."[33] This maternal love is not without its difficulties since it involves identification with the child and the concomitant pain and suffering that accompanies the time of separation from the child as the child begins to develop a sense of self and acquires language. Yet this relationship is so fundamental that

> [a] vestige of the mother can be found in every passionate relationship. When a woman is in a passionate relationship with a man, her dreams or fantasies often depict a ghost of her mother hovering over him. Her painful jubilation often suggests that she is reliving her infantile dependency on her mother's body, the jouissance that this body gave her, and the suffering that frustration or even an intrusion of the mother's body can provoke in the child.[34]

Thus, every relationship in which a woman becomes deeply involved evokes the same welter of experiences that occurred when she was an infant—the influence of one's mother lasts a lifetime. It is in the context of the mother-daughter relationship that Kristeva sees a hope for the recovery of a maternal tongue which will foster a woman's journey along in the struggle to become a subject with a voice. My primary texts are the essays "Motherhood According to Giovanni Bellini,"[35] "The Wheel Of Smiles,"[36] and "Stabat Mater,"[37] supplemented by *Black Sun.*

The fifth chapter will concentrate on the theme of "word" in the context of a "loving relationship" which Kristeva identifies as a partial solution to the situation of abjection. A loving and forgiving other (a functional or substitute mother, in this case a pastor or pastoral counselor) assists the depressed woman to find her voice as she helps the depressed woman to learn to befriend her mother (or internalized maternal images) and overcome the abjection that is a woman-mother's place in Western Christian discourse. The manner in which Kristeva discusses love in the transference relationship will be related to a Christian understanding of *agapé*. Kristeva places great value upon the importance of the Word as well as alluding to the presence of a "protective, loving agency" in the therapeutic relationship.[38] Here I will suggest that there is a compatibility with the way McFague constructs a model of God as "mother"[39] and Kristeva's psychoanalytic understanding of love. Maternal God images such as the ones McFague builds in *Models of God*, will prove helpful in this process and additional positive maternal images may be derived. I discuss the primary texts *Black Sun, In the Beginning Was Love, Tales of Love*, and *New Maladies of the Soul.*

In addition, this chapter will draw conclusions for the pastoral care of women who struggle with depression. Pastoral theologian Christie Cozad Neuger writes, "*Depression* is a very broad term for experiences that range from a passing bad mood to a chronic withdrawal from reality. What really constitutes depression has generated considerable debate and no firm agreement on what causes it or how best to care for those suffering with it."[40] Abuse, economics, low self-esteem and the role religion plays in perpetuating low self-esteem among women are causes of depression that exist in a woman's cultural environment.[41] I will attempt to demonstrate how Kristeva's approach to what she calls borderline experiences (i.e., abjection, love, and melancholia)[42] are instructive for a pastoral theology dedicated to women struggling with depression. This will lead into a proposal in the sixth and final chapter for a theology of "for-giving" as foundational for practice and process in pastoral care.[43]

The sixth and final chapter will incorporate insights from Kristeva's recent *This Incredible Need to Believe* as well as insights from recent literature devoted to the study of forgiveness in theology and psychology. It is my conclusion that Kristeva's understanding of "for-giving" may be a necessary first step in the process of healing self-estrangement that results from a struggle with depression. Indeed, "for-giving" suggests a maternal kind of love that undergirds the process of any counseling relationship in which a person of faith struggles to express and make meaning of his or her suffering and experience healing. While there is a biblical mandate to forgive and much recent psychological literature concludes that those who are able to accept and offer forgiveness actually experience health benefits, forgiveness is a complicated process that often poses difficulties for women who have been abused. Why is this so? Each person has unique capacities for experiencing and practicing forgiveness which I suggest are rooted in our "incredible need to believe" that arises in relation to a "loving and loved third party" whose presence initiates the development of language and our basic "desire to know" and be known—something Kristeva identifies as "our big question mark."[44]

I return to the question I raised at the beginning of this introduction: Why a project focused on Kristeva and women in pastoral theology? In the current feminist literature in pastoral theology, depression among women is addressed by Susan J. Dunlap[45] from a cognitivebehavioral approach while Christie Cozad Neuger[46] uses a narrative approach. There is, at present, an absence of psychoanalytic approaches in the pastoral theology literature which address specifically the issue of depression in women from a feminist perspective. Kristeva represents a major advance in psychoanalytic theorizing on depression among women, (especially, over Melanie Klein's "depressive position" theory) and yet, while Kristeva has gained a significant hearing among those engaged in the "religion and psychology" discussion and feminist theologians, she has yet to be fully admitted into discussions in pastoral theology, and thus, for a pastoral theology of women struggling with depression. I dedicate this work to the numerous voices of "strangers" with whom I sat and listened for hours and whose lives have permanently transformed mine.

Notes

1. Martha J. Reineke, *Sacrificed Lives: Kristeva on Women and Violence* (Indianapolis: Indiana University Press, 1997), 1.
2. Nancy J. Gorsuch, "Gender as Construct and Category in Pastoral Theology: A Review of Recent Literature," *Journal of Pastoral Theology* 10 (2000): 98.
3. Ibid.
4. See for example, Rebecca S. Chopp, *The Power to Speak: Feminism, Language, God* (New York: Crossroad Publishing Company, 1991) as well as C. W. Maggie Kim, Susan M. St. Ville, Susan M. Simonaitis, eds., *Transfigurations: Theology and the French Feminists* (Minneapolis: Fortress Press, 1993).
5. The sources for this information are David Crownfield, ed., *Body/Text in Julia Kristeva* (Albany: State University of New York Press, 1992), ix–xiv and Leon S. Roudiez, ed., *Desire in Language: A Semiotic Approach to Literature and Art,* trans. Thomas Gora, Alice Jardine, and Leon S. Roudiez (New York: Columbia University Press, 1980), 1–12.
6. Crownfield, *Body/Text in Julia Kristeva,* xi–xii.

7. AnneMarie Smith, *Julia Kristeva: Speaking the Unspeakable* (Sterling, VA: Pluto Press, 1998), 3.
8. Ross Mitchell Guberman, ed., *Julia Kristeva: Interviews* (New York: Columbia University Press, 1996), 5.
9. Leon S. Roudiez, ed., *Desire in Language*, 9.
10. Guberman, ed., *Julia Kristeva: Interviews*, 3–7.
11. Ibid., 7.
12. Ibid., 248–49.
13. Julia Kristeva, *Powers of Horror: An Essay on Abjection,* trans., Leon S. Roudiez (New York: Columbia University Press, 1982), vii.
14. Crownfield, *Body/Text in Julia Kristeva,* xii.
15. Ibid., xiv.
16. AnneMarie Smith, *Speaking the Unspeakable*, 3.
17. Julia Kristeva, *This Incredible Need to Believe,* trans. Beverly Bie Brahic (New York: Columbia University Press, 2009).
18. *Contemporary Authors.* s.v. "Julia Kristeva" (New York: Gale, 1997): 247–49.
19. Julia Kristeva, *Murder in Byzantium,* trans C. Jon Delogu (New York: Columbia University Press, 2006). This novel is the only publication in which Kristeva examines her Bulgarian roots through the character Stephanie Delacour who is Kristeva's self-acknowledged alter ego.
20. This text was first published in French as *Séméiotiké* in 1969; the American edition is an abridged version.
21. Other works from this period include: *Language: The Unknown: An Initiation into Linguistics* (1989) was first published as *Le Langage, cet inconnu, Une initiation a la linguistique* under a pseudonym, Julia Joyaux in1969. *Le Texte du Roman* (1970) was not published in English. These works represent major publications that appeared prior to the completion of Kristeva's dissertation, *Revolution in Poetic Language* (1984). This text was first published in French as *La Révolution du langage poétique, L'avantgarde à la fin du XIXème siècle, Lautréamont et Mallarmé* in 1974. *Polylogue* (1977) was published in *Desire in Language* in 1980 as "The Novel as Polylogue."
22. *Powers of Horror: An Essay on Abjection* (1982) was first published as *Pouvoirs de l'horreur, Essai sur l'abjection in 1980. Tales of Love* (1987) was first published in French as *Histoires d'amour* in 1983. It is a collection of essays which is dedicated to eros. Her translator, Leon S. Roudiez notes: "The sociological and cultural investigation of *Powers of Horror* is replaced with a philosophical and theological one." (Tales of Love, vii.) *In the Beginning was Love: Psychoanalysis and Faith* (1987), (based on a lecture series which Kristeva gave at L'Ecole SainteGeneviève, a Catholic school located in Versailles), was first published in French as *Au commencement était l'amour, Psychoanalyse et Foi* in 1985. *Black Sun: Depression and Melancholia* (1989) was first published in French as *Soleil noir: dépression et mélancolie* in 1987. *Strangers to Ourselves* was first published in French as *Etrangers à nousmêmes* in 1988. *Nations without Nationalism* (1993) was first published in French as *Lettre Ouverte à Harlem Désir* in 1990. *New Maladies of the Soul* (1995) was first published in French as *Les Nouvelles Maladies de l'âme* in 1993. This work, like *Tales of Love,* is a collection of essays. *Time and Sense: Proust and the*

Experience of Literature (1996) was first published in French as *Le Temps sensible, Proust et l'expérience littéraire* in 1994. This work combines her interests in psychoanalysis and literary criticism. As noted above, *La révolte intime: Pouvoirs et limites de la psychanalyse* II (*The Intimate Revolt: The Powers and Limits of Psychoanalysis,* vol. 2) was published in French in 1997.

23. The novels are: *The Samurai* (1992) first published in French as *Les Samouraïs* in 1990; *The Old Man and the Wolves* (1994) first published in French as *Le vieil homme et les loups* in 1991; *Possessions: A Novel* (1998) was first published in French as *Possessions* in 1996.
24. Anna Smith, *Julia Kristeva: Readings of Exile and Estrangement* (New York: St. Martin's Press, 1996), 7. As a point of reference, Smith cites the beginning of Kristeva's *Black Sun.*
25. Guberman, *Julia Kristeva: Interviews,* 137–38.
26. See for example, Julia Kristeva, *In the Beginning Was Love: Psychoanalysis and Faith,* with a Foreword by Otto F. Kernberg, trans. Arthur Goldhammer (New York: Columbia University Press, 1987), 23–24.
27. See for example, Guberman, "Julia Kristeva in Person," *Interviews,* 11 as well as Julia Kristeva, "Reading the Bible," in *New Maladies of the Soul,* trans. Ross Guberman, (New York: Columbia University Press, 1995), 115–126.
28. Kristeva, *This Incredible Need to Believe,* 106.
29. Sallie, McFague, *Metaphorical Theology: Models of God in Religious Language* (Philadelphia: Fortress Press, 1982), see Chapter One.
30. Guberman, *Interviews,* 80.
31. Kristeva, *Desire in Language,* 29.
32. Guberman, *Interviews,* 62.
33. Ibid.
34. Ibid., 62–63. A word regarding the meaning of jouissance in Kristeva's writing is in order here. Leon S. Roudiez writes: "Kristeva gives 'jouissance' a meaning closely related to that given the word by Jacques Lacan....What is significant is the *totality* of enjoyment that is covered by the word 'jouissance,' both in common usage and in Lacan; what distinguishes common usage from Lacan's (and Kristeva's as well) is that in the former the several meanings are kept separate and precipitated, so to speak, by the context, whereas in the latter they are simultaneous—'jouissance' is sexual, spiritual, physical, conceptual at one and the same time....In Kristeva's vocabulary, sensual, sexual pleasure is covered by *plaisir*; 'jouissance' is total joy or ecstasy (without any mystical connotation)." Julia Kristeva, *Desire in Language: A Semiotic Approach to Literature and Art,* ed. Leon S. Roudiez, trans. Thomas Gora, Alice Jardine and Leon S. Roudiez (New York: Columbia University Press, 1980), 16.
35. Julia Kristeva, "Motherhood According to Giovanni Bellini," in *Desire in Language,* 237–270.
36. Julia Kristeva, "The Wheel of Smiles," in *New Maladies of the Soul,* trans. Ross Guberman (New York: Columbia University Press, 1995), 154–58.
37. Julia Kristeva, "Stabat Mater," in *Tales of Love,* trans. Leon S. Roudiez (New York: Columbia University Press, 1987), 234–263.
38. Julia Kristeva, *In the Beginning Was Love: Psychoanalysis and Faith,* trans. Arthur

Goldhammer (New York: Columbia University Press, 1987), 3–4; 24–25.

39. Sallie McFague, *Models of God: Theology for an Ecological, Nuclear Age* (Philadelphia: Fortress Press, 1987); see especially, Chapter Four, pp. 101–108.
40. Christie Cozad Neuger, "Women's Depression: Lives at Risk," in Women *in Travail and Transition*, ed. Maxine Glaz & Jeanne Stevenson Moessner (Minneapolis: Fortress Press, 1991), 147.
41. Ibid., 152–53.
42. Guberman, *Julia Kristeva: Interviews*, 20, 30.
43. Portions of this chapter were first presented at a conference held in Richmond, Virginia and will be published as "'Forgiving' and Forgiving: Process and Practice in Pastoral Care," forthcoming in *Pastoral Psychology*.
44. Kristeva, *This Incredible Need to Believe*, xii.
45. Susan J. Dunlap, *Counseling Depressed Women* (Louisville: Westminster John Knox Press, 1997).
46. Christie Cozad Neuger, *Counseling Women* (Minneapolis: Augsburg Fortress, 2001).

CHAPTER ONE

A Crisis in Religious Discourse

Addressing linguistics, philosophy, semiology and psychoanalysis, in the preface to *Desire in Language*, Kristeva writes that "no belief in an all-powerful theory" is tenable.[1] In the introduction to the book, her editor suggests that Kristeva is "[n]ot 'applying' a theory, but allowing practice to test theory."[2] This, I submit, is a vital orientation for any endeavor in pastoral theology. Specifically in this project, I seek to determine how the practice of ministry in a pastoral care and counseling setting tests religious discourse. I contend, as do the authors[3] cited in this chapter, that metaphors create new meanings; therefore, when articulated in a care-giving relationship they have the power to facilitate healing.

It is my thesis that Kristeva's critique of Christian discourse, especially as it relates to feminine depression and melancholia, will bring new insights to those who work with women struggling with depression. I begin with my understanding of what is construed by some as a crisis in religious discourse and then suggest a model for the pastoral theological reflection engaged in throughout this study based on the work of Donald Capps.[4] Since the ultimate goal of this chapter is to relate Kristeva's psychoanalytic understanding of metaphor to a theological perspective on metaphor, I will first outline the importance of models and metaphors in religious discourse. I conclude this chapter by examining briefly Kristeva's metaphor for the developing self—"subject-in-process/on trial"—and juxtapose it with a theological metaphor for the creation of new meaning—"knowledge in process." In brief, the Kristevan metaphor, "subject-in-process/on trial," will serve as a reference point for identity throughout this work.

A Crisis Defined

Sallie McFague identifies four causes of a contemporary crisis in Christian discourse: (1) Christian symbols have lost their power and meaning; (2) the current influence of positivistic science in culture leads to a narrow view of Christian truth; (3) the Christian practice of prayer and contemplation has been lost; and (4) language about God has become repetitious and boring.[5] McFague suggests that nothing short of a revolution in language is necessary. This kind of project meets with resistance, however, because it requires a revolution of one's world view. She advances a remedy for the situation which focuses on a religious discourse that emphasizes personal and relational aspects of language. That is, "[t]o the extent that we know ourselves, our world, and our God, knowledge is profoundly relational and hence, interdependent, relative, situational and limited."[6]

While McFague wrote about this crisis in Christian discourse during the 1970s and 1980s, it is one that certainly continues in the present.[7] In order to be able to restore power and meaning to Christian symbols or revitalize Christian discourse (a project well beyond the scope of this study) an understanding of how metaphors become theological models is first necessary. How metaphors become models *is* germane to this project since I am suggesting that the metaphors Kristeva proposes will bring new insights to bear on the issue of depression in women. I will address this topic in a subsequent section of the chapter in order to suggest how Kristeva's critique of Christian discourse might aid in the task of choosing language which is not boring and repetitious but rather language that has the potential to initiate healing for women struggling with depression because it is reflective of their experience.

Julia Kristeva's work also identifies a crisis in Christian discourse through careful psychoanalytic reflection on selected religious themes. For example, in an interview Kristeva gave in 1988 she remarked that even though people still go to church and believe in God, religion fails to fulfill the promises it makes leaving people like herself to "decompose religious discourse." Nevertheless, she is unwilling to claim that religion is able to be replaced by psychoanalysis despite the fact that analysis offers individuals an opportunity to confess something in order for an analyst to offer hope. Why? Kristeva suggests that "this hope is concomitant with the dissolution of the analytic contract. Believers belong to the name of the father, the community, the church, and an identifiable morality."[8] Thus, the difference between psychoanalysis and religion is that, in the former, the hoped-for outcome is that the relationship between analyst and analyzand will no longer be needed or required, whereas in religion hope is grounded in an enduring relationship that deepens over time.

Like Kristeva, I do not suggest that psychoanalysis can replace religion; I do, however, believe that many insights can be gleaned from her often harsh critique of religion. It is my working hypothesis for this project that just as Kristeva's insights have revitalized interest in psychoanalytic discourse (in Europe at the very least), the insights from her psychoanalytic writings on religious themes compel religious discourse to better reflect women's experiences.

It is impossible to discuss all of Kristeva's writings related to religious themes in a project of this scope. Instead, I will focus on selected writings pertaining to sin (i.e., abjection, alienation and the "stranger"); the place and/or identity of women within a discourse about abjection; abjection as it relates to depression and melancholia, especially in religious women; and the power of the Word and love in their ability to transform lives. I argue, following Kristeva's logic, that it is impossible to understand women's depression if one does not first come to a clear understanding of the negative place that has been assigned to women historically in Western Christianity. Only then can one begin to assist a depressed woman to give voice to her experience by creating new meaning through the adoption of new metaphors. This recognizing of the woman's voice happens, according to Kristeva, in a relationship grounded in the Word and founded in love. I will, in the final chapter, return to Kristeva's understanding of "for-giving" as it relates to forgiving to propose that together these processes, in the context of a therapeutic relationship, represent one possible outcome or direction for pastoral theology which better reflects women's experience in Christian discourse.

Models in Pastoral Theology

How can one relate Kristeva's psychoanalytic insights to a religious discourse that addresses person-to-person relationships as well as God-human relationships in a manner that preserves the integrity of both discourses? In addition, what is the relationship of practice to theory? That is, how does practice shape or reshape theory? With these questions in mind I will provide a brief overview of three models, borrowed from art theory, proposed by pastoral theologian Donald Capps. Then, I will select one which, I believe, is suited to a project which centers on Kristeva's writings. I recognize that my approach is not without limitations. The very fact that I employ one method among others makes this inevitable. As Sallie McFague notes in her study on metaphor, "Since a model offers a path to intelligibility, presumably on the basis of some similarity between the model and the modeled, it is evident that no *one* model can ever be adequate."[9]

Capps uses the work of Rudolf Arnheim[10] as a foundation for his proposal that there are three possible models (i.e., convergence, juxtaposition and structural uniformity) for relating psychology to theology when one considers centric and eccentric forces as they are understood in Arnheim's views on composition in the visual arts. Capps summarizes the significance of these two forces as follows: (1) the centric force or tendency represents a self-centered outlook on life from infancy that endures as a powerful urge throughout life. The self is at the center of all things; and (2) the eccentric force or tendency represents the stance that "one's own center is only one center among others and that the powers and needs of other centers cannot be ignored without peril."[11] Arnheim proposes that the eccentric tendency offers a more realistic worldview which is complemented by the centric one.[12]

To illustrate how the centric-eccentric dynamic becomes visible in art, Capps turns to a discussion of paintings of the Madonna with Child (which makes his discussion even more apropos to this study, since half of chapter four is dedicated to a discussion of Kristeva's writings on the same subject). He observes that the "centric tendency of the painting is usually located in or near the geometric center of the painting" which emphasizes "that the eccentric forces are drawn toward the center."[13] In the example of paintings that portray the Madonna with Child, "invariably...these two figures [are] in the center of the painting. Other personages in the painting—saints, angels, etc.—attend to these two figures strongly emphasizing the centric tendency."[14] More important, perhaps, Capps highlights the fact that the tension between the centric and eccentric tendencies may be located in the geometric center of the painting. Again, he turns to two paintings of the Madonna and Child by da Vinci to make his point. In one, "the boy Jesus [is] looking away from Mary and gazing on the yarnwinder he holds in his hands (symbolic of the cross)" and in another, Jesus looks away from Mary while "clutching a small lamb (representative of his eventual sacrificial death)."[15] This is significant because "[t]hese paintings by da Vinci reflect the tension between centric and eccentric forces as the outer powers invade the center and the center, quite literally, reaches out to them."[16] It is important to remember, here, that the eccentric tendency is representative of the more realistic worldview.

Capps goes on to propose that in pastoral theology these two forces are relevant to the relationship between psychology and theology insofar as he identifies theology with centric forces and psychology with eccentric forces. Thus he concludes that "the very reason pastoral theology turns to psychology is in order to counteract the 'self-centered attitude' to which theology is always susceptible."[17] Fraser Watts (an Anglican priest, former clinical psychologist, and now a lecturer in theology and natural science) is another representative of those who are suspicious of interdisciplinary approaches in pastoral theology that want to privilege theology (a centric force) in a hierarchical relationship with psychology because the integrity of both disciplines is not maintained and the psychological perspective becomes marginalized.[18] Like Capps, Watts desires that the "coming-together of the two disciplines should be on the basis of each one respecting the autonomy and contribution of the other."[19] How then does Capps' proposal maintain the integrity of both disciplines? We shall see. Even though theology is understood as occupying the center of an imagined canvas, Capps does not imply that it is without conflict. Rather, following Arnheim's theory, he suggests that there is a bipolar relationship between psychology and theology which may further illumine the "division *between* competing theological forces" at the center.[20] He concludes then that psychology "may well be the means whereby division created by the conflicting *theological* viewpoints of pastoral theologians may be mediated, even reconciled."[21]

It is precisely this "self-centered attitude" to which theology is susceptible, I suggest, that has helped to foster the oppression some women experience in Christian communities because the theological models used to speak about the nature of God and the nature of human identity ignore the realities of their experiences (which could here be understood as eccentric forces). Moreover, this point addresses my own concerns about a crisis (or a lack, an absence of the feminine) in religious discourse which I believe Kristeva's insights will help address. Kristeva's psychoanalytic critique of Christian discourse, then, may be viewed as a more realistic view of women's experience. In this project, then, Kristeva's writings on feminine identity and depression as they relate to religion may help to liberate the voices of some women who have previously experienced oppression within a Christian community. In other words, her work will have the role of mediator between competing voices.

The first model Capps advances is one of convergence which he maintains exemplifies a modernist viewpoint.[22] It is analogous to a discussion of the depth dimension in a painting. Psychology and theology are viewed as being two separate disciplines which, rather than occupying opposing or parallel paths, are "on convergent paths moving toward an imagined vanishing point."[23] In this model, theology and psychology are employed together to explore a topic in depth. Capps explains that this model "makes *explicit* why psychology would be viewed as requisite to an investigation in pastoral theology,"[24] namely that "the central theme of the subject being investigated is enhanced, made more luminous and powerful, when the eccentric forces within a dynamic field of forces are directed toward, not away from the center."[25] This model is, however, not without its difficulties: (1) the convergence occurs but results in a distortion of each discipline by exaggerating the compatibility between theology (centric force) and psychology (eccentric force); and (2) pastoral theologians learn to compensate for the distortions to such an extent that they become unmindful of the reality that distortions exist.[26] The remedy which Capps advances for dealing with the distortions is for the pastoral theologian to be engaged in some form of practice—either ministering, teaching, or writing—directed at "the problem of [accurately] representing the relationship of theology and psychology."[27]

The second model proposed by Capps is one of juxtaposition, which he maintains represents a postmodernist viewpoint.[28] Whereas the previous model focused on the depth dimension of the painting (i.e., the two forces, theology and psychology, moving toward a point of convergence or a central vanishing point), the second focuses on the surface dimension of the painting and is therefore analogous to a consideration of the frontal plane of a painting. The relationship between theology and psychology here is a parallel one. Insights are gleaned from the fact of their juxtaposition, which Capps compares to a metonymic relationship in poetry.[29] He cites D. Collecott's definition of metonymy; it "'rests on contiguity; it is enough for things to be associated in space for them to be placed together in discourse'."[30] The focus here is not on the depth of the relationship but on the surface relationships. This does not, however, mean that these relationships are not important or meaningful. The surface, after all, is not superficial. Thus, as far as theology and psychology are concerned, they are not, as in the first model, moving toward a point of convergence, but are instead simply set side by side. They both, as it were, "take up space," and the fact that they are located in juxtaposition means that they are relevant to one another, but whether they have an affinity for one another or are repelled by one another depends on many factors, most notably the subject matter of each (which is analogous to the characters who are located side by side in a group portrait, or the natural forms similarly juxtaposed in a landscape painting). Frequently, it is the artists' juxtaposition of persons or natural forms not normally seen together or thought to have any association with one another that creates interest and evokes meaning. In this study, Kristeva's writing is juxtaposed primarily with that of theologians and other psychological theorists in an effort to reap interesting and meaningful insights that will benefit those who minister to women struggling with depression. A robust juxtaposition does not require that psychology be a subordinate conversation partner; rather it does suggest that a ministry of pastoral care will be enhanced as a result of what is learned by placing two distinct disciplines (theology and psychology) side by side in the examination of women struggling with depression. Why? Because the language employed to attend to certain kinds of suffering will be expanded to include the experiences of the sufferer (an eccentric point of view). Since my own stance is that of a pastoral theologian whose theological commitments may at times offer a tendency toward what Capps has identified as a "self-centered" or centric theological perspective, this study intentionally attends to what may be learned by listening attentively to the critiques that Kristeva offers. It may even appear to the reader that psychology occupies a privileged space in the pages that follow as a result.

The third model is one of structural uniformity. It is based on what Arnheim identified as a late or third phase in an artist's work which occurs at the end of a long career. Capps summarizes this phase as follows:

> greater interest is taken in the basic laws that control the observable manifestations of the world. It reflects a shift from hierarchy to coordination. Central to this shift is "the conviction that similarities are more important than differences, and that organization should derive from consensus among equals rather than from obedience to superordinate principles or powers."[31]

Like the second model, this model does not ascribe priority to theology (which, in the first model, is the centric force), but it differs from the second model in that what was juxtaposed in the second model is now considered to be more overlapping, sometimes to the point of being indistinguishable. Thus, the significance of this model is that theology and psychology may be viewed as interchangeable. That is: "One will be as likely to turn to texts by theologians for their psychological as for their theological insights. Conversely, one will turn to psychologists as much for their theological as for their psychological insights."[32] Julia Kristeva's own work could be understood as an example of this third model even if she does not intend to offer theological insights. In "Stabat

Mater,"[33] for example, she reflects on Christian discourse about the Virgin Mary from which one is able to derive a "theology of motherhood" in addition to her intended "psychology of motherhood." On the other hand, the very fact that the major portions of "Stabat Mater" juxtapose the two discourses in separate columns suggests the viability of the second model. Interesting and meaningful insights result not merely from the specific contents of the two columns but also from the very fact of their juxtaposition.

Since I will not be pairing a psychoanalytic theorist with a theologian in a dialogical model in which theology and psychology converge, the first model is not applicable.[34] Neither will I, as the third model suggests, be constructing an original psycho-theological or theo-psychological theory, the sort of achievement that, as Arnheim suggests, is characteristic of artists in late career whose work seems to have become rather undisciplined but, for this very reason, may have unexpected power and meaning. Instead, my project juxtaposes a number of theologians and scientific theorists with Kristeva, in order to draw out the theological insights implicit in selected of her writings and their relevance to a pastoral theology for women struggling with depression. The second model of juxtaposition proposed by Capps, therefore, is the one I have adopted for relating psychology and theology in this project. Again, no one model is considered completely adequate and there are other models used effectively by other pastoral theologians.[35]

It remains to say something regarding how one gets from "here to there." A brief summary of Ian Barbour's[36] study on both scientific and religious models underscores the benefits of using Capps' proposal for a model of juxtaposition. Like the other theorists cited in this chapter, Barbour is also concerned that religious discourse be better related to human experience. His study of models will lead to a discussion of the significance of metaphors in the construction of religious models. This discussion will be based upon some of Sallie McFague's[37] writings and the work of Mary Gerhart and Allan Russell.[38] Indeed, the work of these authors—especially McFague—is indebted to Barbour's work on the importance of metaphors in the construction of both scientific and religious models. By discussing these authors, we will be better positioned to appreciate the significance of Kristeva's work, which reflects a deep appreciation for the power of metaphors for understanding and healing, and for the revitalization of Christian discourse and pastoral practice.

Models: Scientific and Religious

Philosopher of science Ian Barbour is interested in the analogies which can be drawn between religious and scientific models and seeks to demonstrate that they differ only by a matter of degree. Science is not an entirely objective enterprise, nor is religious faith an entirely subjective enterprise. He is also interested in "some of the difficulties in talking about God which are now felt so widely" and offers his work as one means of increasing the awareness of the "*experiential correlates* of theological concepts."[39] His entire project is offered with the hope that it will "renew religious vitality in practice."[40] Thus, his work is especially relevant for the pastoral theologian who, in the case of this project, is concerned that we currently lack a Christian discourse that is sufficiently realistic, sensitive, and powerful to be of assistance to women struggling with depression.

In order to accomplish this goal he maintains that theology must be both confessional and self-critical, and he suggests that it has not been nearly self-critical enough. This, I argue, is what has led to a crisis in Christian discourse.[41] The very fact that a preacher and priest of the caliber of Barbara Brown Taylor would write a book entitled *Leaving Church* and that former religion reporter William Lobdell would write a book entitled *Losing My Religion* seems to indicate that discontent or disillusionment with the centric forces in religious discourse continues to increase.[42]

Barbour maintains that models in science "are mental constructs devised to account for observed phenomena in the natural world. They originate in a combination of analogy to the familiar and creative imagination in the invention of the new."[43] Moreover, they are "partial and provisional ways of imagining what is not observable; they are symbolic representations of aspects of the world which are not directly accessible to us."[44] So, too, he asserts, are religious models analogical, partial, and provisional. One of their main functions is "the interpretation of distinctive types of experience: awe and reverence, moral obligation, reorientation and reconciliation, interpersonal relationships, key historical events, and order and creativity in the world."[45] Thus, a religious model "represents the enduring structural components which myths dramatize in narrative form" and results "from reflection on the living myths which communities transmit.[46] What does he mean by myths? Barbour elaborates: "a myth is a *story which is taken to manifest some aspect of the cosmic order*."[47] Myths "*offer ways of ordering experience, inform man about himself, express a saving power in human life, provide patterns for human actions,* and *are enacted in rituals.*"[48] Thus, myths are not merely interesting stories. They are stories having practical consequences. Also, as Barbour suggests, religious models derive from reflection on these myths.

The manner in which Barbour relates scientific models to religious ones is important because, as noted above, our religious models are not, in his view, sufficiently self-critical, especially in their failure to keep pace with changes in the real world, which for us here, is the "world" of the depressed woman and the pastoral response to this world. A scientific model, given its empirical thrust, needs to have this self-critical dimension built into it, for otherwise it will become an anachronism and need to be discarded altogether.

Correlation is key to understanding how Barbour perceives the relationship between scientific and religious models. Models function in science to "suggest theories which correlate patterns in observational data" while models in religion function to "suggest beliefs which correlate patterns in human experience."[49] Models of both kinds are to be understood as subjective rather than objective since "we cannot isolate uninterpreted experience."[50]

Barbour outlines the similarities and differences between religious and scientific models. The similarities are that they: (1) are analogical in origin; (2) are extensible to new situations; (3) are comprehensible as units; (4) have a similar status (i.e., neither is a literal picture of reality, nor a useful fiction); and (5) are partial and inadequate ways of imagining what is not observable (symbolic representations). The differences include the fact that: (1) scientific models order observations while religious models order experience of individuals and communities; (2) religious models serve non-cognitive functions; (3) religious models elicit more total personal involvement than scientific ones (i.e., a call for decision about matters of ultimate concern); and (4) religious models appear to be more influential than formal beliefs and doctrines derived from them, whereas scientific models are subservient to theories (i.e., religious images have a more direct relationship to experience, especially in worship).[51]

This description of religious and scientific models in their similarities and differences prompts the question: what is their usefulness or status in relation to the world? Barbour presents four distinct ways that scientific models may be related to the world. The first is naive realism which represents scientific thinking until the twentieth century. Thus "scientific theories were [considered] accurate descriptions of 'the world as it is in itself.' The entities postulated in theories were believed to exist, even if they were not directly observable."[52]

Therefore, a "naively realistic view of theories corresponds to a *literalistic view of models.*"[53]

The second view is positivism which flourished in the first half of the twentieth century. From this viewpoint data is "theory-laden" suggesting that there is no "neutral observation-language" which results in models being dismissed because the theories may "be inferred directly from observations by a process of inductive generalization." This second view opposes Barbour's understanding of models in which models are essential to the "origin and continued development of scientific theories" because theories are "the product of creative imagination" and are "mediated through models."[54]

The third view, instrumentalism, one of two models that came into its own in the second half of the twentieth century, agrees with positivism that theories are not representations of the world; "theories should not be judged by truth or falsity, but by their usefulness as calculating devices for correlating observations and making predictions."[55] Moreover, Barbour calls the corresponding view of models within instrumentalism—fictionalism; that is, models "are neither true nor false, but only more or less useful mental devices."[56]

The fourth view, critical realism, which also came into its own in the late twentieth century, is the perspective Barbour prefers. Theories understood from this view are seen as representations of the world which are true and useful. Science is not simply discovery and exploration but is construction and invention; scientists therefore seek to understand as well as predict and control outcomes. Human imagination is important for the formation of theories which "are abstract symbol systems which inadequately represent particular aspects of the world for specific purposes."[57]

By extension these four views on the status of scientific models can be related to religious models.[58] I neither want to literalize nor dismiss religious models; I do not consider them "useful fiction." I concur that they are only partial and inadequate ways of representing particular aspects of the world; moreover they rely on the creativity of human imagination. Thus, like Barbour, I endorse the critical realism position in religious models. This means that I, too, view religious models as representations of the world of human experience, and, because I am especially concerned here with depressed women, I am drawing attention to features of religious models that differ from scientific ones, i.e., that they serve non-cognitive functions, elicit more personal involvement, and have a more direct relationship to experience. The key point here is that, for Barbour, scientific models (in our own case, psychology) and religious models (here, pastoral theology) are similar in some respects but different in others.

How does this relate to the model of juxtaposition that Capps proposes? Recall that this model suggests that psychology and theology are "united by the mere parallelism of the two."[59] Moreover, it is "their juxtaposition [that] is potentially informative."[60] A perspective grounded in critical realism, I suggest, implies that the model is partial and provisional, but it recognizes that both psychology and theology are legitimate theories or "abstract symbol systems" which can be employed to represent particular aspects of human relationships. Theology is the centric tendency which exists in tension with the eccentric tendency—psychology—which as noted above, represents a more realistic worldview. As Barbour observes, "Neither science nor religion is an individual enterprise; a person interprets his experience within a communal tradition."[61] The way to avoid either absolutism or relativism, Barbour maintains, is to assess religious models from a perspective of critical realism.[62] I suggest that Barbour's theory implies that a model of convergence leads to absolutism while a model of structural uniformity in pastoral theology could be construed as leading to relativism. Thus the model of juxtaposition reflects a perspective of critical realism that avoids the polar opposites he defines that still exist in Christianity today: "Commitment alone without enquiry tends to become fanaticism or narrow dogmatism; reflection without commitment tends to become trivial speculation unrelated to real life."[63] Hence, by juxtaposing a psychological model (in this case, the work of Kristeva) and a theological model (in this case, pastoral theology), our hope would be that a more self-critical pastoral theology for women struggling with depression would result.

What is the significance of metaphors for this discussion of models? As has been noted above, Barbour proposes that models are analogical in both science and religion. Metaphors are the fabric that comprises the models insofar as they propose analogies between the way a word is currently understood and a "new context into which it is introduced" while creating a "tension between affirmation and negation" that results from the similarities and differences which compose analogy.[64] A summary of how Barbour understands metaphors, particularly as they relate to religious discourse, is provided below. A metaphor: (1) is a novel configuration produced by the juxtaposition of *two frames of reference*; (2) is a new creation for which there are no rules; (3) arises from the concreteness and individuality of particular experiences; (4) is *not literally true*; (5) is not a useful fiction...with no relation to reality; (6) asserts that there are significant analogies between the things compared; (7) cannot be replaced by a set of equivalent literal statements because it is *open-ended*; (8) often has *emotional and valuational overtones* (unlike a scientific model it calls forth feelings and attitudes); (9) is dynamic (language becomes event); and, (10) influences *perception and interpretation*.[65]

Using light as an example, Barbour suggests that many religious symbols are based on human experience. That is, we see better in the light which comes to symbolize knowledge. God is symbolized as light; for example, the faithful have an experience of being dazzled by the blinding light. What distinguishes the metaphors of religious discourse, say from poetic language, is that "poetic metaphors are used only momentarily, in one context...*religious symbols* become part of the language of a religious community in its scripture and liturgy and in its continuing life and thought."[66] That is to say, the metaphors of religious discourse become permanent insofar as they become models that represent God in theological discourse. Why is this important? Because it has implications for personal religious faith. As Barbour notes, one of the recurrent themes of his book is "the *experiential basis* of religion, which is as essential for renewed religious vitality in practice as for a defensible epistemology in theory. Inherited models are for many individuals today almost totally detached from human experience."[67] This fact points to the reality of the crisis in religious discourse defined at the beginning of the chapter, and issues a particular challenge to the pastoral theologian, for whom the indictment that her model is detached from human experience is an especially devastating one.

Metaphors arise, in part, from human experience, and those which have become models in religion are, at least for some individuals, detached from their experience; one of the chief aims of this project is to determine whether Kristeva's insights, based on an appreciation for the power of metaphorical discourse, will assist in the renewal of religious vitality in practice, especially as it relates to with women struggling with depression. Barbour doesn't end here, however. Continuing on, he pleads for increased awareness of and sensitivity to "experiential correlates of theological concepts" such as sin and salvation which he argues have become "theological abstractions for many persons" even though he believes that "the power of reconciliation overcoming estrangement" is a lived human experience.[68] Metaphors become models that represent the reality of religious experience in human existence. Thus they have the power to shape a person's self understanding in constructive or destructive ways since they are a vehicle for integrating experiences, values, and goals into a person's identity.[69] It is to the destructive effects of Christian discourse upon women that this study speaks. It is my hope that Kristeva's insights can be translated in such a way that new metaphors in Christian discourse will develop which promote creativity and self-integration among women who have been oppressed.

To summarize briefly, what is significant about Barbour's claims for this study is his emphasis upon the partial, provisional and inadequate nature of religious models. Inherited models are often detached from human religious experience. In turn, this detachment from human experience, especially women's experience, has primarily destructive effects on human personality. It is precisely these destructive effects of inherited religious models which I believe Kristeva's writings will help address.

Model to Metaphor and Back Again: McFague

Sallie McFague relies on Barbour's work on religious models for her work on metaphor, using his understanding of critical realism as a method for evaluating the usefulness and appropriateness of metaphors in religious discourse. Like Kristeva, she is concerned with the destructive effects that some inherited traditional models have rendered. McFague acknowledges the necessity of religious models but, in so doing, she also issues an alert contending that religious models tend to "exclude other ways of thinking and talking" leading to a kind of literal understanding which suggests that there is a single understanding of a subject (similar to Barbour's own concern about terms like sin and salvation). This occurs because religious models tend to become more permanent and "object to competition in ways that metaphors do not."[70] The danger which is of primary concern in this study, is the oppression of women which has occurred as a direct result of religious models that "object to competition" thereby excluding women's experience.

In a later work, McFague states that "[a] model is a metaphor that has gained sufficient stability and scope so as to present a pattern for relatively comprehensive and coherent explanation."[71] In an even more recent work, she again points to the difficulty involved with metaphors that become models, noting that "they are often reified, petrified, and expanded so as not only to exclude other models but also to pretend to the status of definitions."[72] Her concern about metaphors which have become models is expressed in yet another form when she differentiates between theological and religious language. Theological language is what she considers a secondary language because it exists to interpret events that primary or religious language seeks to express. She contends that theological language or the metaphors used to construct theological models needs to "gain distance and be different from religious language" because this is what allows us to experience a connection with the sacred.[73] When the space between the two types of discourse collapses, metaphors tend to become literalized—they die because they lose their tension.[74] This describes what I consider to be a contemporary crisis in Christian discourse—one which Barbour suggested was a result of inattention to the correlation of religious experience with theological concepts.

McFague cites the beginning of the demise of metaphor in theological discourse in the eighteenth century which resulted in creative imagination begin consigned to poetry while reason was restricted to the sciences. The end result of this elimination of imagination and metaphor from theological discourse, according to McFague, is Biblical literalism and idolatry. This she contends has led to the "Bible being turned into an idol—perfect and absolute, closed to human interpretation."[75] Here the influence of Barbour upon McFague's work is visible in that her concern with Biblical literalism echoes his criticism of the absolutism of orthodoxy.[76] The concern of this study which is addressed by both of these theorists is that Christian discourse which consists of reified metaphors becomes closed to women's experience.

If McFague is critical of the absence of metaphorical thinking in constructing theological models (or conversely, the presence of literalized metaphors); what then, does a good metaphor look like? In *Speaking in Parables*, McFague asserts that "[a] metaphor is a word used in an unfamiliar context to give us a new insight; a good metaphor moves us to see our ordinary world in an extraordinary way."[77] In *Models of God*, she expands on this understanding of metaphor maintaining that it: (1) is a word or phrase used inappropriately (e.g., arm of the chair, God the father); (2) is unsubstitutable meaning that what is expressed through metaphor cannot be said directly; and (3) "has the character of 'is' and 'is not': an assertion is made but as a likely account rather than a definition."[78] McFague contends that metaphor is the way language works;[79] therefore, it is at the heart of the task of theology, which "is to serve the hearing of God's word, that strange truth that disrupts our ordinary world and moves us—and it—to a new place."[80]

For McFague, metaphors are context dependent and time specific. This means that the dominant metaphors of Christianity are in need of continual revision if they are to reflect any given epoch.[81] This is true, for example, of patriarchy as a root-metaphor in the Christian tradition because it has the power to oppress women both from the perspective of what it does say about women in general and from what it fails to say about women. Women are often defined by this model as being inferior and are left without liberating alternatives by what is omitted in patriarchal understandings of what it means to be a woman and a Christian. We will see just how this is so in later chapters. As McFague reminds us "major models that become world views have subliminal, pervasive power to protect them against criticism" and when they become reified "into objective realities we make them resistant to change and we become prisoners of our own creations."[82] Her solution is to offer metaphors (i.e., God as mother, lover and friend) which recognize the need to speak about salvation as a "destabilizing, inclusive, nonhierarchical vision" for our time and the future. Thus she understands these new metaphors to be associated more directly with qualities often attributed to women including caring, mutuality, attraction, nurturing, supporting, empathy, responsibility, service, self-sacrifice and creativity.[83] This is not to say, however, that these metaphors are necessarily more adequate and more appropriate than older models. McFague readily admits, and I concur that "no language about God is adequate and all of it is improper, new metaphors are not necessarily less inadequate or improper than old ones.[84] My primary interest in these "new metaphors" which are no longer revolutionary is their ability to reflect women's experiences in a pastoral care relationship. Even so, the new metaphors in theology which McFague proposes are sensitive to issues raised by living in a nuclear age that is pluralistic, and share three commonalities: thus Christian faith is (1) seen as destabilizing conventional expectations and worldly standards; (2) inclusive, reaching out to the weak, to the outsider, to the stranger, to the outcast; and (3) antihierarchical and antitriumphalist.[85]

Finally, McFague acknowledges that there is a risk in engaging in the task of theology from this perspective because it is "necessarily tolerant or pluralistic." Thus she concludes "this kind of theology as a whole is a tentative affair and can advance few solid claims in its own behalf. In this sense, it is, I believe, in the tradition of the *via negativa*: finding little to say of God with certainty, it boldly makes it case hypothetically and lets it rest."[86] McFague's heuristic theological constructions derive from her emphasis on the interrelatedness of God, the world and persons. She makes a case for revitalizing theological discourse by searching for new metaphors that derive from human experience. This, I would like to suggest, is a theological method of reflection which is inviting to the pastoral theologian who wants to revitalize Christian discourse by taking the experience of women struggling with depression seriously and on its own terms. In a sense, placing Christian discourse and a Kristevan interpretation of the experience of these women on the same plane (juxtaposition model), both Christian discourse and pastoral practice will benefit. Like Barbour, McFague cautions against literalized models that are built upon dead metaphors and insists that appropriate metaphors are connected to human experience. Metaphor is one place where religious and psychoanalytic discourses intersect. New metaphors which connect women's experience with Christian religious models are needed in order to make sense of their experience and facilitate healing in a pastoral care or counseling relationship. It is my thesis that Kristeva's critique of Christian metaphors will offer new insights that help create new metaphors. Metaphors are open-ended, partial and provisional, or temporary, and this makes them especially good resources for understanding the experience of women struggling with depression and for helping them through pastoral initiatives. A useful way to begin to show this is by focusing on the development of a human self.

Metaphor: A Knowledge-in-Process

This brings us to the work of Mary Gerhart and Allan Russell. Like Barbour, they are concerned to demonstrate that science is neither totally objective, nor religion totally subjective. They, too, focus on how meaning is mediated and give primacy to metaphors in the creation of new meaning. In their study, metaphor is a "knowledge in process" which I suggest is analogous to Kristeva's metaphor of the self—a "subject-in-process/on trial." First I will summarize briefly Gerhart and Russell's extensive study of "metaphoric process" and then conclude by drawing parallels with the manner in which Kristeva discusses metaphor in relation to the "subject-in-process/on trial."

Mary Gerhart, a professor of religious studies, and Allan Russell, a professor of physics, are very interested in the relationship between religious and scientific models. I suggest that they take Barbour's work a step further since their concern is not solely the objective/subjective split but the complete dichotomization of science and religion. They describe this dichotomy simply as science tending generally to concern itself with "how" questions while religion has concerned itself primarily with "why" questions. It is this kind of dichotomization which they hope their theory of metaphor will help to bridge.

They offer a theory of metaphor as "knowledge-in-process."[87] For them, metaphor above all else is a "process of creating new meaning."[88] They contend that "only in acts of metaphor...is the tension between original knowledge and its concept sufficiently sustained so that something genuinely new results."[89] One of their purposes in studying metaphor is to determine "the way in which knowledge grows and changes and the reasons why the understandings that we achieve are surrendered so reluctantly."[90] Knowledge, in their view, is always in process. Therefore, "[k]nowledge-in-process for the individual knower is best understood in terms *not of how the answers change* but how the *questions* do."[91] Also, in both science and religion, "knowledge-in-process is best perceived in historical horizon-shifts...in the occurrence of new and significantly distinct forms of understanding."[92] Meaning then is mediated and only "said to be constitutive when it has become stabilized for any given generation."[93] Thus, in their discussion of stabilized meanings (which might also be construed as dominant metaphors), they explain why individuals yield only reluctantly and slowly to new meanings. They contend that when meanings are destabilized in the manner suggested by McFague that "one's horizon of understanding as previously constituted may be so threatened that one may, out of fear, reject theoretical understandings."[94] Thus the resistance or reluctance is not created by a stabilization of meanings necessarily but rather by anxiety caused when accepted meanings are challenged or destabilized by something new. When this observation is applied, for example, to McFague's quest for new metaphors that reflect our time, it might explain why some will want to reject her theological proposals. Again, if one accepts the premise that religious and psychoanalytic discourses intersect in metaphor, then the process of choosing metaphors used to correlate patterns in human religious experience with meaning warrants careful consideration.

What Gerhart and Russell consider unique about their theory is their focus on the *process* involved in making metaphors rather than on a linguistic *form*.[95] Crucial to this focus is a distinction between metaphor and analogy. They differentiate between analogy and metaphor as follows:

> The finding of analogies may arrange or rearrange the concepts that populate our fields of meanings, but the metaphoric process reforms fields of meanings themselves. There is a sense in which analogies are found—they either exist or do not exist. Metaphors, by contrast, are created.[96]

The turning point for Gerhart and Russell comes from the manner in which the metaphors are *created*. Their primary concern in this regard is how knowledge changes as a result of engaging in a metaphoric process. Metaphoric process creates new meanings and changes theoretical structures of meaning while analogy only extends meanings which already exist. Thus a metaphoric process is a "distortion of the fields of meanings."[97] In contrast to analogy, the metaphorical process can result in a sea-change in understanding; everything has changed. More has occurred than the mere extension of previous boundaries.

Gerhart and Russell summarize the significance of analysis of metaphor for theology as follows: (1) one can use the tension to contradict one's ordinary world of meanings and to conclude in paradox; (2) one can succumb to the tension, allowing it to bring about a horizon-shift so sudden and radical that self-continuity is sacrificed; and (3) one can mediate the new meaning, allowing it to transform the new incompatibility within the self's steady horizon-growth.[98] By extension, it can be said to have the same importance for pastoral theology. I would like to suggest that their third point carries the most weight for pastoral theology since steady growth and transformation toward a healthy self and healthy relationships are often the focus of a pastor's relationship with individuals in a care-giving relationship.

The goal for Gerhart and Russell is that the subject (i.e., the knowing person) is able to arrive at "an instance of cognitive self-transcendence or knowledge-in-process" by reflecting on the status of questions asked in any inquiry.[99] Knowledge-in-process is itself a metaphor for the way knowledge grows and changes. While self-transcendence is not a given, it is a process in which knowledge is key as we "move away from our immediate understandings" by means of comparison but this does not protect us from slipping into naïveté or a form of gnosticism (here understood as the religious equivalent of begging the question), or even uncritical pluralism which ultimately "inhibit further understanding and further horizon-growth."[100] Here, too, their project reflects the work of Barbour but then travels a step beyond. To be avoided is the literalization or trivialization of religious metaphors. Like McFague, Gerhart and Russell acknowledge that "the idea of metaphor is unsubstitutable" since "[t]hat which is intrinsic to the metaphor, namely the insistence (in the face of resistance) that what the metaphoric insight discloses is the way things are is perhaps most clearly seen in the prophetic statements of any age."[101]

This idea that "metaphor is unsubstitutable" provides the foundation for the rest of this project which is concerned with the way metaphors are chosen in pastoral care and counseling relationships with women struggling with depression. I suggest that many of the traditional religious metaphors chosen have often exacerbated women's struggles and the work of the various theorists discussed thus far demonstrates why at least some Christian discourse (the Christian discourse which is the fabric of a pastoral care and counseling relationship) is in need of revision. It remains to see if knowledge changes in a manner analogous to the way the self develops through the creation of new metaphors. And this brings us, finally, to Kristeva.

A Kristevan Metaphor: The "Subject-in-Process or on-Trial"

For Kristeva, any speaking/thinking subject (person) is always in process or on trial since the French word *procès* always has a legal connotation. This understanding of identity development points to the struggle or conflict involved in becoming. In fact, in Kristeva's theory, the speaking subject is also a divided subject that is always in motion or changing.[102] She acknowledges that her metaphor "corresponds exactly to the Freudian idea of psychic life as founded on the death drive and on Eros,"[103] and thus recognizes that the woman who is moving toward self-transcendence does so as a "divided subject," as one who seeks life but also experiences the pull and weight of death. Thus, her understanding of the person as a subject who is always in process or on trial "assumes that we recognize, on the one hand, the unity of the subject who submits to a law—the law of communication, among others; yet who, on the other hand, does not entirely submit, cannot entirely submit, does not want to submit entirely."[104] The urge to revolt arises from the aggression or violence of the death drive as easily as it does from the desire for pleasure or jouissance. As a result of the contest or trial of becoming a speaking subject we gain a "vision of the human venture as a venture of innovation, of creation, of opening, of renewal."[105] The journey to become a self resembles the process outlined by Gerhart and Russell for the expansion of knowledge. Whether the speaking subject is male or female, the law in Kristeva's discourse is represented by the paternal or Word of the father. This, of course, means that there is no real discourse which represents the maternal or the feminine. A female subject's process of development, then, will be an even greater "trial" since there is no language which describes precisely the realities of her experience, especially her religious experience. Moreover, the subject-in-process—man or woman—is living in the midst of an historical crisis which Kristeva describes as occurring at the levels of authority or democracy, religion, and language in its relationship to sexual identity. A power that once, perhaps, belonged to the "priest," Kristeva now locates in the person of the therapist, one who can be a "stabilizing apparatus" in the face of the current crisis.[106]

This power to restore and renew is in the hands of the analyst because she, according to Kristeva, is the one who restores amatory discourse to its central place in the process of becoming a speaking subject. The analyst does so by countering the death drive with the language of love—of life—in relationship with the depressed woman for whom the death drive has become so dominant that she loses her interest in speech. "Lover's discourse" which was once foundational for the construction of Christian discourse has become so commonplace in "churches that are filled with people who go there to hear that God loves them"[107] that it has been relegated to the domain of psychotherapy. This begins to reflect McFague's criticism that the metaphors of patriarchy in theological discourse have become dead metaphors which no longer help us to interpret religious experience but rather resist change and thereby make us "prisoners of our own creations." What makes psychoanalytic discourse unique and the successor to religious discourse, Kristeva contends, is its ability to be "a scene of metaphor production" as well as a "scene of *provisional* interpretation." Interpretation or knowledge in a therapeutic relationship is provisional rather than absolute as the analyst aids in the process of restoring meaning (and affect) to the speech of the depressed. Moreover, Kristeva understands:

> *Love is something spoken, and it is only that:* poets have always known it. From now on amatory styles will be spread out before us like different historical embodiments of the metaphoricalness that is essential to loving states: like stylistic variants of the *cure*, another name for *life*, which the Western subject has experienced for two thousand years.[108]

Kristeva is describing transference love which is the ground for therapeutic change but she, perhaps more than most, recognizes that this language was once the sole privilege of the church and religious discourse.

This, I submit, is already an accurate theological insight advanced by the psychoanalytic theorist. Thus Kristeva identifies what is absent currently in religious discourse—metaphor and provisional interpretation. These were both identified as integral elements for the development of religious models earlier in the chapter. The self will develop and heal in a relationship where new meanings and interpretations are offered, just as knowledge changes through the creation of new metaphors. In each case, something new challenges our perception of reality while it promotes growth and transformation. I suggest that if the clergy heed Kristeva's call for a restoration of amatory discourse which according to her definition rests on the use of metaphor, the "priest" need not be replaced by the therapist; rather she can work alongside of the therapist.

If the "subject-in-process" demonstrates how Kristeva uses metaphor, what claims does she make about metaphor per se? She proposes: "Let us call metaphor, in the general sense of a *conveyance of meaning*, the economy that modifies language when subject and object of the utterance act muddle their borders."[109] For Kristeva, then, the accent in metaphorical language is upon motion, that is, in the act of speaking itself in relation to another speaking subject. She writes: "The utterance is precisely what seems to me, from the position of an analyst, the only basis for meaning and significance in discourse."[110] It isn't simply the act of speaking aloud that provides the space for meaning and healing but the relationship between the listener and the one who speaks. The metaphor, then, is created in a relationship (her emphasis here being the transference relationship established in an analytic relationship). As Kristeva maintains: "The 'being who acts' could exist only for a subject in symbolic *contact*, that is to say in motion, in *transference* with another."[111] An important place of intersection for psychoanalytic and Christian discourse is the creation of metaphors and the new meanings they generate.

Conclusions

We have seen that no one model will be adequate or complete. Donald Capps' model of juxtaposition will be the governing one for this project since it is congruent with Barbour's position of critical realism which avoids absolutism on the one hand, and relativism on the other. Key to this juxtaposition of psychoanalytic and Christian discourse is the metaphor, especially the Kristevan metaphor of "the subject-in-process." My decision to focus on women struggling with depression is especially appropriate in this regard, for they as individuals seek revitalization of which Christian discourse is also in need. My project is based on the conviction that such revitalization may occur by "muddling the borders" between religious and psychological discourse, which is the second model's equivalent of the first model's movement toward a convergence in a single vanishing point.

Metaphor is unsubstitutable in this project because it is a building block for models and as McFague contends it is the way we think. For Kristeva, metaphor is a basic essential for life and the analytic cure; it is the language of love that awakens desire in those who struggle with depression. Following Gerhart and Russell, metaphor throughout this study will be understood as a "knowledge-in-process" which is more life-changing than analogy. Good metaphors do not merely effect increments of knowledge but rather revolutionize its very structures. They are partial and provisional ways of imagining what is not observable; from the perspective of critical realism, the importance of creative human imagination is recognized. Moreover, in religious discourse, metaphors suggest beliefs which correlate with patterns in human experience. They involve more than the tension in the relationship between two interpretations of a metaphorical utterance; they are about the relationship between the speaking subject and the Other in the moment of utterance. As McFague proclaims, "[s]omething *new* is being said about reality."[112]

Dead metaphors (i.e., metaphors which have lost their tension or "inappropriateness") account, in part, for a crisis in religious discourse of which both Kristeva and McFague are aware and to which they are attempting to respond. This crisis is also acknowledged by Barbour as well as Gerhart and Russell though their interest in metaphoric language is centered more on the eventual construction of models. Metaphor is the way language works; it is the way we think. Metaphors provide at the very least a partial model for the way knowledge changes and grows. As McFague argues, it is nonmetaphorical thinking which has led to literalism and idolatry, thus creating a crisis for the "subject-in-process" within religion in general and Christianity in particular. What follows is offered in the spirit of a reformist perspective.[113] It is hoped that something new will be said about reality by offering a close reading of selected texts by Kristeva, using the metaphor of the "subject-in-process" as my continuing point of reference.

Notes

1. Julia Kristeva, *Desire in Language: A Semiotic Approach to Literature and Art*, ed. Leon S. Roudiez, trans. Thomas Gora, Alice Jardine and Leon S. Roudiez (New York: Columbia University Press, 1980), ix.
2. Ibid., 1.
3. Those authors who will be cited in addition to Kristeva are: Ian Barbour, Sallie McFague, Fraser Watts, and Mary Gerhart and Allan Russell. The work of pastoral theologian, Donald Capps, will also be cited not to support the case for metaphor and creation of meaning but rather to establish a method for juxtaposing the various authors cited.
4. Donald Capps, "The Lessons of Art Theory for Pastoral Theology," *Pastoral Psychology* 47:5 (1999): 321–346.

5. Sallie McFague, *Metaphorical Theology: Models of God in Religious Language* (Philadelphia: Fortress Press, 1982), see Chapter One.
6. Ibid., 194.
7. Christie Cozad Neuger, *Counseling Women: A Narrative, Pastoral Approach* (Minneapolis: Fortress Press, 2001), 10–13, 68. Neuger doesn't label the situation a crisis but is concerned about language which both reflects and creates reality, especially when "the language of the culture does not carry the experience or perspective of women or others of nondominant cultural status, then the culture will not operate in the best interests of those groups. And, not only are the people in these groups deprived of empowerment and full participation in the culture, but the culture is damaged too." (68)
8. Ross Guberman, ed., *Julia Kristeva: Interviews* (New York: Columbia University Press, 1996), 10. See also 68–69.
9. Sallie McFague, *Metaphorical Theology*, p. 74.
10. Rudolf Arnheim, *New Essays on the Psychology of Art* (Berkeley: University of California Press, 1986); *The Power of the Center: A Study of Composition in the Visual Arts*, the new version, (Berkeley: University of California Press, 1988); *The Split and the Structure: Twenty-Eight Essays* (Berkeley: University of California Press, 1996) as cited by Donald E. Capps, "The Lessons of Art Theory for Pastoral Theology," *Pastoral Psychology* 47:5 (1999), 321–46.
11. Rudolf Arnheim, *The Power of the Center: A Study of Composition in the Visual Arts*, new version, (Berkeley: University of California Press, 1988), 2, as cited by Capps, "The Lessons of Art Theory for Pastoral Theology," 330.
12. Ibid.
13. Capps, "The Lessons of Art Theory for Pastoral Theology," 330.
14. Ibid.
15. Ibid., 330–31.
16. Ibid., 331
17. Ibid.
18. Fraser Watts, "Relating the Psychology and Theology of Forgiveness," in *Forgiveness in Context: Theology and Psychology in Creative Dialogue*, eds. Fraser Watts and Liz Gulliford (New York: T & T Clark, 2004) 3–4.
19. Ibid., 4.
20. Capps, "The Lessons of Art Theory for Pastoral Theology," 332.
21. Ibid., 333.
22. Ibid., 341.
23. Ibid., 336.
24. Ibid., 337.
25. Ibid.
26. Ibid., 338.
27. Ibid.
28. Ibid., 341.
29. Ibid., 340.
30. Ibid.

31. Rudolf Arnheim, *New Essays on the Psychology of Art* (Berkeley: University of California Press, 1986), 288, as cited by Capps, "The Lessons of Art Theory for Pastoral Theology," 342.
32. Ibid.
33. Julia Kristeva, "Stabat Mater," *Tales of Love*, trans. Leon S. Roudiez (New York: Columbia University Press, 1987), 234–64.
34. Capps, "The Lessons of Art Theory for Pastoral Theology," 337. He notes that the most common model for a dissertation in pastoral theology is the first model.
35. For example, a good illustration of a model which claims that psychology and theology may exist in a complementary relationship based on complementarity in scientific models is Deborah van Deusen Hunsinger's *Theology and Pastoral Counseling: A New Interdisciplinary Approach* (Grand Rapids: Eerdmans, 1995). This model corresponds most closely to the "convergence" model as described by Capps. Another example in the field of practical theology that corresponds closely to the "convergence" model is offered by James E. Loder and W. Jim Neidhardt in *The Knight's Move: The Relational Logic of the Spirit in Theology and Science* (Colorado Springs: Helmers and Howard, 1992).
36. Ian G. Barbour, *Myths, Models, and Paradigms: A Comparative Study in Science and Religion* (New York: Harper & Row, 1976).
37. Sallie McFague TeSelle, *Speaking in Parables: A Study in Metaphor and Theology* (Philadelphia: Fortress Press, 1975); *Metaphorical Theology: Models of God in Religious Language* (Philadelphia: Fortress Press, 1982); *Models of God: Theology for an Ecological, Nuclear Age* (Philadelphia: Fortress Press, 1987).
38. Mary Gerhart & Allan Russell, *Metaphoric Process: The Creation of Scientific and Religious Understanding* (Fort Worth: Texas Christian University Press, 1984).
39. Barbour, *Myths, Models and Paradigms*, 179.
40. Ibid., 178.
41. Ibid., 181.
42. Barbara Brown Taylor, *Leaving Church: A Memoir of Faith* (San Francisco: HarperCollins, 2007) and William Lobdell, *Losing My Religion: How I Lost My Faith Reporting on Religion in America—and Found Unexpected Peace* (New York: Collins, 2009).
43. Barbour, *Myths, Models, and Paradigms*, 6.
44. Ibid., 7.
45. Ibid.
46. Ibid., 27.
47. Ibid., 19, emphasis in original. See pp. 19–28 for more detail.
48. Ibid., emphasis in original.
49. Ibid., 49.
50. Ibid., 53.
51. Ibid., 69.
52. Ibid., 34.
53. Ibid., 35.
54. Ibid., 35-36.
55. Ibid., 36.

56. Ibid., 37.
57. Ibid.
58. In fact, Sallie McFague does just that in *Metaphorical Theology*, 131–133.
59. Capps, "Lessons of Art Theory for Pastoral Theology," 339.
60. Ibid.
61. Barbour, *Myths, Models, and Paradigms*, 147.
62. Ibid., 177.
63. Ibid., 136.
64. Ibid., 12.
65. Ibid., 13–14.
66. Ibid., 15.
67. Ibid., 178.
68. Ibid., 179.
69. Ibid., 175.
70. Sallie McFague, *Metaphorical Theology*, 24.
71. McFague, *Models of God*, 34.
72. Ibid., 39.
73. McFague, *Metaphorical Theology*, 119.
74. Ibid., 38.
75. Ibid., 77.
76. Barbour, *Myths, Models, and Paradigms*, 177.
77. McFague, *Speaking in Parables*, 4.
78. McFague, *Models of God*, 33.
79. McFague, *Metaphorical Theology*, 37.
80. McFague, *Speaking in Parables*, 41.
81. McFague, *Models of God*, 56–57.
82. McFague, *Metaphorical Theology*, 150.
83. McFague, *Models of God*, 56.
84. Ibid., 35.
85. Ibid., 47–48. Indeed, one of Kristeva's metaphors for woman is stranger. I will address her use of this metaphor in the next chapter but want to suggest that not only does Christian faith need to reach out to the outsiders and the strangers but the Christian community needs to listen to the voices of the strangers insofar as Western Christianity needs to recognize that both collectively and individually it is also estranged from itself. In so doing, the discourse of Western Christianity will be compelled to change.
86. Ibid., 40.
87. Mary Gerhart and Allan Russell, *Metaphoric Process: The Creation of Scientific and Religious Understanding* (Forth Worth: Texas Christian University Press, 1984).
88. Ibid., 98.
89. Ibid., 51.
90. Ibid., 59.
91. Ibid., 62, my emphasis.
92. Ibid., 63.
93. Ibid., 64.

94. Ibid.
95. Ibid., 94.
96. Ibid., 113.
97. Ibid., 119.
98. Ibid., 125–26.
99. Ibid., 129.
100. Ibid.
101. Ibid., 160.
102. Julia Kristeva, *Revolution in Poetic Language*, trans. Margaret Waller (New York: Columbia University Press, 1984), 131, 155. See also, for example, Julia Kristeva, *Desire in Language*, 17; 136–37 and Julia Kristeva, *Revolution in Poetic Language*, trans. Margaret Waller (New York: Columbia University Press, 1984), ix. Waller notes that *le sujet* is the speaking/thinking agent whose "identity, never become, ever becoming, questioned and questionable, is always on trial (*en procès*)."
103. Guberman, ed., *Julia Kristeva: Interviews*, 26.
104. Ibid. Anne-Marie Smith offers a helpful summary of what the "subject-in-process" means within Kristeva's work: "Like any subject the subject-in-process of writing is a subjectivity in revolt against constraint and against the signifier which announces fixed identity. So the subject's quest for identity, as subjectivity, brings into play a never-ending struggle between the social—the arena in which one can speak and be heard—and the need to speak one's singularity." See, *Speaking the Unspeakable*, 24.
105. Guberman, *Interviews,* 26.
106. Ibid., 37.
107. Ibid., 68, my emphasis.
108. Julia Kristeva, "Throes of Love: The Field of Metaphor," *Tales of Love*, trans. Leon S. Roudiez (New York: Columbia University Press, 1987), 276–77, emphasis in original.
109. Ibid., 268. Elsewhere she writes: "To transpose corresponds to the Greek *metaphorein*, to transport; language is, from the start, a translation, but on a level that is heterogeneous to the one where affective loss, renunciation, or the break takes place." See Julia Kristeva, trans. Leon S. Roudiez, *Black Sun: Depression and Melancholia* (New York: Columbia University Press, 1989), 41.
110. Kristeva, "Throes of Love: The Field of Metaphor," 274.
111. Ibid.
112. McFague, *Metaphorical Theology*, 133.
113. Reformist here is understood in the manner in which McFague defines it as follows: "Revolutionary feminists, however, propose that women's experience is the major source for 'naming' new religious metaphors and models that will be commensurate with that experience, a view not shared by the reformers. Revolutionary feminists are primarily concerned with the search for self-identity—the becoming of women—and for movement from nonbeing within the patriarchal model to a new naming of the self and the divine....Can an immanental, exclusively feminist perspective be absorbed into the Christian paradigm? It is doubtful, in my opinion, that it can be, nor is revolutionary feminist theology interested in making it commensurate with the tradition. *The critical act,*

at least from a reformist perspective, is to see the genuine insights it offers for needed revision in that paradigm" my emphasis. *Metaphorical Theology*, 155–56.

CHAPTER TWO

The Stranger in Our Midst: Sin, Abjection and Self-estrangement

Introduction

In the first chapter, I explored the potential for the role of metaphors in constructing theological models. In this chapter, I will examine closely two of Kristeva's key metaphors—the abject and the stranger—to help revitalize Christian theological reflection on the nature of sin, especially as it relates to the situation of women struggling with depression. In turn, I suggest that the work of pastoral counselors who provide care to women struggling with depression will be strengthened and enhanced when it is informed by Kristeva's metaphors of the abject and the stranger. How is this so? I believe that these metaphors expand and deepen a Christian understanding of sin thus leading to more expansive possibilities for healing.

Before examining Kristeva's writing, I will summarize the understanding of sin that informs this study. Then I will explore how Kristeva's metaphors of the abject—or abjection—and the stranger (sometimes referred to as the alien, the foreigner, or the voyager) bring new insights to this understanding, leading to important new applications relating to the female "subject-in-process." Even as her writings bring new insights to an understanding of sin, so they also shed new light on the rituals employed in Christian communities to absolve sin. In *Powers of Horror,* Kristeva explores the relationship of the abject to celebrations of the Christian Eucharist and rituals of confession as one way to resolve the condition of biblical abomination. In *Strangers to Ourselves*, she considers the recognition of the "stranger within" as a possible means to strengthen community and put an end to violence against the foreigner. Since Kristeva examines the role of the foreigner in religious communities, her insights, by extension, can be applied to contemporary Christian churches. These two texts serve as the primary focus for this chapter.

In concentrating on the metaphorical meanings of abjection and "the stranger," I will demonstrate, first, how Kristeva views the development of abjection from a secular meaning—filth—to a sacred one—defilement. I will look briefly at how this notion of abjection led to a replacement of the violence of sacred sacrifice with a ritual of purification, the most import of which is, for Kristeva, the Eucharist. As Cleo McNelly Kearns observes, the sacraments are central in Kristeva's psychoanalytic account of the Christian tradition.[1] Yet it is in the power of discourse—"the talking cure"[2]—that Kristeva locates the greater potential for healing and transformation. Here, her concern is with the liberating power of therapeutic discourse construed as confession. The question that I raise here and will return to in the fifth chapter is: How does Kristeva's interpretation of confession vis-a-vis the Eucharist offer sustaining power to liberate a woman's voice in order that her self-estrangement and depression can begin to heal?

Kristeva suggests that the terms exile, foreigner, stranger, and alien apply to women, for women live at the borders of society. They live at the borders of society because they do not have equal access to power with men. Thus, anyone who is "other," a stranger in our midst, confronts women "with the possibility or not of *being an other*."[3] In addition, life with "the stranger" confronts us with the fact that "[s]trangely, this foreigner lives within us: he is the hidden face of our identity, the space that wrecks our abode, the time in which understanding and affinity founder."[4] This "stranger within," I suggest, is a metaphor for a Christian understanding of sin as self-estrangement or self-alienation. Kristeva maintains, however, that recognizing this stranger within bears hope for the future disappearance of the stranger as foreigner—represented as an enemy on the outside. That is, once we have recognized the stranger who resides within (the contents of our unconscious mind), there will no longer be a need to direct violence at an enemy on the outside. Recognizing the stranger within is the foundation for reconciliation with an "other." A brief explanation of how sin is being understood here follows.

Sin: A State of Estrangement

I propose that an understanding of sin as a universal condition of alienation or estrangement is preferable to one which accentuates disobedience or rebellion, particularly for women who have internalized cultural and religious representations of abjection and exile.[5] Why? Disobedience and rebellion do not take psychopathology or the plight of one who has been subjected to intimate violence into serious consideration. Disobedience and/or rebellion emphasize volition with regard to sin, suggesting that individuals are always and at all times in control of their instincts while they simultaneously and consciously refuse God's gift of grace.[6] Thus, sin construed as disobedience and rebellion does not fully consider the realities of human experience or the differences that exist from person to person with regard to ability and capacity for choice. Moreover, sometimes the very actions deemed sinful may be what finally enable an abused woman to leave an abusive situation.

Against this view of sin as disobedience or rebellion, Paul Tillich views sin as estrangement, which "describes the disruption of an essential unity and consequently a destructive situation."[7] This view of sin as a disruption includes disruption of interpersonal relationships, self-relationships, human-divine relationships and community relationships in ways that lead to estrangement "in the communion of the knowing and the known, as well as of the loving and the loved."[8] Some feminist theologians, however, are not content with this understanding of sin as alienation or estrangement. Mary Potter Engel argues that these concepts are too vague to help women who are victims of abuse. She claims that sin is more accurately defined as a "distortion of the self's boundaries," "a perversion of love for another into false love or sentimentality," or "a distortion of the dynamic tension between freedom and dependence."[9] Her chief criticism of sin understood as alienation or estrangement is that it implies reconciliation with the abuser which suggests, for example, that "any victim who is struggling to create a separate identity for herself is wrong."[10]

In my view, her criticism is accurate only if reconciliation is understood solely as an event which occurs between a victim and one who perpetrates violence. Rather, reconciliation needs to be understood first and foremost as a healing of the self. This corresponds either to a disruption in the unity of a self or the distortion of a self's boundaries which need to be restored. As Tillich observes, reconciliation is one concept among a group of concepts including regeneration, redemption and atonement, justification and sanctification that "resists all attempts at precise definition and systematic ordering."[11] Each one of these concepts points to a type of healing of the distortion of a self's boundaries by "means of a different symbolic material and with a different emphasis"; reconciliation frequently "*designates the reunion of a personal or personified being with an object or a state of things and not with another person.*"[12] As noted in the previous chapter, no one model is ever complete or adequate. Nevertheless, for the purpose of this study, sin is understood as a condition of estrangement or alienation. The terms alienation and estrangement loom largely in Kristeva's writing. Anna Smith addresses, in part, why they do:

> [T]o renew thought, Kristeva believed that one must renew terminology; this is how to break out of the restrictive habits prescribed by the old definitions, for these terms used in new contexts come to have other meanings, possessing an alterity or novelty...the concept of estrangement...linked to Kristeva's discourse of exile...will take on resonances of the failure and subsequent renewal of identity and language.[13]

This recalls the manner in which Sallie McFague contends that metaphor works in theology. A discussion follows of how this understanding of sin may be expanded and deepened by Kristeva's metaphors of the abject and the foreigner or stranger.

Abjection: Women's Experience of Self-Estrangement in Christianity

Abjection: A Feminine Boundary of Alienation and Estrangement

According to Kristeva, living in a state of abjection is like living "at the border of my condition as a living being."[14] Thus "[t]he abject has only one quality of the object—that of being opposed to *I*."[15] The object referred to here is the lost or maternal object; according to Kristeva, it is lost during the process of language acquisition in the pre-oedipal triangle.[16] It is this oppositional quality of the abject which "perpetuates the bounds of the self."[17] The maternal object becomes identified with the abject as an infant becomes aware of the separation from its mother, and this is especially devastating for a female child, as the maternal object is the member of the oedipal triangle with whom she most closely identifies. To portray this self-identification, Kristeva associates abjection in its most elementary and archaic forms with the symptoms of bulimia which she describes as a type of food loathing:[18]

> Along with sight-clouding dizziness, *nausea* makes me balk at that milk cream, separates me from the mother and father who proffer it. "I" want none of that element, sign of their desire; "I" do not want to listen, "I" do not assimilate it, "I" expel it. But since the food is not an "other" for "me," who am only in their desire, I expel *myself*, I spit *myself* out, I abject *myself* within the same motion through which "I" claim to establish *myself*.[19]

It is only upon "abjecting" the mother's body both psychically and physically that the female child begins to develop a self. Thus a woman learns a form of self-loathing in the process of becoming a speaking subject.

As Noëlle McAfee notes, "while this [the abject] is termed primary repression, it is not a one-time event."[20] Why? The abject returns in "fleeting encounters, fleeting because we flee, horrified of falling back into the maternal body, where no difference—and thus no subjectivity—is possible."[21] This detail of "expelling myself" in order to become an "I" leads Kristeva to conclude that "it is thus that *they* see that 'I' am in the process of becoming an other at the expense of my own death....I give birth to myself amid the violence of sobs, of vomit."[22] Abjection is "death infecting life" which is caused not by a lack of cleanliness or health but by that which "disturbs identity, system, order."[23] This "death infecting life" is what Martha J. Reineke has termed "death-work," which is an elaboration of Freud's death drive.[24]

What is it that creates the disturbance? For Kristeva, it is the first loss experienced by a "subject in process" or the initial loss of the maternal object experienced in early childhood. Abjection of self then is a culminating experience for the speaking subject in which "it is revealed that all its objects are based merely on the inaugural *loss* that laid the foundations of its own being" so much so that abjection of self demonstrates that "all abjection is in fact recognition of the *want* on which any being, meaning, language, or desire is founded."[25] The "want" is the want of the mother who has to be "abjected" in order for her child to become a self. Without this want or experience of abjection, the boundaries of the self do not form and language is not acquired. Abjection, then, is the ultimate form of self-estrangement predicated upon the loss of the maternal object. Yet, according to Kristeva, identity formation and language acquisition will not occur unless a "subject-in-process" endures the trials of self-abjection.

Abjection is especially reflected in language, for that which has been abjected is the mother. It occurs when the child knows nothing except semiotic language, with all the experiences that come to expression in semiotic form.[26] Because the maternal object is first and foremost identified with the semiotic, the female child experiences the greatest self-estrangement. While Kristeva refers to the consequences of such self-estrangement in *Powers of Horror* in male pronouns, her continued use of the symptoms of bulimia are more suggestive of female experience: "Fear cements his compound, conjoined to another world, thrown up, driven out, forfeited. What he has swallowed up instead of maternal love is an emptiness, or rather a maternal hatred without a word for the words of the father; that is what he tries to cleanse himself of, tirelessly."[27] Fear "permeates all words of language with nonexistence...ghostly glimmer."[28] Finally, "discourse will seem tenable only if it ceaselessly confront[s] that otherness...a deep well of memory that is unapproachable and intimate: the abject."[29] This ceaseless confrontation is the substance and essence of what happens in the therapeutic conversation—an encounter with the abject. Because it is permeated by fear, language fails women struggling with depression; therefore, that which is most needed for the healing of self-estrangement is often inaccessible. The journey out of abjection occurs through a relationship based on love which involves the transformation of the subject.[30]

In psychoanalytic terms, the abject, for Kristeva, becomes "the 'object' of primal repression" or "the ability of the speaking being, always already haunted by the Other, to divide, reject, repeat."[31] Abjection is then, a "precondition of narcissism" or a "kind of narcissistic crisis."[32] This is so because it is at the place of yearning for the maternal object that "desire expatriates the *ego* toward an *other* subject and accepts the exactness of the ego only as narcissistic."[33] Narcissism is "never the wrinkleless image of the Greek youth in a quiet fountain"; rather, it "appears as a regression to a position set back from the other, a return to a self-contemplative, conservative, self-sufficient haven."[34] What precipitates this narcissistic crisis? Kristeva identifies two possible origins—either "too much strictness on the part of the other" or the "lapse of the other"—both of which give rise to an appearance of the abject "in order to uphold 'I' within the Other. The abject is the violence of mourning for an 'object' that has always already been lost."[35] Thus the "subject-in-process/on-trial" will not become an "I" without this experience of abjection—an experience of mourning for the lost maternal object. This is significant for religion and religious discourse since abjection "persists as *exclusion* or taboo...but drifts over to more "secondary" forms such as transgression....It finally encounters, with Christian sin, a dialectic elaboration, as it becomes integrated in the Christian Word as a threatening otherness."[36] I suggest that this "threatening otherness" which Kristeva identifies in the

Christian Word–sin–foreshadows the alien place that women often occupy in Christian discourse that both feels alien and, in fact, alienates them. This experience of alienation, often an experience of self-alienation, contributes to women's struggle with depression.

Abjection: Alien Language or the Root of Women's Depression

We have seen thus far that, for Kristeva, the maternal (or feminine) is associated with the abject. An experience of the abject is an experience of primal repression without which a "subject in process" is unable to acquire language or become a self. But a price is paid for this. The abject becomes, in Western Christianity, an experience of "threatening otherness" which locates the feminine within the discourse about sin.

For Kristeva, it is the lost, mourned, maternal object or a "confrontation with the abject" that sets verbalization in motion because a child stops nursing and the mouth that was once filled with the mother's breast is now filled with words that elaborate upon a painful loss or want, and "the aggressivity that accompanies it, by *saying*....Language learning takes place as an attempt to appropriate an oral "object" that slips away."[37] Thus, the move to symbolic language is an act of rejection, replacing the original orality with a new orality based on verbalization. While Kristeva does not elaborate upon this reference to her mother here, there is a brief allusion to her memory of her mother in childhood in "Stabat Mater" which describes vividly her own experience of being enveloped with maternal love (prior to separation) as well as the experience of the violence and hatred of the abject:

> Concerning that stage of my childhood, scented, warm, and soft to the touch, I have only a spatial memory....Fragrance of honey, roundness of forms, silk and velvet under my fingers, on my cheeks. Mummy. Almost no sight–a shadow that darkens, soaks me up, or vanishes amid flashes. Almost no voice in her placid presence. Except, perhaps, and more belatedly, the echo of quarrels: her exasperation, her being fed up, her hatred.[38]

Since this commentary appears in the left-hand column of "Stabat Mater" where Kristeva writes in a very personal style about her own experience of giving birth, I suggest that this is one brief literary allusion to her own experience of abjection as a child. This is significant since it occurs in a text which locates the experience of abjection within Christian discourse. Here, Kristeva heralds her description of melancholia in *Black Sun*.[39]

As Kristeva notes, "discourse is substituted for maternal care" and there is an "ascendancy of the Other" which "takes over where narcissism leaves off"; fear and fascination are the results.[40] Abjection is, finally, a "limit that turns the speaking being into a separate being who utters only by separating,"[41] and this raises the question for Kristeva: "How does such a limit become established without changing into a prison?"[42] She continues her discussion at this point by describing how the condition unfolds in an analytic transference relationship. It is the "first authentic feeling of a subject in the process of constituting itself."[43] For the borderline patient, the limit becomes a prison which Kristeva calls "a fortified but empty castle." Abjection is overcome by learning to overcome fear and falsehood (false selves) in a process of object-relating which raises desire. She states: "When the fortified castle of the borderline patient begins to see its walls crumble, and its indifferent pseudo-objects start losing their obsessive mask, the subject-effect—fleeting, fragile, but authentic—allows itself to be heard in the advent of that interspace, which is abjection."[44] On the one hand, then, the person who has not journeyed out of abjection lives with what Kristeva calls a "powerless outside"; on the other hand, there is an "impossible inside." This limit of abjection, I contend, is a prison for all women in a Western—particularly Christian—culture since all women are potential mothers and the maternal body represents what is prohibited. As we shall see in the next section, there Kristeva pinpoints a direct association between the feminine and the abject in Christian discourse in language used to describe sin.

To illustrate the self-alienating effects of abjection, Kristeva introduces the borderline patient, in a discussion that has direct bearing on the possible roots of depression—especially, for those women who struggle with it who have been raised in the various cultures of Western Christianity.[45] For the borderline patient, there is a disconnection or dissociation from meaningful object relations as well as drive representations (i.e., *eros* and *thanatos*).[46] Language is thus alien to the borderline patient for whom

> [o]nly seldom is metaphor included in his speech; when it is, more than with anyone else, it is a literal one—to be understood as metonymy for unnameable desire. "I displace, therefore you must associate and condense for me," says such an analysand, who, in short, is asking the analyst to build up an imagination for him.[47]

A rebirth or passage from the void that is abjection results from "a speech that is recovered, rediscovered as belonging to him."[48] Elsewhere Kristeva has commented that she is interested in borderline situations of subjectivity—abjection, for example—for "we are all involved in pathology...we pass through abjection or melancholy."[49] This is noteworthy because Kristeva's analysis of the speech of the borderline patient is directly applicable to the speech of the depressed as she frequently uses these terms interchangeably. Some individuals, however, get stuck in these borderline situations; it is these very same individuals who come seeking help from clergy of whom this project speaks. Attentiveness to the themes and questions Kristeva raises will, I believe, enable the "stranger" to find and use her voice. She will be able to assert her strength without relinquishing her place of difference. How does Kristeva perceive religion's answer to abjection?

Abjection and the Maternal: From Filth to Sacred Defilement

The religious answer to abjection and the limit it represents is defilement, taboo or sin.[50] While Kristeva's writing on this subject is, to an extent, a revision of Freud's *Totem and Taboo*,[51] this will not be my focus here. Rather, my concern is a woman's place in religious discourse which Kristeva describes as a "*confrontation with the feminine* and the way in which societies code themselves in order to accompany as far as possible the speaking subject on that journey. Abjection or the journey to the end of the night."[52] Kristeva's primary concern here is not the manner in which the mother-son incest prohibition contributes to the structure of the social order.[53] Instead she is concerned here with the manner in which the self develops as it confronts the abject (feminine) as well as with what occurs when the sacred confronts and codes the feminine as abject in religious ritual. The experience of abjection as noted above is not a one-time event; therefore her continuing interest in the development of the abject, particularly within Christianity, is related to the journey that each "subject in process" takes through abjection in order to become a self. For women, especially, it is often a journey that does not lead to the "end of the night" but to the despair of melancholy.[54]

A few words regarding how Kristeva uses Freud are necessary at this point in order to follow her argument. She claims: "If the *murder* of the father is that historical event constituting the social code as such, that is, symbolic exchange and the exchange of women, its equivalent on the level of the subjective history of each individual is therefore the *advent of language*."[55] If one accepts Freud's thesis (and Kristeva's) that the prohibition against the murder of the father as well as mother-son incest constitutes the beginning of the social code, then the advent of language constitutes the beginning of the history of a "subject-in-process." This is important when related to the feminine place in discourse, since, as Kristeva informs us, the mother is categorized as abject.[56] "Warding off danger" is central to the task of religious rituals founded on the prohibition; they function to "ward off the subject's fear of his very own identity sinking irretrievably into the mother."[57]

The abject or filthy object is excluded and becomes sacred defilement on the basis of a religious prohibition. Defilement "is what is jettisoned from the '*symbolic system*.'"[58] What is excluded as filthy represents in some fashion a boundary or a limit which if crossed would threaten the inner and outer boundaries of a speaking subject.[59] Kristeva asks: "Why does *corporeal waste*, menstrual blood and excrement, or everything that is assimilated to them, from nail-parings to decay, represent—like a metaphor that would have become incarnate—the objective frailty of symbolic order?"[60] Her answer leads us to the "war between the sexes" in that "ritualization of defilement is accompanied by a strong concern for separating the sexes, and this means giving men rights over women."[61] Whereas tears and sperm, even though they belong to the physical borders of the body, have no polluting value, menstrual blood which signifies sexual difference is viewed as a threat to phallic power; consequently the other sex, the feminine, becomes synonymous with radical evil.[62] While menstrual blood is associated with life and the incest taboo, excrement represents death and decay or the taboo against murder. It is also linked to the maternal or feminine inasmuch as "maternal authority is experienced first and above all, after the first essentially oral frustrations, as sphincteral training."[63] This is significant because it defines the maternal space or authority—where language is acquired—as something already defiled; language then sets up a separation and an order which represses maternal authority.[64]

Food, for Kristeva, is perhaps the most archaic form of abjection. Is it also identified with the feminine? Food has polluting value only as an oral object and to the "extent that orality signifies a boundary of the self's clean and proper body. Food becomes abject only if it is a border between two distinct entities or territories" (i.e., nature/culture; human/nonhuman).[65] How is it related to the maternal? She asserts: "[F]ood is the oral object (the abject) that sets up archaic relationships between the human being and the other, its mother, who wields a power that is as vital as it is fierce."[66] Thus, menstrual blood, excrement, and food are linked to the maternal and are abject.[67]

The pure/impure distinction in Kristeva's economy is not archetypal. It describes the process of differentiation of the "subject-in-process" as summarized in the following observation she makes with regard to the Indian caste system:

> The pure/impure opposition represents (when it does not function as metaphor) the striving for identity, a difference. It appears instead of *sexual difference*...it acts as a *separating value* peculiar to the symbolic function itself (sacrificer/sacrifice/God; subject/thing/meaning). The hierarchy founded on the pure and the impure displaces (or denies) the difference between the sexes; *it replaces the violence of sacrifice with the ritual of purification.*[68]

In other words, the "subject-in-process" differentiates from the maternal object during sphincteral training which, in Kristeva's view, involves the struggle or "trial" for a "clean and proper self."[69] The mother, however, is also associated with menstrual blood or impurity; the violence felt toward her is either displaced or denied through a ritual of purification in the ideal. In reality, however, she is still often the victim of violence. Thus, mother, who needs to be cleansed herself, is responsible for the speaking subject's development of a "clean and proper self." The key here is Kristeva's emphasis on the impure/pure distinction in relation to difference, differentiation and identity. More will be said about Kristeva's understanding of the ritual of purification later in this chapter, but the important point here is her association between the abject as it relates to what is impure and the striving for identity which is a striving for separation from the abject, the feminine or the maternal. The maternal is loathed; therefore, the maternal often experiences the violence of sacrifice.[70]

In her reading of *Oedipus at Colonus*, Kristeva notes that there is a first estrangement introduced between knowledge and the Law. This is significant because, "*I who knows am not the Law*;" and therefore, "If the Law is in the Other, my fate is neither power nor desire, it is the fate of an estranged person: my fate is death."[71] Thus, abjection is assigned to the person who is not identified with the Law. If, in the former examples (menstrual blood, excrement, food), recourse is made to rituals to purify abjection, it is "in the *sayings* of Oedipus concerning divine Law as well as Theseus that [abjection] is assumed."[72] Now, the issue is not exclusion (as it was in the case of defilement) but the charge of transgression. Thus, in the estrangement of knowledge and the Law, a "bridge has been built toward another logic of abjection: it is no longer defilement to be excluded ritually as the other facet of the sacred (social, cultural, one's own) but *transgression* due to a misreading of the Law."[73] What, then, corresponds to the purification effected by ritual? It is the ability to speak out of this abjection:

> The border between abjection and the sacred, between desire and knowledge, between death and society, can be faced squarely, uttered without sham innocence or modest self-effacement, provided one sees in it an incidence of man's particularity as *mortal and speaking*. "There is an abject" is henceforth stated as, "I am abject, that is, mortal and speaking."[74]

It is here that Kristeva begins to trace the interiorization of the abject. Defilement is no longer a threat from the outside but the inside. Transgression is a result of one's misdeeds or transgressions of the Law. A "subject-in-process/on-trial" is a knowing and speaking subject. Estrangement results when there is a separation or disconnection between what one knows and what one does.

Abjection: From Sacred Defilement to Sin

The background for Kristeva's discussion of a Christian understanding of sin is provided by her discussion of "biblical abomination," particularly as it appears in the Hebrew Bible. As she understands it, the biblical view on impurity

> is permeated with the tradition of defilement...it *points to* but does not *signify* an autonomous force that *can* be threatening for divine agency. I shall suggest that such a force is rooted, historically (in the history of religions) and subjectively (in the structuration of the subject's identity), in the cathexis of maternal function—mother, women, reproduction.[75]

The Levitical code accents the impure over and against the pure, describing the distance or separation between God and people. Therefore, "the place *and* law of the One do not exist without a *series of separations* that are oral, corporeal...relating to fusion with the mother."[76] There is a movement away from murder understood as religious sacrifice to sacrifice which is also governed by rules and prohibitions. At the center of the prohibitions, one finds objects related to the maternal (e.g., food, menstrual blood) that cause impurity. Blood becomes "a fascinating semantic crossroads, the propitious place for abjection where *death* and *femininity*, *murder* and *procreation*, *cessation of life* and *vitality* all come together."[77]

The place of abjection converges on the maternal because the logic of separation identifiable in the Levitical code "persists in positing an agency that is *other* than that of the nutritious, the sanguine, in short the 'natural' maternal."[78] The abject, with its religious, sacred overlay orders the cult, controls desire and directs the drives. Thus, "[t]he abject tears me away from the undifferentiated and brings me into subjection to a system."[79] The "subjective interiorization of abjection" is an accomplishment of the New Testament. Citing the work of René Girard, Kristeva suggests that through the death and resurrection of Christ, "sin is visited upon all members of the community...it thus prepared them for a...society without violence."[80]

In reality, we do not inhabit a society without violence. The association of the maternal object with the abject in religious discourse results in a continuing identification of women with defilement, waste and transgression. In turn, women continue to be the victims of violence. Women occupy a "strange" place and are estranged from themselves and the community as a result. As noted above they are "dirty" and thus loathed while at the same time they are responsible for the success or failure of a nascent subject's struggle for a "clean and proper self." The discourse of Western Christianity continues to situate women in the place of the abject, therefore contributing to an oppression that often leads to their struggles with depression. Even though Christian discourse is partially responsible for women's oppression and their subsequent silence, Kristeva's understanding of the importance of rituals of purification as well as Christian confession and the Eucharist point to the potential positive value in religious discourse (even if these Christian rituals no longer work for her on a personal level). A discussion of these Christian rituals follows.

Abjection: From Sin to Religious Rituals of Purification

Kristeva theorizes that, when Christ breaks with the Jewish taboos (e.g., table fellowship with the unclean), "a new arrangement of differences is being set up, an arrangement whose economy will regulate a wholly different system of meaning, hence a wholly different speaking subject...[A]bjection is no longer exterior. It is permanent and comes from within."[81] Citing numerous examples from the gospels (e.g., Mark 7:6, Matthew 15:11), she focuses on Jesus' criticism of the Pharisees that their faith is centered on outward appearances (suggesting too close of a link with orality) rather than inward transformation. This means that the threat to the speaking subject now comes from within: "For evil, thus displaced *into* the subject, will not cease tormenting him from within, no longer as a polluting or defiling substance, but as the ineradicable repulsion of his henceforth divided and contradictory being."[82] The focus in Christianity, as in Judaism, still centers on orality which the New Testament attempts to "rehabilitate by rendering it guiltless."[83] Thus it isn't what enters a person from the outside that leads to defilement but what comes forth from the inside of a person which renders him or her impure. (See for example, Matthew 15:11 and 23:27–28.)

In her analysis of the story of the Syrophenician woman in Mark 7, Kristeva asserts that "[t]he nutritive opening up to the other, the full acceptance of archaic and gratifying relationship to the mother...is here the condition for another opening—the opening up to symbolic relations, true outcome of the Christic journey."[84] With regard to a Christian understanding of sin, then, "[s]wallowed up, one might say reabsorbed, Christian defilement is by that token a revenge of paganism, a reconciliation with the maternal principle."[85] Though reunited with the speaking subject, this maternal principle is not finally rehabilitated in the New Testament nor by Christian theology according to Kristeva. What is accomplished is the shift from a quest after what defiles to a search within that identifies error in thoughts and speech.[86]

Thus, in the Christian context, it is no longer a substance but an action on the part of the speaking subject which leads to impurity. Kristeva analyzes the miracle stories in Mark of the multiplication of the bread and fish (Mark 6:38–44 and 8:14–21). In their context, these two miracle stories serve as bookends to Jesus' discourse on what defiles a person. This is significant insofar as the action of multiplication itself is no longer what is important but rather satisfying hunger aimed at the spirit and the *meaning* of Jesus' action is of utmost importance. She links the multiplication of loaves to her understanding of the Eucharist (which is influenced by the Roman Catholic concept of transubstantiation) concluding that the narrative of the Eucharistic prayer "by surreptitiously mingling" the themes of "devouring and satiating" tames the tendency toward cannibalism even as it "invites a removal of guilt from the archaic relation to the first pre-object (ab-ject) of need: the mother."[87] Thus the pre-cognitive desire to devour the maternal object is satisfied by pure nourishment from the *body* of Christ. Why is this important?

Kristeva locates the significance of the Eucharist in a primal fantasy of devouring the abject (the mother). In this way, the interiorization of impurity becomes complete in Christianity through the celebration of the Eucharist. How is this so? Kristeva suggests that the "*division* within Christian consciousness finds in that fantasy [devouring the mother], of which the

Eucharist is the catharsis, its material anchorage and logical node. Body and spirit, nature and speech, divine nourishment, the body of Christ, assuming the guise of a natural food (bread), signifies me both as divided (flesh and spirit) and infinitely lapsing."[88] Humanity is infinitely lapsing or sinful. Sin "remains the only token of difference from the sublimity of Christ...even if its remission is always promised, [sin] remains the rock where one endures the human condition as separate."[89] One means of ritual purification is accomplished through communion which "temporarily gives back innocence....To eat and drink the flesh and blood of Christ means, on the one hand, to transgress symbolically the Levitical prohibitions, to be symbolically satiated...and to be reconciled with the substance dear to paganism."[90] The maternal which was "abjected" or vomited up is swallowed once again. Is the sin which is released feminine?

Kristeva answers with a qualified yes: "The brimming flesh of sin belongs, of course, to both sexes, but its root and basic representation is nothing other than feminine temptation."[91] Considering the story of the Fall in Genesis, there are two possibilities: "The one locates it in relation to God's will and in that sense causes it to be not only original but coexistent with the very act of signification; the other places it within the femininity-desire-food-abjection series." In at least one sense, then, *Powers of Horror* traces the relationship of the feminine to the abject or what is eventually interiorized as sin. Adam's sin can be read as consuming desire both for food (the fruit of the tree) and woman (sexual covetousness). Here Kristeva's reading of Christianity is that it "does not cut off the abject" as "Christian sin ties its spiritual knot between flesh and law."[92] Abjection is also the "requisite for reconciliation, in the mind," because it occupies the place "between the flesh and the law."[93]

Conversely, release from if not remission of sin happens in the speech act. That is, "'[c]onfessing sins,' 'remitting sins'—such phrases are probably liturgic in origin, but in themselves they already define sins as *inherent in speech* and slated for *release*."[94] Confession, though, involves more than acknowledging and remitting sins, for there is also the act of bearing witness:

> *I acknowledge* and *I bear witness*: in those terms Christians *confess*, hence avow their faith in Christ, as they will later their trinitary [*sic*] faith. Already Christ had "confessed" in this way before Pontius Pilate. The avowal of faith is thus from the very start tied to persecution and suffering....Speech addressed to the other, not sinful speech but the speech of faith, is pain; this is what locates the act of *true communication*, the act of avowal, within the register of persecution and victimization.[95]

As avowal of faith occurs within this register of persecution and victimization, it follows that there is a profound link between the speech of faith and the experience the maternal.[96] An avowal of faith is a powerful speech act, as it "brings my most intimate subjectivity into being for the other."[97] Kristeva relates this to ascetic monastic practices (i.e., bewailing, prayer, atonement and confession) emphasizing that speaking is a necessity for the remission of sins. This is because it completes the interiorization of sin (a form of abjection), and "with the ultimate interiorization of sin within discourses, by the final postulate that does away with an offense because of its enunciation before the One. An enunciation that amounts to a denunciation."[98]

While Kristeva may appear here to undermine the power of the speech act known as confession—viewing it as a denunciation in a negative sense—it is not the case that she deems confession to have little value. Rather, her concern is the abuses which have occurred in the history of the church as a result of the practice of confession—abuses which include condemnation, censorship and other forms of punishment that exacerbate the suffering of the one who confesses. Nevertheless, Kristeva acknowledges that "on the fringes of mysticism, or in rare moments of Christian life," it is possible for "the most subtle transgression of law, that is to say, the enunciation of sin in the presence of the One," to "reverberate not as a denunciation but as the glorious counterweight to the inquisitorial fate of confession."[99] These occasional moments which Kristeva designates as "glorious counterweights" to the Church's abuses of confession, especially during the Inquisition, are to be found in signs or painting, music and words. Citing Mark 16:17,—"And these signs shall follow them that believe; in my name shall they cast out devils; *they shall speak with new tongues*,"—she concludes that speech or "spoken sin as fortunate" locates power not in a judging God but in discourse itself; hence "the Word became flesh."[100] While, in her view, Christianity has suffered a crisis which has transferred that power of speech from the priest to the therapist, Kristeva does not claim that the power of Word cannot be reclaimed in religion.

Powers of Horror is a study of the development of abjection as it relates to the religious and social coding of women. Abjection becomes filth which in turn becomes defilement, which leads eventually to ritual purification and matricide. Calling this her Rosetta stone, Reineke contends that Kristeva demonstrates why violence against women is intractable in a sacrificial economy that is exemplified by Western Christianity.[101] Reineke is particularly interested in the lives of female medieval mystics and notes that the very bodies of women "carry potential for order and meaning" as well as "disorder and chaos" so much so that "[m]enstruation, reproduction, and aging all testify to the triumphs and tragedies of existence."[102] How does this lead to violence against women? Reineke asserts that "because religions choose symbols not only to distinguish order from disorder, but also to effect order and control disorder, the female bodies are associated most closely with life and death processes, *authority asserted over their bodies is power asserted over the very forces of creation.*"[103] Reineke's summation of the female situation echoes Kristeva's analysis of biblical abomination. This authority asserted over female bodies in the name of religion continues to contribute to women's oppression. In order to help women succeed in their struggles against oppression and the depression that ensues from it, we first need to understand their situation of powerlessness.

The maternal matrix represents a boundary for a nascent subject and as a result is forever associated with or identified with the abject. Any woman—as a potential mother—is linked permanently to what is defiling, estranging or sinful. Even so, Kristeva recognizes that the female body and the maternal can be gazed at without loathing as long as "we recognize ourselves as always already altered by the symbolic—by language," and provided that "we hear in language—and not in the other, nor in the other sex—the gouged-out eye, the wound, the basic incompleteness that conditions [our] indefinite quest."[104] Thus, if language creates an initial estrangement, it is also language which provides the way out of the abject or "journey to the end of night" and which will finally resolve the oppression women have experienced as a direct result of their association with the abject. Where does this journey take us? For Kristeva, the journey through language enables us to identify and welcome the stranger within.[105] In order to understand how welcoming this stranger within assists women out of the double-bind Kristeva identifies, it is first necessary to consider what she means by the stranger. For this, we turn to her more recent work, *Strangers to Ourselves.*[106]

A Woman's Liberation from Self-Estrangement: Recognition of the Stranger Within

Woman: A Silent Stranger in a Foreign Land

In *Strangers to Ourselves*, Kristeva writes compellingly about the stranger with her own experience as a foreigner in France always in the background.

The foreigner represents consciousness of difference,[107] a border,[108] is a "stranger to his mother,"[109] experiences hatred,[110] does not speak one's mother tongue—"that language of the past that withers without ever leaving you,"[111] and is often, legally speaking, an alien.[112] The realm in which the foreigner resides is one between two languages or the realm of silence: "It is not the silence of anger that jostles words at the edge of the idea and the mouth; rather it is the silence that empties the mind and fills the brain with despondency, like the gaze of sorrowful women coiled up in some nonexistent eternity."[113] Kristeva alludes here to her earlier work in *Black Sun*, focusing on the loss of a mother-tongue, and silence as the realm where sorrowful women reside gazing out at the rest of the world but not participating in it. Here is clear evidence of the melancholia and depression that results from the absence of a language which represents women's experience. It may not be readily apparent how the identification of the stranger or foreigner provides a pathway out of abjection for women since, thus far, the "stranger" still seems to situate women in a place which is no place; that is, in the realm of sorrowful silence between two languages. What may be said, however, is that the experience of being a foreigner or homeless is universal for both men and women.[114]

In essence, the foreigner belongs to no place, no particular time, and no particular love. The only protective shield which exists for the foreigner or stranger is indifference.[115] This indifference, often interpreted as aloofness, "is only the resistance with which he succeeds in fighting his matricidal anguish."[116] No matter what the individual differences are, Kristeva suggests that foreigners (who have chosen to live as exiles) "add to their passion for indifference a fervent extremism that reveals the origin of their exile. For it is on account of having *no one* at home against whom to vent their fury...they wander about the world, neutral but solaced for having developed an interior distance from the fire and ice that had seared them in the past."[117] The development of this interior or emotional distance from every relationship that stirs emotional pain (since it is a reminder of the lost mother), leads the foreigner to become a "[m]elancholy lover of a vanished space"[118] or a "dreamer making love with absence, one exquisitely depressed."[119]

Kristeva further differentiates foreigners into two irreconcilable groups determined by the manner in which they live out their attachment to a lost space (the first of which for all individuals is the maternal matrix). There are the ironists who "waste away in an agonizing struggle between what no longer is and what will never be—the followers of neutrality, the advocates of emptiness."[120] There are also the believers who "transcend: living neither before nor now but beyond, they are bent with a passion that although tenacious, will remain forever unsatisfied."[121] These believers who long for another always promised land often ripen into skeptics.[122] The foreigner as believer, especially the female believer, is of most concern in this study.

While the foreigner is continuously aware of emptiness and/or unsatisfied desire, this sense of absence (a wandering in space) is balanced by the occasional meetings in which foreigners engage. Such meetings are "[a] crossroad of two othernesses...a mutual recognition...[which] owes its success to its temporary nature."[123] Kristeva's images of the encounters between foreigners are reminiscent of a Eucharistic feast, a hospitality ritual, especially in that the encounter begins with table fellowship:

> The meeting often begins with a food fest: bread, salt, and wine. A meal, a nutritive communion. The one confesses he is a famished baby, the other welcomes the greedy child....But this table corner, where they gulp with such pleasure, is covered with the paths of memory...the hospitality merrymakers also become united for a while through the spirit.[124]

In *Powers of Horror*, the Eucharist was represented as a "communion" which could remit the feminine abject or sin. Kristeva returns to this theme in *Strangers to Ourselves*, emphasizing that this banquet, which occurs outside of time, is for the foreigner, a utopia.[125] It is a utopia owing to the strange familiarity of the words, a nutritive communion which includes confession and a unity in the spirit.

That this depiction of a meeting contains religious allusions is more than coincidental. In fact, upon her own arrival in France on Christmas Eve, 1965, Kristeva attended midnight mass.[126] Her first meeting as a foreigner, then, was just such a nutritive communion. In an interview Kristeva states: "Foreigners must confront a ghost from the past that remains hidden in a secret part of themselves."[127] This meeting, I suggest, may have been a confrontation of her own ghost from the past, one perhaps associated with taking communion with her father before dawn in Saint Nedelia's.[128] In any event, her portrayal of the meeting of foreigners in language reminiscent of the Eucharist supports Cleo McNelly Kearns' view that, even "as the sacraments are at the heart of Christian ecclesiastical tradition, so they are at the heart of Kristeva's psychoanalytic and structuralist account of that tradition. Indeed her own strategies of analytic listening and aesthetic play are seldom more acute than when directed to sacramental practices and their rationales."[129] Kearns cites, for example, the chapter in *Powers of Horror* in which Kristeva's analysis of

Confession and Communion shows them to be at least partial means for "redeeming" the maternal.

I suggest that, in *Strangers to Ourselves*, "the meeting" carries forward a Eucharistic motif as metaphor. Concerned with feminist sacramental theology, Kearns suggests, following Aquinas, that a sacrament is "a sign or seal of a sacred thing" or, in a Kristevan fashion, that it "creates a *sujet en procès*."[130] While the ability of the Eucharist to create a subject-in-process overstates the case, I do believe, as Kristeva suggests, that Communion has the potential to assist a "foreigner" in her confrontation of a ghost from her past, one that resides in the unconscious. Insofar as Communion is a "sign of a sacred thing," it has transformative power to assist a subject-in-process.

Everyone, Kristeva asserts, has the experience of being a foreigner even if only temporarily as a tourist. What is the power or meaning of this experience? She claims that the "metaphorical value of the word 'foreigner' first leads the citizen to a feeling of discomfort as to his sexual, national, political, professional identity. Next it impels him to identify—sporadically, to be sure, but nonetheless intensely—with the other."[131] The native feels guilty about the hatred which is stirred up inside by the mere presence of the foreigner. Identification with the foreigner is a conscious act made to assuage the guilt and restore one's own "clean and proper self." It isn't just acceptance of the other which is crucial but an ability to *be in the other's place.* Confrontation with the foreigner leads, then, to a confrontation with the ghost from the past and an ability to "imagine and make oneself other for oneself."[132]

Noting that foreigners, being uprooted, create symbolic communities, Kristeva finds a basis for the emergence of religious fundamentalism within communities of exiles as

> "the religion of the abandoned forbears is set up in its essential purity and one imagines that one preserves it better than do the parents who have stayed 'back home.'...Fundamentalists are more fundamental when they have lost all material ties, inventing for themselves a 'we' that is purely symbolic; lacking a soil it becomes rooted in ritual until it reaches its essence, which is sacrifice."[133]

If in our more mobile and open societies individuals continue to feel more and more like excluded foreigners, they may invent a symbolic "we" based on a sacrificial ritual. In other words, they invent a "we," one in which women are often victimized because this "we-ness" is often founded on a sacrificial economy—one which has matricide as an organizing principle.

Kristeva believes that the reason an individual chooses existence as a foreigner is related to the "dark origins" of the life and death drives. Abandoning one's maternal tongue and native land are choices made in the service of repressing the insatiable love for a lost mother and the hatred, in a woman's case, is born toward herself. Concerning the origin of a foreigner—family, blood, and soil—she proclaims that the foreigner is a "courageous and melancholy betrayer" of her origin. Moreover, "[h]is origin certainly haunts him...but it is indeed *elsewhere* that he has set his hopes, that his struggles take place, that his life holds together today. *Elsewhere* versus the origin, and even *nowhere* versus the roots...the absconder is an orphan consumed by his love for a lost mother."[134] Those that now wander as foreigners without a voice or a language to express their pain, are setting their hopes "elsewhere" because "they are consumed by love for a lost mother." They reside in an "impossible elsewhere" but belong nowhere. Again, the emphasis on a lost mother as well as the repetition of melancholy, maternal tongue, dead language, and dead mother[135] recall Kristeva's thesis in *Black Sun*. Foreigners play a key role in revitalizing religion especially, according to Kristeva, when "a people" has an "ethical concern." Thus "[t]he image of the foreigner comes in the place and stead of the death of God and, with those who are believers, the foreigner is there to bring him back to life."[136] In other words, the image of the foreigner as the stranger provides a boundary that serves to solidify the identity of a community, even if that boundary suggests anxiety, dread, exile, and/or hatred. What happens when that foreigner is a woman? The woman is an object of intense loathing.

While the abject is closely linked to the feminine and the maternal for Kristeva, the experience of a foreigner is a universal one. Abjection is a form of estrangement, but so too, is the experience of a foreigner.[137] It is helpful at this point to recall how Kristeva differentiates between abjection and the uncanny strangeness of being a foreigner; abjection is: "[e]ssentially different from 'uncanniness,' more violent, too, abjection is elaborated through a failure to recognize its kin; nothing is familiar, not even the shadow of a memory."[138] While the limit that a foreigner represents may strengthen a community's identity, the foreigner pays a high price. For like the maternal abject object, the foreigner is often the focus for displaced rage and violence. If our discussion of Kristeva's association in *Powers of Horror* of the woman (as actual or potential mother) with the abject showed how women are especially subject to depression, her portrayal of the foreigner in *Stranger to Ourselves* enables us to see how women may, in a similar manner, be the object of rage and violence.[139]

Foreigners: Representation of a Facet of Violence

In Kristeva's view, foreigners represent an "intrusion of the *other* in the homogeneity of a family or a group."[140] Group identity is achieved by excluding what is dissimilar. At first, it might appear that the position of difference is the goal of human autonomy; yet, in the end the foreigner is a stranger who challenges identity.[141] At the "dawn of civilization," the first foreigners, the Danaïdes, were women. Their legend represents the end of an endogamous society (i.e., marriage within the group) and the beginning of an exogamous one (i.e., marriage with outsiders). More important, however, "the very ambivalence [the legend of the Danaïdes] ascribes to those foreigners recognized the necessity for the violence of passion (or, on the social plane, the validity of extirpation, or wrenching away, of foreignness itself) as foundation for the basal family alliance."[142] Thus, strangeness or foreignness is the political facet of violence which underlies civilization. Strangeness was the mark of women who as brides were viewed as foreigners; it demarcates the beginning of antagonism between the sexes and continues to connect women with the abject, the foreign and violence/sacrifice.[143]

Over time, the designation "foreigner" or "stranger" became associated with "the barbarian" who was identified with moral inferiority; the term came to refer exclusively to evil, cruelty and savageness.[144] Kristeva traces the meaning of the word through ancient Greek civilization and demonstrates how the Stoics changed the meaning of foreigner (i.e., a foreigner was one who was unable to interpret the laws of Providence and therefore, an exile) while also exhibiting a certain acceptance and/or tolerance of foreigners through a type of "conciliation" (*oikeiosis*). These gains foreshadowed the early Christian understanding of *agape* in that "[t]he distinction of the *other* is immediately outweighed by the apology of the *self* within an ethics that caught a glimpse of otherness only to deny it."[145] The practice of accepting foreigners into the polis led to the establishment of

> "identifying criteria that transcended politics by putting forward cultural and symbolic factors. With such criteria...Christianism was founded by preaching to foreigners, merchants, and fringe elements. But nascent Christianism was no longer located within the bounds of the city; instead, it appealed to an invisible spiritual community: *the Ecclesia took the place of the Polis.*"[146]

The hopefulness that Kristeva perceives with the recognition of the stranger, begins with tolerance of the dissimilarity that necessarily occurs in an *Ecclesia* that gives the exogamous principle a spiritual valence, one that transcends all artificial boundaries. This is a hopefulness that can be sought in a Christian community, at least in the ideal. Violence did not, however, come to an end with this extension of the Stoic "conciliation" towards the foreigner; neither has it ceased today.

The Stranger as Pilgrim and the Reality of Estrangement

Kristeva locates the foundation of Christian hospitality in Yahweh's covenant with Israel. She provides a brief word study of "stranger" in Hebrew before analyzing the story of Ruth, noting that the Hebrew *ger*, "stranger," is problematic in that it includes the sense of "convert." She distinguishes between two types of strangers or foreigners: (1) the foreigner who retains his (*ger* is masculine) identity as foreigner but follows Hebrew law; and (2) the foreigner who is naturalized by converting to Judaism.[147] This differentiation of two types of foreigners is confirmed in *A Hebrew and English Lexicon of the Old Testament*;[148] however, *ger* is translated primarily as a "sojourner," indicating a temporary presence only intimated by Kristeva in her observation that the first type of resident stranger who is obedient to Hebrew Law nonetheless retains his foreign identity. The English translation is mostly a literal rendering of her French, which, however, would have been strengthened had the translator chosen the word "sojourner" over "stranger."[149] The choice of sojourner would further strengthen her case that the Christian community of faith was bounded by its strangeness even though it had no physical borders, as it was conceived as an invisible spiritual community.

Moreover, Kristeva associates the foreigner with wandering. In this regard, the story of Ruth is significant for her, as it supports her view of the movement from defilement attributable to a substance from the outside of a person in Judaism to Christianity's understanding of sin as something coming from within. As a Moabite, Ruth introduces an element of foreignness into the very roots of Jewish royalty, reminding "those unable to read that the divine revelation often requires a lapse, the acceptance of radical otherness, the recognition of a foreignness that one might have tended at the very first to consider the most degraded."[150] Kristeva's reading of Ruth's sojourn recalls the notion of the abject as related to a primal fantasy of devouring (evoking yet again a Eucharistic image). She states:

> The faithful devour the foreigner, assimilate him and integrate him under the protection of their religion's moral code, which both integrator and integrated support. Covered by such religious ideals, devouring fantasies are not expressed and the guilt they might give rise to is avoided....If David is *also* Ruth, if the sovereign is *also* a Moabite, peace of mind will then never be his lot, but a constant quest for welcoming and going beyond the other in oneself.[151]

This sets the stage for her discussion of estrangement in Paul (and Augustine) and begins to illuminate why the recognition of the stranger (and the stranger's voice) provides a helpful solution to those already identified as abject, alien, estranged and foreign.[152] Using 1 Corinthians 9:20 as a springboard, Kristeva sets out to define the Christian community as one which is already *other*, that is, "a community of those who were different, of foreigners who transcended nationalities by means of a faith in the Body of the risen Christ."[153] The composition of the Christian community consisted of sojourners: people on the margins of society, women and foreigners "who remained bound to their native culture, nevertheless created among themselves *bonds* of solidarity, mutually welcoming each other in holy places where, precisely, the foreigner was safe from any affront."[154] This may help to explain why women have sought safety within the Church despite the fact that it is frequently an inhospitable place for women. More important, "as the foreigner is Christ himself, to welcome him is to be welcomed in God."[155] Hospitality is central to the definition of the community's identity. Kristeva cites numerous passages from the Pauline corpus to support her point that there is no exclusion in the ecclesial community founded by Paul; rather there is a new creation where all are citizens and saints.[156]

In her discussion of the therapeutic potential in Paul's presentation of exile and pilgrimage, Kristeva asks: "What was there in the ecclesiastical community thought up by Paul that could have sufficient appeal to weld the foreigners of that heterogeneous universe?"[157] By way of an answer, she suggests that Paul perceived a link between the Church, the Risen Christ, and the Eucharist. Kristeva suggests that Paul did more than address the material discomfort of foreigners, he also "spoke to their *psychic* distress and he proposed, instead of an insertion in a social set aimed at satisfying their needs, a journey between two dissociated but unified spheres that they could uncover in themselves: a journey between 'body' and 'soul.'"[158] Kristeva identifies this as a better solution than others available at the time (Eastern religions and/or legal appeals) because "the Pauline church assumed the foreigner's passion-inspired division, deeming his being torn apart between two worlds to be a split less between two *countries* than between two *psychic domains* within his own impossible unity."[159] The wandering engaged in by this sojourner was not from one geographic place to another but rather a wandering that took place between flesh and spirit, life and death. The "we" of community is formed only as a result of "that splitting that all wanderers are urged to discover within themselves and in others, after they first recognized themselves in Christ."[160] Thus, Kristeva credits Paul with being both an adept politician and psychologist.

As far as Paul's psychological intuitions are concerned, the words which "stage" the Church—Resurrection and Eucharist—become therapeutics of exile and distress. This leads Kristeva to claim that the Church is founded "on the logic of desire in which one is led to identify with a splitting that henceforth is no longer dangerously set (like the foreigner's melancholy distress), but is, thanks to Christ, experienced as a transition toward a spiritual liberation starting from and within the concrete body."[161] This theme of splitting brings to mind the manner in which Kristeva describes the "woman-mother" in *Powers of Horror* (and "Motherhood According to Giovanni Bellini" which will be discussed in chapter four). Here, then, the resurrected Christ is experienced as a solution for healing the splitting each subject-in-process experiences. The celebration of the Eucharist, the internalization of his body and blood, may therefore be understood as a reconciliation with the lost maternal object precisely because it includes a primal fantasy of devouring.[162] In effect, Christ restores what was originally lost. The subject-in-process and on-trial—an emerging subject of desire—is now embarked upon a journey. The experience of this journey, says Kristeva, is "not that of a material tourism, but a *theory* of spiritual contemplation and mutation."[163] This sets the stage for her discussion of the reunion that is the antithesis of estrangement.

Here, Kristeva looks briefly at Augustine, maintaining that "[t]he adventure he advocated could not do without the two focuses: estrangement and reunion, want and desire—and never one without the other."[164] The journey begun with Paul now becomes a pilgrimage, one which transforms the foreigner into a religious pilgrim. The differences that compose strangeness "in love are not to be erased but forgiven."[165] The wandering of the pilgrim (as opposed to the sojourner or foreigner) is now a gift called *caritas*. This means that "[t]he alienation of the foreigner ceases within the universality of the love for the other."[166] Moreover, "[i]dentification with the absolute subject, Christ, brings foreigners together."[167] Such *caritas* "is not dependent upon reciprocity and cannot be understood in the realm of debt, dependency, and gratitude."[168]

However, this ideal faded quickly as human needs began to conflict with the absolutes of religion and states or nations in such a way that the "fate of the foreigner in the Middle Ages—and in many respects also today—depended on a subtle, sometimes brutal, play between *caritas* and the political jurisdiction."[169] Once again, the foreigner would become a boundary or a "borderline." This time, however, boundaries were drawn along the lines of Christianity. Instead of the universality that was originally intended, generosity or hospitality was limited to those foreigners who were Christian.

Kristeva identifies two prevalent attitudes towards foreigners by the time of the Middle Ages: (1) a Christian one "with its advantages and abuses, now protective, then persecutive"; and (2) a political one that "was modified along with the evolution of feudalism toward a centralized feudal State which submitted the foreigner to economic demands...(either, 'the foreigner is in excess,' or 'we need the foreigner')."[170] The stranger, always a foreigner was often a target of abuse, both political and religious. In effect, the foreigner is both excluded and responsible for exclusion particularly along religious boundaries since

> "dissidence within the faith was perceived as a political threat against this new, certainly fragile unit, which was no longer the polis but the empires....Religious transcendency...was, from the start, subjected to the political interests with which one religion identifies as against the others. One foreigner drives out the other."[171]

There was and continues to be a differentiation between "settled" and "temporary foreigners." Today we call the settled strangers resident aliens.[172] Although the experience of being a resident alien is not limited to women, even those who reside in their "mother land" are resident aliens to the extent that they are associated with what is abject.

Why should we be concerned with the status of the foreigner? Because "we are all in the process of becoming foreigners in a universe that is being widened more than ever, that is more than ever heterogeneous beneath its apparent scientific and media-inspired unity."[173] Differences such as sex, age, profession, or religion are not one and the same with foreignness, although they may "support it or add to it."[174] A foreigner is in essence defined by being excluded from a "social group structured about a given kind of political power."[175] Insofar as women in a Western Christian culture have only limited access to political power, they remain foreigners.

From Pilgrim to Voyager

Kristeva continues her discussion of the stranger by presenting other historical images of foreignness from the Renaissance through the Enlightenment, noting, for example, that the sojourn which had become a pilgrimage now becomes a voyage.[176] While the voyager role was associated with exploration, especially over uncharted seas, it was quickly applied, metaphorically, to an inner process. This idea of voyager as metaphor is used by one of Kristeva's interpreters, Anna Smith, to describe a privileged place for women:

> "Her constant moving from place to place that enables her to view everything as strange may actually help her to mediate more productively the relation between body and language. Accordingly, she must keep the subjective unity of the 'I' in a productive tension with the strangeness of what Kristeva calls 'maternal rhythm.'"[177]

Thus, the female voyager is the female intellectual who travels in space, time, and language who "[h]aving a closer contact with the mother's body...[is a] potential advocate of the mother-tongue's pluralising of meaning."[178] In other words, the female voyager's relationship to the abject maternal body or place of strangeness grants her a certain privilege; she is no longer estranged from language but lives as an exile or foreigner within it. This presents the opportunity for new meanings to be opened up in language. Kristeva's own voyage into this strangeness leads finally to a discussion of Freud's essay on the uncanny (or *unheimliche*).[179] The confrontation with death, with the contents of repression, is in Kristeva's understanding a confrontation with the feminine as we shall see.

The Stranger Within: An Uncanny Strangeness

At the end of her own voyage into strangeness, Kristeva meets with Freud. She comments on Freud's own wandering and his encounters with political and cultural foreignness:

> Freud's personal life...conditions his concern to face the other's discontent as ill-ease in the continuous presence of the "other scene" within us. My discontent in living with the other—my strangeness, his strangeness—rests on the perturbed logic that governs this strange bundle of drive and language, of nature and symbol, constituted by the unconscious, always already shaped by the other. It is through unraveling transference—the major dynamics of otherness, of love/hatred for the other, of the

> foreign component of our psyche—that, on the basis of the other, I become reconciled with my own otherness-foreignness, that I play on it and live by it.[180]

As McAfee observes, this strangeness is "the cause and effect of our own self-formation."[181] Her understanding of the uncanny in Kristeva's thought is helpful here:

> [T]he uncanny strangeness of abjection is not only a side-effect of (primary) repression but is itself a mechanism by which the I is formed and maintained. The abject not only threatens the I, it constitutes it, setting bounds of the self. By pushing one out of the *chora* (undifferentiated being) into the symbolic realm, it allows one to experience difference, where subjectivity becomes possible, where one enters into language and the economy of desire.[182]

Recognizing the stranger within is the journey, voyage, or pilgrimage of a subject-in-process. In light of this observation, Kristeva raises the question upon which a sense of hopefulness is founded: "How could one tolerate a foreigner if one did not know one was a stranger to oneself?" Hence the title for her work, *Strangers to Ourselves.* Already in this question, Kristeva alludes to the power of the word spoken and heard in love.[183] At this point, however, the question serves to launch her discussion of *unheimlich* in Freud's writing.

Citing Freud, Kristeva notes that "'the uncanny is that class of the frightening which leads back to what is known of old and long familiar,' which, as far as Freud was concerned, was confirmed by Schelling who said that 'everything is *unheimlich* that ought to have remained secret and hidden but has come to light.'"[184] An investigation into uncanny strangeness is, for Kristeva, "an investigation into *anguish* generally speaking and, in a fashion that is even more universal, into the *dynamics of the unconscious.*"[185] The *other* is not an enemy on the outside but is one's own and proper unconscious (the impossible inside) that may be tainted by strangeness. The language Kristeva employs here is reminiscent of the language of abjection from *Powers of Horror.* Thus, "[a]bjection is the expression of both a division (between the subject and its body) and a merging (of self and Other, the social)."[186] Moreover, "the builder of the *other* and in, the final analysis, of the *strange* is indeed repression itself and its perviousness."[187] What circumstances lead to repression and thus the experience of uncanny strangeness when the repressed is brought to light? For Kristeva, the most important is confrontation with death. This is because the

> "fear of death dictates an ambivalent attitude: we imagine ourselves surviving (religions promise immortality), but death just the same remains the survivor's enemy, and it accompanies him in his new existence. Apparitions and ghosts represent that ambiguity and fill with uncanny strangeness our confrontations with the image of death."[188]

In addition to the confrontation with death, Kristeva adds the confrontation with the feminine as experiences which lead to repression. Consistently, Kristeva demonstrates that the maternal and the feminine are associated with negativity, the repression of which leads to self-estrangement.

Anna Smith notes that Freud's understanding of uncanny is central to Kristeva's understanding of estrangement; *unheimlich* translated literally from the German is "unhomely." She points out: "Infinitely more powerful than any intellectual sensation of novelty, uncanniness has a more visceral quality capable of arousing irrational responses in the individual."[189] Kristeva and Smith both remark upon the significance of the womb, which, in Freud's essay, is a first home that later evokes a fear of being buried alive. This leads to an association of the mother's body with estrangement and death.[190] Uncanny strangeness is linked to anguish but it does not merge with it. Thus, if "anguish revolves around an *object*, uncanniness...is a *destructuration of the self* that may either remain as a psychotic *symptom* or fit in as an *opening* toward the new, as an attempt to tally with the incongruous."[191] An "opening toward the new" is significant since it suggests that through this opening the foreigner as *other* might be tolerated.

Kristeva proposes that "uncanniness occurs when the boundaries between *imagination* and *reality* are erased. This observation reinforces the concept...of the *Unheimliche* as a crumbling of conscious defenses, resulting from the conflicts the self experiences with an other."[192] We encounter what is estranged from the self (through repression) as a result of an encounter with an other—a stranger, a foreigner. We are estranged not from the foreigner (on the outside) but from that which was once familiar but has been repressed (a self-estrangement). A reunion with this portion of the self is what allows for a potential end to one's self-alienation or estrangement, of the foreigner within.

This does not, however, erase the association of women with that which is "strange," and this as potential victims of violence. On the contrary, to the extent that a woman-mother represents that which has been repressed, she is the object of violence designed to prohibit the return of that which was repressed. In other words, her victimization is very much a symptom of the self-alienation of the "other." As Kristeva describes the encounter with the foreigner, it is typically violent, comprised of a catastrophic aspect. Instead of recognizing that the foreigner is oneself, one depersonalizes the foreigner, abjecting it as other. Thus, while "we cannot suppress the symptom that the foreigner provokes...we simply must come back to it, clear it up, give it the resources our own essential depersonalizations provide, and only thus soothe it."[193] Unfortunately, recognition that our depersonalization of the foreigner is a depersonalization of ourselves is not the sole or even primary response individuals have when confronted by the foreigner. Individuals who have power, for example, are likely to respond very differently. For those with "acknowledged power and a resplendent image," uncanniness "is changed into management and authorized expenditure: strangeness is for the 'subjects,' the sovereign ignores it, knowing how to have it administered."[194] This abjection of one's own uncanny strangeness, one's own repressed self, introduces the possibility of acting from paranoia, producing mental impoverishment and, in more extreme forms, overt acts of murder.[195] We have the ability to choose how we respond "when we are assailed by the strange." We can choose whether "to worry or to smile." How we decide "depends on how familiar we are with our own ghosts."[196]

Kristeva concludes her discussion of uncanny strangeness by reflecting on the "stranger within us." Encounters with foreigners do not arouse the same level of terrifying anguish which is "provoked by death, the female sex, or the 'baleful' unbridled drive."[197] Thus, by recognizing that the foreigner is within us, we are invited "not to reify the foreigner, not to petrify him as such" but to "discover our disturbing otherness."[198] That is, "If I am a foreigner, there are no foreigners."[199]

On Recognizing "The Stranger's Voice"

What makes Kristeva's discussion of "the stranger within us" important for a pastoral theology for women struggling with depression? It illustrates how the foreigner is the return of the abject which in the end is associated with the woman-mother. It suggests how the maternal object is implicated in the self-alienation that is illumined by the metaphor of the stranger. Kristeva's brief answer to this question lies in her response to an interview question:

> I am very attached to the idea of the woman as irrecuperable foreigner...starting with this permanent marginality, which is the motor of change. I think that for me femininity is exactly this lunar form, in the way that the moon is the inverse of the sun

> of our identity. From this point of view, perhaps we women have it more than the men, but the men have it also. And to try to preserve this part as unreconcilable permits us perhaps always to be what Hegel called the eternal irony of the community. That is to say, a sort of separate vigilance that keeps groups from closing up, from becoming homogenous and so oppressive. That is, I see the role of women as a sort of vigilance, a strangeness, as always to be on guard and contestatory.[200]

Women themselves treat the "feminine" as the stranger within them—as somehow alien—and therefore, know the importance of being vigilant against such self-alienation. Men, on the one hand, may be able to project this self-alienation and attack violently the woman-mother they have repressed. On the other hand, women are all potential mothers so the woman-mother they repress is themselves leading to an intensified self-alienation that manifests itself in depression, a form of self-inflicted violence. When women claim their voices, they serve a role that guards against oppression and violence, even as they speak from their individual and unique positions of foreignness.

By retracing Kristeva's steps through abjection and strangeness, I have attempted to demonstrate how the traditional metaphors used to describe women in both Christian and psychoanalytic discourse occupy a negative and marginalized space that is associated with the maternal body. Yet the metaphor of the stranger, while it may be a bane, also proposes a blessing for women when they speak and their voices are recognized. "The stranger" offers the possibility of bringing to an end the experience of foreignness for all people. As Anna Smith observes,

> unless those marginalised by culture *speak* their marginalisation, they remain trapped in narcissism. Women and aliens for instance have the potential to enrich cultural life because they stand for difference, yet without the resources of language creatively or analytically disposed, their potentially subversive signs of difference melt away.[201]

Ironically, just what the "stranger" needs most—language and a voice—often fails her. It is the task of the pastoral theologian or pastoral care-giver to help restore the voice that has been lost or worse never been developed. In order to do this, we need to allow ourselves to be "affected by the estranging qualities of abjection." As Smith contends: "For unless analysts and critics permit their discourse to be affected by the estranging qualities of abjection, then speech will not be transformative, renewing or sublime, but will block the productive forces that have assisted in its birth."[202] This applies to pastors and pastoral counselors as well. We have an opportunity to renew speech in Christian community through relationships that are founded in love, but first we need to recognize the stranger within. The potential that Anna Smith identifies for women to enrich cultural life remains as yet untapped; it does so in part, I suggest, because, as Kristeva contends, there is an absence of a maternal discourse. Some might want to argue that the solution lies in the introspective process of psychotherapy. Without a language to give voice to the process, however, the woman remains "coiled up in some nonexistent eternity."[203] Her solution will be explored in the fourth chapter. In the next chapter, I will examine her depiction of women and the feminine as described by the "melancholic-depressive composite." These are the women who remain silent, gazing sorrowfully at the world from their place which is nowhere.

Notes

1. Cleo McNelly Kearns, "Kristeva and Feminist Theology," *Transfigurations: Theology and the French Feminists*, eds. C. W. Maggie Kim, Susan M. St. Ville, Susan M. Simonaitis (Minneapolis: Fortress Press, 1993), 71.
2. Julia Kristeva, "Within the Microcosm of 'The Talking Cure'," in *Psychiatry and the Humanities: Interpreting Lacan*, vol. 6, trans. Thomas Gora and Margaret Waller, eds. Joseph H. Smith and William Kerrigan (New Haven: Yale University Press, 1983), 33–48.
3. Julia Kristeva, *Strangers to Ourselves*, trans. Leon S. Roudiez (New York: Columbia University Press, 1991), 13.
4. Ibid., 1.
5. Mary Potter Engel, "Evil, Sin and Violation of the Vulnerable," in *Lift Every Voice: Constructing Christian Theologies from the Underside*, eds. Susan Brooks Thistlethwaite and Mary Potter Engel (New York: Harper and Row, 1990), 157. For example, she writes: "Many battered women are trapped in abusive relationships because they have been raised to believe that disobedience to their husbands is unbiblical and sinful....Our children also suffer when we define sin as disobedience. One of the most indelible lessons children learn at home, school and church is 'Honor thy father and thy mother.' Because this is often the only notion of sin drilled into them, they find it hard to understand, let alone resist, the violent and violating actions of their parents or other elders toward them."
6. Nancy J. Ramsay, "A Story of Freedom's Corruption: Sin as a Response to the Human Condition," in *Theology and the Interhuman: Essays in Honor of Edward Farley*, ed. Robert R. Williams (Valley Forge: Trinity Press International, 1995), 204.
7. Paul Tillich, "Estrangement and Reconciliation in Modern Thought," *The Meaning of Health*, ed. Perry LeFevre (Chicago: Exploration Press, 1984), 2.
8. Ibid.
9. Engel, "Evil, Sin and Violation of the Vulnerable," 160–63.
10. Ibid., 160.
11. Tillich, "Estrangement and Reconciliation in Modern Thought," 1.
12. Ibid., my emphasis.

13. Anna Smith, *Julia Kristeva: Readings of Exile and Estrangement* (New York: St. Martin's Press, 1996), 20.
14. Julia Kristeva, *Powers of Horror: An Essay on Abjection,* trans. Leon S. Roudiez (New York: Columbia University Press, 1982), 3.
15. Ibid., 1.
16. Julia Kristeva, *Black Sun: Depression and Melancholia,* trans. Leon S. Roudiez (New York: Columbia University Press, 1989), 27–28. Or, Kristeva, *Powers of Horror,* 32.
17. Noëlle McAfee, "Abject Strangers: Toward an Ethics of Respect," in *Ethics, Politics, and Difference in Julia Kristeva's Writing,* ed. Kelly Oliver (New York: Routledge, 1993), 118.
18. *Diagnostic and Statistical Manual of Mental Disorders,* 4th ed., (Washington, DC: American Psychiatric Association) 539; "Anorexia Nervosa is characterized by a refusal to maintain a minimally normal body weight. Bulimia Nervosa is characterized by repeated episodes of binge eating followed by inappropriate compensatory behaviors such as self-induced vomiting; misuse of laxatives, diuretics, or other medications; fasting; or excessive exercise."
19. Kristeva, *Powers of Horror,* 2–3.
20. Noëlle McAfee, "Abject Strangers: Toward an Ethics of Respect," 118.
21. Ibid.
22. Kristeva, *Powers of Horror,* 3.
23. Ibid. See also, Elizabeth Gross, "The Body of Signification," in *Abjection, Melancholia and Love: The Work of Julia Kristeva,* eds. John Fletcher and Andrew Benjamin (New York: Routledge, 1990), 80–103; especially pages 86–93 where she discusses "abject bodies." Her reading of Kristeva supports my interpretation.
24. Reineke, *Sacrificed Lives,* 25. Reineke claims to take her cue from Kristeva citing an essay published in 1983, "Within the Microcosm of the 'Talking Cure'," in *Psychiatry and the Humanities: Interpreting Lacan,* vol. 6, trans. T. Gora and M. Waller, ed. Joseph H. Smith and William Kerrigan, (New Haven: Yale University Press, 1983), 33–48. Commenting on Freud's term "death drive" or "death instinct," Reineke states: "I prefer the term *death-work. Death-work,* unlike other words that Kristeva summons to define the labor of the unconscious, emphatically evokes the social and cultural landscape crucial to the functions of negativity. The term *death-work* serves as a reminder that the human practice of absence, a worldly elaboration by the subject of alterity, estrangement, and lack, is oriented toward mortality. In the face of the subject's desire for the fullness of being, which humans historically have linked with immortality, the subject finds that full presence forever eludes it." (25)
25. Kristeva, *Powers of Horror,* 5.
26. See also Cleo McNelly Kearns, "Kristeva and Feminist Theology," *Transfigurations: Theology and the French Feminists,* 65. She offers a concise statement differentiating between the symbolic and the semiotic which are key concepts in Kristeva's work: "*Symbolic,* for Kristeva, describes the rational, conscious, socially negotiable level of a signifying practice, while *semiotic* describes its corporeal, associative, less conscious, and more drive-patterned other face." Kearns acknowledges that "these terms can be very confusing to Anglo-Americans, for whom the term *symbol* carries a good deal of the

connotations of materiality, associative meaning, and sensuality that Kristeva would place on the side of the semiotic." Once one understands how Kristeva is using them, however, it is clear why she associates the semiotic with the maternal object as experienced in the first years of life, and the symbolic with paternal qualities of rationality, low, and conscious processes.

27. Kristeva, *Powers of Horror*, 6.
28. Ibid.
29. Ibid.
30. Kristeva, *In the Beginning Was Love*, 3; for example: "This mobilization of two people's minds and bodies by the sole agency of the words that pass between them sheds light on Freud's famous remark, in *The Future of an Illusion,* that the foundation of the cure is 'our God Logos.' It also recalls the words of the Gospels: 'In the beginning was the Word' (John 1:1) and 'God is love' (1John 4:8)." See also Rebecca Chopp's "From Patriarchy into Freedom," in *Transfigurations: Theology and the French Feminists*, eds. C. W. Maggie Kim, Susan M. St. Ville, Susan M. Simonaitis (Minneapolis: Fortress Press, 1993), 39. Chopp maintains that transformation of subjectivity not adaptation or restitution is central in Kristeva's works.
31. Kristeva, *Powers of Horror*, 12.
32. Ibid., 13–14.
33. Ibid., 14, Kristeva's emphasis. Kelly Oliver's discussion in *Reading Kristeva: Unraveling the Double Bind* (Indianapolis: Indiana University Press, 1993), 55–57, of the "abject mother" is helpful here. She notes that the abject is something repulsive, a relationship to a boundary and "threatens the unity/identity of both society and the subject." This threat has its origins in "what has been prohibited by the Symbolic order, what has been prohibited so that the Symbolic order can be. The prohibition that founds, and yet undermines, society is the prohibition against the *maternal body*, (my emphasis) whether it is the oedipal prohibition against incest formulated by Freud, the prohibition against the mother's desire...formulated by Lacan, or the prohibition against the semiotic chora formulated by Kristeva. All of these prohibitions are directed against the maternal body....On the level of personal archeology, abjection shows up as the struggle to separate from the maternal body." (55–56) For Kristeva, as Oliver notes: "Human life, human society, is founded on the abject separation of one body from another at birth. This separation, like subsequent ones, is labored but necessary. This primary separation, which founds and prefigures symbolic separation, is prior even to the maternal authority that separates the infant's body into drives and satisfactions. The prototypical abject experience, then, is the experience of birth itself. It is at the birth of the child, and not before, that the identity of the human subject is most visibly called into question. Before the umbilical cord is cut, who can decide whether there is one or two?" (57)
34. Kristeva, *Powers of Horror*, 14.
35. Ibid., 15.
36. Ibid., 17.
37. Ibid., 41.
38. Kristeva, "Stabat Mater," *Tales of Love*, 250.

39. I will return to this experience in the next chapter.
40. Kristeva, *Powers of Horror*, 45.
41. Ibid., 46.
42. Ibid.
43. Ibid., 47.
44. Ibid., 48. "Subject-effect" in this instance may be understood as desire for the opposite sex or more generally, as desire for an object relation.
45. See Christie Cozad Neuger, *Counseling Women* (Minneapolis: Fortress Press, 2001), 149–177. She cites statistics that indicate twenty-five percent or more of all women will struggle with depression at some point in their lives. Neuger emphasizes that those who counsel with these women need to "find ways to deconstruct the diminishing and disempowering messages fed to women that destroy self-esteem and agency and work in a myriad of ways against the possibility of abundant life for women." (170) One of those diminishing and disempowering messages is the association of the feminine with the abject.
46. Kristeva, *Powers of Horror*, 49.
47. Ibid., 50.
48. Ibid. It is curious to me that Kristeva, here, describes the speech of a male patient since a borderline diagnosis is more often (i.e., 75% of the time) rendered for women. This could be a result of the fact that she views experiences of abjection, love and melancholia as borderline situations which everyone must pass through as part of the struggle to become a self.
49. Guberman, *Interviews*, 30.
50. Kristeva, *Powers of Horror*, 48.
51. Kearns, "Kristeva and Feminist Theology," *Transfigurations*, 57.
52. Kristeva, *Powers of Horror*, 58–59. Feminine in this context is understood by Kristeva as "far from being a primeval essence," it "is a coming face to face with an unnameable otherness—the solid rock of jouissance and writing as well."
53. Elizabeth Gross, "The Body of Signification," 86–87. She highlights the difference between Freud and Kristeva as follows: "What is new about Kristeva's position is her claim that what must be expelled from the subject's corporeal functioning [the abject] can never be fully obliterated but hovers at the border of the subject's identity, threatening apparent unities and stabilities with disruption and possible dissolution. Her point is that it is impossible to exclude the threatening or anti-social elements with any finality. They recur and threaten the subject not only in those events Freud described as the 'return of the repressed'—that is, in psychical symptoms—they are also a necessary accompaniment of sublimated and socially validated activities, such as the production of art, literature, and knowledges, as well as socially unacceptable forms of sexual drives."
54. Woman's depression and melancholia will be addressed in the next chapter. Kristeva does suggest, in part, that a woman is more susceptible to these conditions "because a woman cannot have a mother-substitute as an object of desire in the way that a man can." Kelly Oliver, *Reading Kristeva*, 64 and Kristeva, *Black Sun*, 81–83.
55. Kristeva, *Powers of Horror*, 61.
56. Ibid., 64.

57. Ibid.
58. Ibid., 65.
59. Ibid., 69.
60. Ibid., 70.
61. Ibid.
62. Ibid. 71.
63. Ibid.
64. Ibid., 72. While the maternal and the feminine are not synonymous in Kristeva's thought, in her description of the social coding of women as abject, all women are viewed as potential mothers. See also, Elizabeth Gross, "The Body of Signification," 92. As Gross observes: "The cultural horror of menstruation...is not straightforwardly linked to the horror sexual *difference*. Menstruation does not simply differentiate female from male; rather it marks the differences between men and *mothers* (or potential mothers). The horror of menstruation links women to a (presumed) natural maternity without acknowledging women's sexual specificity. Menstrual blood is the living matter that helps to sustain and bring forth life. Horror of menstrual blood is a refusal to acknowledge the subject's corporeal link to the mother. It is a border separating one existence, the mother's body, from another, the foetus, which both is and is not distinct from it. It marks the site of an unspeakable and unpayable debt of life, of existence, that the subject (and culture) owes to the maternal body."
65. Kristeva, *Powers of Horror*, 75.
66. Ibid., 75–76.
67. She discusses the Indian caste system, *Oedipus the King* as well as *Oedipus at Colonus*, the transgression of the Levitical code in Judaism and the concept of Christian sin. See especially, Chapters Three and Four in *Powers of Horror*.
68. Kristeva, *Powers of Horror*, 82.
69. Reineke, *Sacrificed Lives*, 97.
70. Ibid. 73, 86. Reineke's thesis is: "linguistic and cultural codes, especially religion, are structured by a sacrificial economy oriented toward matricide." (73)
71. Kristeva, *Powers of Horror*, 87.
72. Ibid., 88.
73. Ibid.
74. Ibid.
75. Ibid., 91.
76. Ibid., 94.
77. Ibid., 96.
78. Ibid., 103.
79. Ibid., 111.
80. Rene Girard, *Des Choses cachees depuis la foundation du monde* (Paris: Grasset, 1978), 203–05, as cited in Kristeva, *Powers of Horror*, 111. See also Donald Capps, *The Child's Song: The Religious Abuse of Children* (Louisville: Westminster John Knox Press, 1995), 68.
81. Kristeva, *Powers of Horror*, 113.

82. Ibid., 116.
83. Ibid., 114.
84. Ibid., 115. Kristeva interprets this passage as a mother-daughter reconciliation that occurs when the mother simultaneously opens her heart up to Christ and "fills" her daughter with a privileged food—one supposes the Word of Christ.
85. Ibid., 116.
86. Ibid., 117.
87. Ibid., 118.
88. Ibid.
89. Ibid., 120.
90. Ibid., 119.
91. Ibid., 126.
92. Ibid., 127.
93. Ibid., 127–28.
94. Ibid., 120.
95. Ibid., 129.
96. I will focus on the need for a maternal discourse in Christian discourse in the fourth chapter.
97. Kristeva, *Powers of Horror*, 129.
98. Ibid., 130.
99. Ibid., 131.
100. Ibid.
101. Reineke, *Sacrificed Lives,* 32, 96.
102. Ibid., 108.
103. Ibid., my emphasis.
104. Kristeva, *Powers of Horror*, 88–89.
105. Ibid., 177. Reineke's reading of the stranger supports this conclusion.
106. Julia Kristeva, *Strangers to Ourselves*, trans. Leon S. Roudiez (New York: Columbia University Press, 1991).
107. Kristeva, *Strangers to Ourselves*, 1.
108. Ibid., 4.
109. Ibid., 5.
110. Ibid., 13.
111. Ibid., 15.
112. Ibid., 41.
113. Ibid., 16.
114. Kristeva's various interpreters agree on this point. See for example, Anna Smith, *Julia Kristeva: Readings of Exile and Estrangement* (New York: St. Martin's Press, 1996), 97; Noëlle McAfee, "Abject Strangers: Toward an Ethics of Respect," *Ethics, Politics, and Difference in Julia Kristeva's Writing*, ed. Kelly Oliver (New York: Routledge Press, 1993), 116–34.
115. Kristeva, *Strangers to Ourselves*, 7.
116. Ibid., 9.

117. Ibid.
118. Ibid.
119. Ibid., 10.
120. Ibid.
121. Ibid.
122. Ibid.
123. Ibid., 11.
124. Ibid.
125. This is particularly significant for women as will be demonstrated in the next chapter. Women live in a time that Kristeva identifies as monumental or eternal as opposed to the linear time of history.
126. Marilyn Edelstein, "Metaphor, Meta-narrative, and Mater-Narrative in Kristeva's 'Stabat Mater,'" in *Body/Text in Julia Kristeva: Religion, Women, and Psychoanalysis*, ed. David Crownfield (Albany: State University of New York Press, 1992), 46. In note three, Edelstein cites Kristeva's "My Memory's Hyperbole," trans. Athena Viscusi, in *The Female Autograph*, ed. Domna C. Stanton, Special Issue, *New York Literary Forum* 12–13 (1984): 263.
127. Guberman, *Interviews*, 4.
128. Ibid., 138.
129. Cleo McNelly Kearns, "Kristeva and Feminist Theology," *Transfigurations: Theology and the French Feminists*, 71.
130. Ibid., 75.
131. Kristeva, *Strangers to Ourselves*, 19.
132. Ibid., 13.
133. Ibid., 24.
134. Ibid., 29–30.
135. Ibid., 36.
136. Ibid., 40.
137. McAfee, "Abject Strangers," 122–23. Her interpretation of Kristeva supports this position: "she is not discussing xenophobia...for she is not describing a *fear* of foreignness as much as a *dread* of foreignness....Dread (or anxiety) signals an encounter that threatens the border between undifferentiated being and subjectivity." And, "Kristeva is describing the foreigner in a way that recalls the abject. While she never explicitly equates the foreigner with the abject, she gives ample room for such a reading."
138. Kristeva, *Powers of Horror*, 5. Although more will be said later in this chapter regarding Kristeva's understanding of uncanniness, a brief citation of what she means here will suffice: "that which *is* strangely uncanny would be that which *was* (the past tense is important) familiar and, under certain conditions (which ones?), emerges. A first step was taken that removed the uncanny strangeness from the outside where fright had anchored it, to locate it inside, not inside the familiar considered as one's own and proper, but the familiar potentially tainted with strangeness and referred (beyond its imaginative origin) to an improper past. The other is my ('own and proper') unconscious." See Kristeva, *Strangers to Ourselves*, 183.

139. There is general agreement among Kristeva scholars that the experience of being a female (or of femininity) is closely associated with being a foreigner or an exile and the object of violence. This occurs as a direct result of Kristeva's own experiences as a foreigner in France. See chapter four in Anne-Marie Smith, *Julia Kristeva: Speaking the Unspeakable* (Sterling, VA: Pluto Press, 1998).
140. Kristeva, *Strangers to Ourselves*, 41.
141. Ibid., 42.
142. Ibid., 46. Kristeva notes that the bride in Greece was always thought of as a foreigner or suppliant—a suppliant before the gods. The status of the Danaïdes was never assured and their father Danaüs, even though he received a home, recognized that they were never fully assimilated into the Greek *polis*.
143. Ibid.
144. Ibid., 51.
145. Ibid., 59.
146. Ibid., 63.
147. Ibid., 68.
148. Francis Brown, S. R. Driver, Charles A. Briggs, ed. *A Hebrew and English Lexicon of the Old Testament* (Oxford: Clarendon Press, 1951), 158. See also, William L. Holladay, ed., *A Concise Hebrew and Aramaic Lexicon of the Old Testament* (Grand Rapids: Eerdmans Publishing Company, 1971), 63–64. Here *ger* is also translated as sojourner as well as alien and exile. The person who sojourns does so because he or she seeks shelter for self and family.
149. Julia Kristeva, *Étrangers à nous-mêmes* (Paris: Gallimard, 1988), 100.
150. Kristeva, *Strangers to Ourselves*, 75.
151. Ibid., 75–76.
152. McAfee, "Abject Strangers," 123. The manner in which McAfee relates the abject to primary repression and the foreigner to secondary repression is insightful: "The foreigner is the return of the abject, our encounter with the nothing—especially insofar as the foreigner is a manifestation of no origin, an other tongue, an abyss or gulf, the frail borders of our psyche, and an encounter with the other within us....If it were a primary repression, it would signal a repression/forgetting of undifferentiated being. If it were a secondary repression, it would mark the creation of the difference between self and other. Both repressions make subjectivity possible: the first through creating the *possibility* of difference, the second through *differentiating* subject from object."
153. Kristeva, *Strangers to Ourselves*, 77.
154. Ibid., 79.
155. Ibid.
156. Ibid., 80. See for example, Ephesians 2:11–13; 2:19–20; 4:24; Galatians 6:15; Colossians 3:10.
157. Ibid., 81.
158. Ibid.
159. Ibid., 81–82.
160. Ibid., 82.

161. Ibid.
162. Anna Smith, *Julia Kristeva: Readings of Exile and Estrangement*, 49. She notes the significance of Communion for Kristeva observing the importance of the aspect of loss and renewal in relation to the mother-tongue.
163. Kristeva, *Strangers to Ourselves*, 83.
164. Ibid.
165. Ibid., 84.
166. Ibid.
167. Ibid., 85.
168. Ibid.
169. Ibid.
170. Ibid., 88–89.
171. Ibid., 90.
172. Ibid., 41, 92.
173. Ibid., 104.
174. Ibid., 96.
175. Ibid.
176. Ibid., 114.
177. Smith, *Julia Kristeva: Readings of Exile and Estrangement*, 59. In order to provide a sense of what Kristeva means by maternal rhythm I include here remarks that she made about feminine identity and what she calls the "woman effect" or "maternal function" with regard to language acquisition in an interview: "By emphasizing the biological and physiological characteristics of feminine identity, one could see it as a symbolic effect of the way the subject experiences social cohesiveness, power, and language....In our monotheistic-capitalist societies, 'the woman effect' entails a specific relationship to both *power* and *language*, or, if you will, to the power of language....I have called this modality of the linguistic (and social) functioning of language the '*semiotic*.' The semiotic is heard in rhythms, intonation, and children's echolalia as well as in artistic practice and in discourse that signifies less an 'object' than a jouissance." *Julia Kristeva: Interviews*, ed. Ross Guberman, 104–05.
178. Ibid., 68.
179. Sigmund Freud, "The 'Uncanny'," trans. James Strachey, Vol. XVII, S.E. (London: Hogarth Press, 1919), 219–252.
180. Kristeva, *Strangers to Ourselves*, 181–82.
181. McAfee, "Abject Strangers," 125.
182. Ibid., 119.
183. Julia Kristeva, *In the Beginning Was Love: Psychoanalysis and Faith*, trans. Arthur Goldhammer (New York: Columbia University Press, 1987), 60–61. She states: "Therapy as deployment of language in all its complexity, variety, and functionality integrates concern ...with the Ideal....Its vital efficacy is inseparable from its ethical dimension, which is commensurate with love: the speaking being opens up to and reposes in the other."

184. Sigmund Freud, "The Uncanny," in *The Standard Edition of the Complete Psychological Works of Sigmund Freud,* 17: 220 and 225 as cited by Kristeva, *Strangers to Ourselves,* 183.
185. Kristeva, *Strangers to Ourselves,* 182.
186. Gross, "The Body of Signification," 92.
187. Kristeva, *Strangers to Ourselves,* 184.
188. Ibid., 185.
189. Anna Smith, *Readings of Exile and Estrangement,* 27.
190. Ibid., 44; Kristeva, *Strangers to Ourselves,* 185.
191. Kristeva, *Strangers to Ourselves,* 188.
192. Ibid.
193. Ibid., 190.
194. Ibid.
195. Ibid.
196. Ibid., 191.
197. Ibid.
198. Ibid., 192.
199. Ibid.
200. Guberman, ed., *Interviews,* 45.
201. Smith, *Readings of Exile and Estrangement,* 185.
202. Ibid., 156.
203. Kristeva, *Strangers to Ourselves,* 16.

CHAPTER THREE

Struggle Against the Sun: The "Melancholic-Depressive Composite" in Women

Thus, there is no choice but to struggle eternally against the sun; the "I" is successively the sun and its opponent, language and its rhythm, never one without the other.

–Julia Kristeva, *Desire in Language*

In the second chapter, we saw that the association of woman with the foreigner or the stranger is both her bane and her blessing. She represents a border or boundary for the nascent subject-in-process/on-trial[1] when a third party enters the mother-child relationship and language is acquired; she also inhabits a border land since language is associated with the Law of the father.[2] Following Kristeva's logic, the on-going struggle "against the sun" for women is first, the struggle against the maternal object which at some level is a struggle against the self; and second, the struggle to reclaim a discourse with meaning that neither obliterates women's differences nor reifies their place among the abject. Kristeva describes this struggle to both achieve a specular (or mirror) identification with the mother and introject the maternal body (and self) in *Black Sun* as "an inversion of matricidal drive into a death-bearing maternal image" which is, in fact, "more difficult, if not impossible. Indeed, how can She be that bloodthirsty Fury, since I am She (sexually and narcissistically), She is I? Consequently, the hatred I bear her is not oriented toward the outside but is locked up within myself."[3] In other words, a depressed woman is unable to express her feelings verbally or through any other means (e.g., art, music, etc.) because she is, in essence, paralyzed by the death-bearing maternal image which is also a representation of herself.[4] (One needs to remember that all women are at least potential mothers in Kristeva's view.)

As I suggested in the last chapter, discourse, particularly Western religious discourse, represents an alien tongue for women even as it associates the feminine with sin. Noticeably absent, especially in Protestant theology is a maternal discourse. This leads Kristeva to ask: Does the rise of feminism in Protestant countries result from an absence of discourse about the Virgin/Maternal?[5]

Kristeva is critical of avant-garde feminists who would reject the notion of motherhood completely. This does not mean, however, that she wholly embraces the view of women or mothers that has traditionally been offered by the Christian church. In her view, the church has erred in the opposite direction from avant-garde feminists. While she recognizes that the absorption of femininity within maternity is specific to many civilizations, "Christianity, in its own fashion, brings it to its peak."[6] In other words, motherhood has been "consecrated" as *the representation* of the feminine. Her questions about the reduction of the feminine to the maternal, however, do not end here. She wonders if this reduction of the feminine to the maternal "represents no more than a masculine appropriation of the Maternal, which, in line with our hypothesis, is only a fantasy masking primary narcissism? Or else, might one detect in it, in other respects, the workings of enigmatic sublimation?"[7] To underscore her point she observes that for both Freud and Da Vinci, "the taming" of the maternal or of primary narcissism is necessary for artistic or literary accomplishment. This reduction of the feminine which occurs within Christianity and results in women's oppression, then, is the result of a masculine fantasy.[8] For Kristeva, this perspective leaves several questions unanswered:

> What is there, in the portrayal of the Maternal in general and particularly in its Christian, virginal, one, that reduces social anguish and gratifies a male being; what is there that also satisfies a woman so that a commonality of the sexes is set up, beyond and in spite of their glaring incompatibility and permanent warfare? Moreover, is there something in that Maternal notion that ignores what a woman might say or want?[9]

This last question—"Is there something in that Maternal notion that ignores what a woman might say or want?"—is the primary focus for most of chapter four. In order to be able to explore this question, I will begin first in this chapter with Kristeva's proposal for a maternal discourse. This will entail, first, a summary of what she has to say regarding feminine identity, focusing primarily on *About Chinese Women.* Then, I will focus on the time and place that women occupy in religious discourse. Here, too, my primary text will be *About Chinese Women,* supplemented by her essay, "Women's Time." This will lead to a discussion of the importance that Kristeva envisions for a maternal discourse relevant to women struggling with depression. My primary text will be *Black Sun* supplemented by *About Chinese Women* and a published interview Kristeva gave shortly following the French publication of *Soleil Noir* (*Black Sun*).

Feminine Identity

In *About Chinese Women,* Kristeva devotes the first part of the book to an examination of her own position as a Western female writer. She writes that women

> "have the luck to be able to take advantage of a biological peculiarity to give a name to that which, in monotheistic capitalism, remains on this side of the threshold of repression, voice stilled, body mute, always foreign to the social order...it is the lot of the feminine to assume the role of *waste,* or of the hidden work-force in the relationships of production and the language which defines them."[10]

Here Kristeva introduces the themes which would later become central in *Powers of Horror, Black Sun,* and *Strangers to Ourselves*: the feminine is foreign to the social order; assumes the role of waste or the abject; and, dwells in a hidden realm of silence where paternal law is defining. Her expressed aim in this portion of *About Chinese Women* is to question the tradition which has defined women in this way for more than two thousand years.

In her essay, "Women's Time," Kristeva returns to this theme of women's difference, stating that "the time has perhaps come to emphasize the multiplicity of female expressions and preoccupations so that from the intersection of these differences there might arise, more precisely, less commercially and more truthfully, the real *fundamental difference* between the two sexes."[11] In other words, Kristeva argues for a more nuanced understanding of women so that a more truthful conversation may be engaged about the fundamental differences between the lived experience of men and women. Later she cites Lacan's comment in "God and the Jouissance of Woman":

> There is no such thing as Woman'. Indeed, she does *not* exist with a capital 'W', possessor of some mythical unity—a supreme power, on which is based the terror of power and terrorism as the desire for power. But what an unbelievable force for subversion in the modern world! And, at the same time, what playing with fire![12]

Here, in endorsing Lacan, Kristeva reminds us of the hopefulness of woman's difference; that is, the ability to be a creative force for change in the world based upon her strangeness or difference. It is also a creative force fraught with danger, for women are signified as "playing with fire."

Kristeva locates the beginning of the "war between the sexes" in the creation narrative in Genesis. Since woman is made from the very thing missing from man—a rib—God created man and woman by *dividing* them. Moreover, "the Biblical woman will be wife, daughter, or sister, or all those things at once. She will *rarely have a name.* Her function is to assure procreation....with the law of the community, with its political and religious unity, she has no direct relation: God...speaks only to men."[13] The suggestion here is that "woman" has no name, therefore no identity and no relationship with God except through men, even as men have enjoyed the power to construct language which constructs identity.

Unity within the religious community is represented by the God of monotheism. Woman comes, then, to represent the removal of a threatening desire from the community. Thus, "you have woman who is speechless, but who appears as the pure desire of speech, or who insures, on the human side, the permanence of the divine paternal function: that is, the desire to propagate the race."[14] "Woman" is nameless and speechless. This reality leaves women excluded from both knowledge and power. Citing the story of Eve and the serpent as the best example of women's exclusion from "the single true and legislating principle, from the Word," Kristeva states

> the serpent stands for the inverse of God, since he invites Eve to transgress God's prohibition. But it is also this very desire to transgress which Adam represses, which he dares not act out, which is his shame: the sexual symbolism helps us understand that the serpent is that which, in God or Adam, remains outside or beyond the sublimated content of the Word. Eve has no relationship except with that—precisely because she is its opposite, the "other race."[15]

Thus women, from the beginning, are assigned the role of living as exiles outside the realm of the Word and power. Women exist not simply as the opposite sex but live as an excluded race of people, excluded primarily from knowledge and power which then leaves them speechless and gives rise frequently to a struggle with depression.

What options or alternatives exist for women inside Christianity if, as Kristeva claims, women are excluded from knowledge and power in patrilineal (western, modern) societies, societies "governed by a monotheism whose essence is best expressed in the Bible: the paternal Word sustained by a fight to the finish between the two races (men/women)"?[16] For Kristeva there are only two opposite and extreme options: (1) virginity (association with the Word); and/or, (2) martyrdom (expiation of carnal pleasure). Virginity was and is "represented by Mary and imitated by female monastic orders."[17] Thus, there is only a false recognition of a woman's sexual difference or "maternal *jouissance*";[18] moreover, "we see that what Christianity recognizes in a woman, what it demands of her in order to place her within its symbolic order, is this: while living or thinking of herself as a virgin impregnated by the Word, she lives and thinks of herself as a male homosexual."[19] If, on the other hand, a woman does experience heterosexual carnal pleasure it needs to be expiated through martyrdom. Thus,

> if a woman is not virgin, nun, and chaste, but has orgasms and gives birth, her only means of complying with the symbolic paternal order is to engage in an endless battle between her sexual maternal body and the symbolic prohibition—a battle that will take the form of guilt and mortification, and will culminate in masochistic jouissance.[20]

This seems to be the only viable but rather unhealthy alternative open to women in Western Christianity, since as Kristeva observes, even Augustine maintains that no one would dare prefer virginity to martyrdom.[21] That is, no woman would dare to prefer a sexless life or life without maternal *jouissance*. If she chooses her sexuality, however, she also chooses masochism in a Western Christian culture according to Kristeva.

A third alternative, however, is available to women as mothers in the Christian community who prepare their children for baptism.[22] In her psychoanalytic examination of the feminine in Christianity, Kristeva focuses on this alternative, and explores the role of the mother and the function of language.[23] With respect to the role of the mother, a woman can only participate in the socio-symbolic order of community by bearing children "in the name of the father." Thus the primary purpose of bearing children is to prepare them for baptism and membership in Christian community. Here, too, a woman's jouissance, her sexual difference and accompanying joy in that difference is denied. Suffering and sacrifice, then, are understood to be associated with jouissance for women. In other words, Christianity assigns women a place which leaves them with two options, according to Kristeva—"two great Christian feminine archetypes"—the ecstatic and the melancholic.

Kristeva cites Theresa of Avila as an example of an ecstatic for whom "the mother is denied and her attributes are displaced onto the symbolic father. The woman then submits herself to a sexually undifferentiated androgynous being."[24] The melancholic is exemplified by Catherine of Siena (especially her treatise on the sensual delight of tears) for whom "submission to the father is experienced as punishment, pain, and suffering inflicted upon the heterogeneous body."[25] Both of these types, Kristeva notes, can exist within one individual. Again, what is significant here is that, for Kristeva, it is within one of these two extremes only that a girl in a monotheistic capitalist social structure will have access to knowledge, power and symbolism. In a certain sense, then, as gender is currently socially constructed, girls and young women are assigned a place as their identities develop which assures that they will be viewed as "sick." In a word, they are identified with what is abject.

In describing one of her women patients, Kristeva indicates that, as women are identified with that which is abject, their very language or "mother tongue" becomes alien to them. In healthy women speech is a "second nature" but for those who suffer from depression speech is

> like an alien skin; melancholy persons are foreigners in their maternal tongue. They have lost the meaning—the value—of their maternal tongue for want of losing the mother. The dead language they speak, which foreshadows their suicide, conceals a Thing buried alive. The latter, however, will not be translated in order that it not be betrayed; it shall remain walled up within the *crypt* of the inexpressible affect, anally harnessed, with no way out.[26]

The effect of their alienated language upon women is that their mourning for the maternal object tends to become an implosive gesture that is often suicidal. Indeed, Reineke sees in the above cited passage an explanation for the current status of women in the social order: "That the Symbolic order does not pose the attraction for women that it does for men thus accounts for the unsettled prospects of women in the social order and for the seriousness with which they may consider other options."[27]

The Symbolic order—language—that which often offers hope or compensation is that which is refused by men and women who struggle with melancholia. Again, what makes this different for women is the reality that the symbolic order is less attractive for women than men because it represents a male-oriented paternal structure; therefore, I suggest there is less incentive for them to engage in what Kristeva has called the "speaking cure." As Ewa Ziarek has observed concerning Kristeva's description of melancholia:

> If mourning is a "normal," or normative, stage in learning language, melancholia registers a certain crisis in symbolic mediation. It undermines the process of translating the other into a linguistic totality...Kristeva defines melancholia as an inability to lose the primordial other but then she immediately qualifies her description as a refusal to accept any compensation for that loss, especially in terms of symbolic mastery.[28]

Melancholia is, then, an inconsolable grief that resists attempts to be defined or ameliorated in speech. In this, Ziarek detects not a "disorder of the subject" but "a powerful critique of the desire to master alterity through the order of representation."[29] Thus even though it seems contradictory, a woman's refusal to "master alterity" may at times actually be a hopeful sign of personal strength which will lead her back to health. Why? Women seek a language that truly depicts their experience as other, as stranger, or foreigner. Ziarek concludes:

> Melancholia points to an irreducible excess of alterity disrupting the order of representation. This excess of alterity—being overwhelmed by the other—indicates a breakdown of the mechanism of mediation in the symbolic order. Indeed in the way Kristeva orchestrates her description, melancholia registers an encounter with the other without the intermediary of the third term, understood as a paternal signifier, phallus, or the symbolic order. Although maternal alterity remains in this case unnameable, exterior to the order of signs, it leaves its imprint both on the discourse and on the speaking subject—it signals itself in language as blank spots or dissociation of form.[30]

As noted in a previous citation from *Black Sun* (see footnote 2 above), women's first experience with the other (the woman-mother) is more immediate; therefore the feminine "subject-in-process/on trial" may be more immediately and intensely overwhelmed by the other who in Kristeva's words is "I am She." Building upon Ziarek's interpretation of Kristeva, I suggest that feminine melancholia is not, then, a disorder of the subject but rather her critique of the restraints placed upon her developing identity in early childhood by the social order. It is one manner in which the "subject-in-process/on trial" struggles to find her voice and a discourse which reflects her experience.

Silence, then, is one possible interpretation of feminine identity. There is, however, another possibility. Following upon the work of Alice Jardine, Diane Jonte-Pace concludes that woman or the feminine "will always be posited as the ultimate limit to any discourse articulated by man."[31] Moreover, she goes on to suggest that the representation of "limit" by the feminine leads to the gendering of absence (i.e., death as opposed to life) as feminine.[32]

What, then, does Kristeva say with respect to a woman's relationship to the symbolic order and its significance for the "subject-in-process?" At best it is a conflicted relationship. Either a woman identifies with the paternal order, thereby renouncing her difference or she identifies with the maternal body but consequently loses access to knowledge and power which are acquired through the paternal symbolic order. Neither option seems to present a hopeful process of becoming a subject. And yet, for Kristeva, it is precisely from her place as a stranger or foreigner, here in a male dominated discourse, that a woman can find hope. Claiming her difference will in the end lead to a position of strength, whereas simply acquiescing to the "law of the father" even with its offer of knowledge and power will lead to ultimate destruction. Thus, against those who view nuns, revolutionaries, and feminists as liberated women, Kristeva thinks otherwise. She associates them with Electra, as they are "militants" to be sure, but "militants in the cause of their fathers."[33] She concludes that a woman may take pleasure in a paternal ordering of life if she has first identified with her mother and

> imagines herself to be the repressed and sublimated content of the culture rising through its cracks. If, on the other hand, she has failed to identify with the mother, and—as victim or militant—found her one superficial, backward, and easily severed hold on life in the symbolic paternal order, its dissolution can be her death.[34]

Thus, a woman whose sole connection with the social order and life is founded upon a male discourse identified with her father and therefore, not with her unique experiences as a woman, faces the possibility of suicide when that discourse fails her. As was demonstrated in the last chapter, a woman's violence tends to erupt as an implosion in the form of self-mutilation (eating disorders, for example) or suicidal threat whereas men often externalize and direct these impulses toward others. The difficulty, as viewed by Kristeva, is that there is not currently an adequate maternal discourse inside or outside the bounds of religious discourse which expresses a woman's particularity.[35]

Thus far in Kristeva's economy, feminine identity is equated with negativity. The meaning of woman is abject, absence, alterity, death, difference, ecstatic, melancholic and silence.[36] For Kristeva, the crucial question with regard to feminine identity is a *symbolic* question. She states: "Sexual difference–which is at once biological, physiological and relative to reproduction–is translated by and translates a difference in the relationship of subjects to the symbolic contract which *is* the social contract: a difference, then, in the relationship to power, language and meaning."[37]

"Women's Time" or Women's Place?

This discussion of the meaning of woman as it has evolved in Western culture in relationship to the paternal symbolic order (especially the paternal symbolic of Western Christianity) leads Kristeva to a discussion of women's place in time. She notes that the paternal symbolic order is a temporal order. This means: "If *I* don't exist except in the language I address to another, I am only *present* in the moment of that communication."[38] This time is linear time–the time of history and politics. The paternal symbolic order or "the verbal order of communication" defines past, present and future. In other words, "[t]here is no time without speech. Therefore, no time without the father. That's what the father means: sign and time. It is understandable, then, that what the father doesn't say about the unconscious, what sign and time repress in the impulses, appears as their *truth*...and that this truth can be imagined only as a woman."[39] Here it is important to remember that Kristeva refers to the individual father of prehistory (the third party in the pre-oedipal triangle) whose voice initiates the inaugural loss of the woman-mother. One may also hear faint echoes of the "Word of the Father" (and John's gospel) in this description as well. Thus, the feminine is viewed by Kristeva as standing outside time while being linked to the unconscious, "a curious truth." Elsewhere she observes that "when evoking the name and destiny of women, one thinks more of the *space* [the womb] generating and forming the human species than of *time*, becoming or history."[40] Why? Women do not enjoy equal access to language, knowledge or power.

A woman's so-called fortune then amounts to a double bind or cultural trap.[41] She is permitted to engage in what is considered "marginal speech" in the realms of philosophy, religion and science, and possibly experiences jouissance through pregnancy, which interrupts linear time. As Kristeva notes, the "endless 'Madonnas with Child'" point to the reality that artists have exalted this atemporal truth (i.e., the unconscious) which they suspect "springs from the side of the mother...by finding its symbol in the female body."[42] Thus,

> once it [truth] is given form—as a woman, for example—the 'truth' of the unconscious passes into the symbolic order, it even over-shadows it, as fundamental fetish, phallus-substitute, support for all transcendental divinity. A crude but enormously effective trap for feminism: to acknowledge us, to make us into the truth of the temporal order, so as to keep us from functioning as its unconscious 'truth,' formless beyond true, and false, beyond present-past-future.[43]

To illustrate her point she offers a brief study of Tiepolo's painting, *Time Disrobing Truth*.[44] The painting is enigmatic because it isn't easy to discern if it is a rape scene or Time and Truth engaged in coitus. The painting represents the artist's fantasy "where a woman, intended to represent Truth, takes the place of the phallus...she ceases to act as atemporal, unconscious, splitting, destroying, and breaking the temporal and symbolic order; rather, she substitutes herself for it as solar mistress, priestess of the absolute."[45] Why is this important for Kristeva? "When Truth is stripped in order to be presented as itself, 'truth' is lost within itself; for in fact it has no self; it only rises between the cracks of an identity."[46] Only when women identify with values[47] identified as masculine do they gain access to power (e.g., politics); the suggestion here is that only then will they have a recognizable identity which of course, amounts to a false self (in the case of this painting, the woman becomes a substitute phallus).

Parallel to the two extremes Kristeva identifies for religious women (i.e., ecstatic and melancholic), she identifies two extremes for the place of women in the temporal order: either we identify with the masculine, becoming the most passionate of bureaucrats (e.g., women ministers!) or subversives; or we "remain in an eternal sulk before history, politics, society: the symptoms of their failure, but symptoms betrothed to marginality or to a new mysticism."[48] Kristeva wants a solution which allows a woman access to knowledge and power without requiring that she deny or reject her feminine/maternal side. Kristeva suggests that the most hopeful way through the difficulty of either extreme—identifying with the masculine or accepting our feminine role passively with an occasional hysterical symptom—is to listen. It is a distinctive kind of listening that will assist a woman to avoid the trap of either extreme insofar as she recognizes "the unspoken in speech, even revolutionary speech;

by calling attention at all times to whatever remains unsatisfied, repressed, new, eccentric, incomprehensible, disturbing to the *status quo*."[49] She recognizes, however, that at this point in history this is unlikely to happen, for what she has identified here is "an impossible dialectic," or a "constant alternation between time and its 'truth,' identity and its loss, history and the timeless, signless, extra-phenomenal things that produce it."[50]

In "Women's Time," Kristeva revisits the discussion she began in *About Chinese Women* where history (and politics) is described as linear and as paternal time in contrast to feminine time which is interpreted as monumental time or eternity, and as cyclical time (surrounding the repetition of the cycle of reproduction).[51] As noted above, she sees the place that women occupy more as a space than a time. She offers numerous examples to support her argument. These include the manner in which children acquire the symbolic function or language which Kristeva maintains is conditioned by "the permanence and quality of maternal love" that gives rise to

> the first spatial references which induce the child's laugh and then induce the entire range of symbolic manifestations which lead eventually to sign and syntax...they all converge on the problematic of space, which innumerable religions of matriarchal (re)appearance attribute to 'woman', and which Plato, recapitulating in his own system...designated by the aporia of the *chora*, matrix space nourishing, unnameable, anterior to the One, to God and, consequently, defying metaphysics.[52]

Thus, motherhood is separated from the feminine by a space—the maternal matrix—the *chora*. Strictly speaking, Kristeva provides reference here to that era in motherhood before the woman becomes an object and prior to the infant's becoming a subject.[53] Unlike Freud, Kristeva does not gender an infant—male or female—as masculine.

Indeed, in her earlier essay, "Motherhood According to Giovanni Bellini," Kristeva already had distinguished the feminine from motherhood. In the following passage, motherhood is more specifically described as the time of pregnancy itself. This, however, is not a time but a space:

> Cells fuse, split, and proliferate; volumes grow, tissues stretch, and body fluids change rhythm, speeding up or slowing down. Within the body, growing as a graft, indomitable, there is an other. And no one is present, within that simultaneously *dual and alien space*, to signify what is going on. "It happens, but I'm not there." "I cannot realize it, but it goes on." Motherhood's impossible syllogism.[54]

The significance of Kristeva's emphasis on space and eternity over against linear or historical time with respect to the feminine is related to the manner in which she defines woman or feminine as "other," as "difference." Woman is the stranger who stands outside of time and speaks from an "impossible elsewhere." Not only must women contend with an alien tongue, they must also contend with an alien space.

Although Kristeva says that she does not intend to "leave the door wide open to religion and mysticism"[55] with her conception of time as it relates to female subjectivity, there can be no doubt that she does, in fact, open the door for religious discourse to assist in resolving an unavoidable contradiction. She reiterates that "female subjectivity as it gives itself up to intuition becomes a problem with respect to a certain conception of time: time as project, teleology, and prospective unfolding...as departure, progression, and arrival...the time of history."[56] That is, time as it is described here belongs to history, language and a patrilinear culture but women exist in a marginalized space outside of linear time analogous to an unavoidable contradiction that results when "the hysteric...who suffers from reminiscences would rather recognize his or her self"[57] in monumental time or eternity. There is an unavoidable contradiction or antagonism because linear time is the time of language as enunciation and is, therefore, necessary for giving voice to suffering. Women's time which she likens to "space-time in infinite expansion,"[58] then, seems to offer no possibility for enunciation. Kristeva then opens the door to religion and mysticism in her assessment of the antinomy identified above:

> Within the bounds of a given civilization, however, this antinomy of psychic structures becomes an antinomy among social groups and ideologies. Indeed, the radical viewpoints of certain feminists are akin to the discourse of marginal spiritual or mystic groups, as well as, interestingly enough, to the concerns of modern science.[59]

Later in this same article she suggests that "beyond the socio-political level where it is generally inscribed (or inscribes itself), the women's movement–in its present stage, less aggressive but more artful–is situated within the very framework of the religious crisis of our civilization."[60] In other words, Kristeva is critical of some feminists whose drive for power amounts to the same kind of cultural oppression for women who choose not to conform to it as the "Law of the father" constituted in an earlier Western culture dominated by

Christianity. What is most desired is a kind of feminism which celebrates the singularity of each woman in her uniqueness.

Does Kristeva allude to a solution here? That is to say, if the crisis in religious discourse, as identified by Kristeva, is to be resolved, will an answer be revealed at the intersection of religious and psychoanalytic discourse for the struggle of women *in* time as opposed to outside of linear time? Indeed, as Kristeva brings "Women's Time" to a close she proposes just such an answer in the form of a question: "What discourse, if not that of a religion, would be able to support this adventure which surfaces as a real possibility, after both the achievements and the impasses of the present ideological reworkings, in which feminism has participated?"[61] And yet, Kristeva's writings neither support a feminism that is guilty of an inverted sexism, nor would they support a goddess religion. Her proposal is for the restoration of a maternal discourse. This leads us to a discussion of the importance of the maternal tongue as it relates to the hope a maternal discourse offers women—particularly those who struggle with depression.

Melancholia and the Maternal Tongue

I return again to Kristeva's early work, *About Chinese Women*, in which she lays the foundation for much of her later work that pertains to a discussion of the sacred and the feminine as these relate to one's maternal tongue and a maternal discourse. The absence of a maternal discourse, particularly in Protestantism, leaves women with two extreme choices. They can either become what her interpreters describe as a "homologous woman" (i.e., one who identifies with the Word and Law of the Father)[62] or they can succumb to melancholia, a kind of living death that for some leads to suicide. In fact, as Kristeva examines the "call of the mother" for women in *About Chinese Women*, she reflects on the suicides of women writers (e.g., Virginia Woolf). The following passage sets the tone for her foray into female depression long before she wrote *Black Sun*:

> For a woman, the call of the mother is not only a call beyond time, beyond the socio-political battle. With family and history at an impasse, this call troubles the Word. It generates voices, 'madness', hallucinations. After the superego, the ego, that fragile envelope, founders and sinks. It is helpless to stave off the eruption of this conflict, of this love which has bound the little girl to her mother and then lain in wait for her—*black lava*—all along the path of her desperate attempt to identify with the symbolic paternal order. Once the moorings of the ego begin to slip life itself can't hang on: slowly, gently, death settles in. *Suicide without a cause, or silent sacrifice for an*

> *apparent cause which, in our age, is usually political*: a woman can carry off such things without tragedy, without even drama. She can carry them off as though it were simply a matter of making an inevitable, irresistible, self-motivated transition, rather than feeling a *well-fortified front*.[63]

The "black sun" or "struggle against the sun" has not yet appeared but there is "black lava" that envelopes the little girl as she struggles to become a speaking subject independent of the woman-mother. The "well-fortified front" brings to mind the "empty but fortified castle" descriptive of the speech of the "abject" woman or "borderline patient" in *Powers of Horror*. In this instance it is precisely that "well-fortified front" which prevents the counselor from reaching into the "impossible elsewhere" to assist a woman in her journey back into time and speech. There is already in this passage a trace of the refrain of matricide that appears throughout *Black Sun* (e.g., "how can She be that bloodthirsty Fury, since I am She...She is I? Consequently, the hatred I bear her is not oriented toward the outside but is locked up within myself").[64]

In her very brief study of the Russian poet, Maria Tsvetaieva, Kristeva compares the suicide of men to women suggesting that, whereas for men it is a desire to be more powerful than God, for women it isn't a desire for power or death but rather "not to be" which in the final analysis is "to be God."[65] What is the significance of this difference which Kristeva proposes? She writes that men have the ability to "imagine an all-powerful though always insignificant mother"; moreover they are able to "lean on her and be guided by her through the social labyrinth," but not without their "own running ironic commentary."[66] Women are not able to rely upon their mothers in this same manner which results in a girl relying upon her own resources. Thus Kristeva claims that the inability to rely upon the woman-mother leads to a "so-called female homosexuality, identification with men, or a tight rein on the least pre-oedipal pleasure. And if no paternal 'legitimization' comes along to dam up the inexhaustible non-symbolized impulse, she collapses into psychosis or suicide."[67] The options allowed for a woman within the paternal symbolic order of society cast her, at best, as a victim; at worst, she slips from depression into death if she does not "identify with the father and strive for access to the Word and to time."[68]

Kristeva's solution to this double-bind is foreshadowed at a surprising place in her writing—the beginning of her record of the interviews she conducted with Chinese women. Here she proclaims that if a woman lacks faith in God then she "validates her existence by believing in man."[69] This is the double bind for women and Kristeva's solution requires that a woman

> perceive that both 'man' and 'God' are metaphors for unity, cohesion, social continuity—metaphors for language. Thus, when her will becomes so disturbed that she can no longer believe in language or appropriate it for herself, a woman begins to do or write something of her own. An impossible mission, since language *exists*, it remains the same; and for a woman it is more neutralizing and more impressive than for anyone else.[70]

As we shall see in the fifth chapter, writing is an aesthetic practice (a type of forgiveness) that provides a way out of the "frozen speech" for the depressed. A woman uses the language that exists but only makes it her own and creates new meanings when she becomes frustrated with the *status quo* and accepts or interiorizes her difference. She gives voice to her experience and creates something which is her own through the metaphors she chooses. A woman's inability to appropriate or believe in language leads us to a discussion of how keenly Kristeva perceives the loss of the maternal object in relation to the importance of a maternal tongue, especially as it pertains to feminine depression.

Melancholia—"A Sun That Remains Black"

One might wonder how Kristeva came upon the title—*Black Sun*—for her volume dedicated to feminine depression and melancholia. The answer is provided in her discussion of Nerval's poem, "El Desdicahdo," (i.e., disinherited).[71] She borrows the image from a line in his poem that refers to a "dead star" which represents "the image of the muse, also that of a lofty universe, of the cosmos, which is higher still than the medieval tower or the presently wrecked destiny."[72] The full meaning of this metaphor in Kristeva's writing is evident in the following:

> As a result of the absorption of the "dead star" into the "lute," the "Black Sun" of "Melancholia" emerges. Beyond its alchemical scope, the "Black Sun" metaphor fully sums up the blinding force of the despondent mood—an excruciating, lucid affect asserts the inevitability of death, which is the death of the loved one and of the self that identifies with the former (the poet is "bereft" of the "star").[73]

The "dead star" of the first stanza of the poem is linked by Kristeva to the "you" who brought solace to the poet in the second stanza. The "dead star," then, suggests the dead mother for whom the melancholic mourns.[74] The last line of the first stanza, "Bears the Black Sun of Melancholia" is interpreted by Kristeva as follows:

> The verb "bears" points to that bursting out, that reaching the signs of darkness, while the learned word *melancholia* serves to bespeak the struggle for conscious mastery and precise meaning....*Melancholia* belongs to the celestial realm. It changes darkness into redness or into a sun that remains black, to be sure, but is nevertheless the sun, source of dazzling light.[75]

The "black sun" represents the "unthinkable nature" of the solar source of light in that "melancholia and depression acknowledge that at the heart of human experience lies an inconsolable grief over the perpetually estranged nature of existence."[76] Depression and melancholia represent in some form, an eclipse of the sun, of the very light that gives warmth to our being. Indeed in one of her more recent works, *This Incredible Need to Believe*,[77] a photograph of a solar eclipse provides the artwork for the book jacket connecting her previous work to this present work because faith itself, according to Kristeva, develops from a "shadowy zone." Kristeva seems to be correct when she observes that "*naming the sun* locates [Nerval] on the threshold of a crucial experience, on the divide between appearance and disappearance, abolishment and song, nonmeaning and signs."[78] The sun, even if it remains black, assures that the struggle to give voice to the inconsolable grief over losing the mother continues.

Kristeva locates the beginning of this "perpetually estranged nature of human existence" in the pre-oedipal relationship that a child has with the mother, "If I did not agree to lose mother, I could neither imagine nor name her."[79] This means that a girl, in order to be able to enter the world which is governed by the "Law of the father," needs to agree to give up her mother (or maternal object). Then, and only then, does she gain access to the world of knowledge and power through paternal discourse. The symbiotic relationship with the mother has to be broken by a third party. The mother is not given up permanently but is recovered through language—the ability to call out to her, "Mama." Thus the beginning of the journey to become a speaking subject

> starts with a *negation* (*Verneinung*) of loss, along with the depression occasioned by mourning. 'I have lost an essential object that happens to be, in the final analysis, my mother,' is what the speaking being seems to be saying. 'But no, I have found her

> again in signs, or rather since I consent to lose her I have not lost her (that is the negation), I can recover her in language."[80]

Depressed persons are unique in that they are unable to recover her in language (because they never agreed to give her up) and instead want to cling to their mothers. Again, in an often cited passage she states: "Depressed persons, on the contrary, *disavow the negation*: they cancel it out, suspend it, and nostalgically fall back on the real object (the Thing) of their loss, which is just what they do not manage to lose, to which they remain painfully riveted."[81] Thus, as John Lechte points out, "Rather than expressing emotion and affect, the subject *becomes* these: melancholics, in short, act out what needs to be elaborated in signs and symbols formed in response to the loss of the object (mother)."[82]

It might seem to the reader who is unfamiliar with Kristeva's work that she blurs the boundary between depression and melancholia. In an interview she gave shortly following the French publication of *Black Sun,* she drew a distinction by distinguishing between three types of melancholia and then defining what she identifies as a "melancholic-depressive composite." The three types of melancholia are: (1) "melancholia as a serious affliction characterized by a slowing-down of psychic and motor functioning"; (2) a less serious form of despondence "that often alternates (as does the psychiatric version) with states of excitement"; this is "a neurotic state known as depression"; and (3) a melancholia in the broadest sense of the term, i.e., melancholia as a 'distant soul,' as 'spleen,' and as nostalgia depicted in literature and art: "This third form of melancholia is still an illness, but it takes on an element of beauty that can be quite sublime. As I say in my book, beauty is born in the land of melancholia; it is a source of harmony that goes beyond despair."[83] In this same interview she gave her rationale for a melancholic-depressive composite:

> [E]ven though important differences exist between melancholia and depression, they have at least two things in common. First, they are both characterized by a *divestment of social bonds* and the ceasing of all relationships. It is as though melancholic and depressed people were saying, "No, we're not interested in your society, your activities, or your language. We are different from that; we do not exist; we are dead." Second, they both detail a *devaluation of language*...the speaker always gives the impression that he neither believes in it nor inhabits it, that he is outside language and inside the secret crypt of his silent pain.[84]

Thus, the world of the depressed (and the melancholic) might be described as the land of the living dead. This land, inhabited by those who reject language presents a unique and difficult challenge to the psychoanalyst or pastoral counselor insofar as this type of care works through speech to gain access to an individual's pain. Kristeva's solution is to emphasize "the importance of the voice and of other signs that are not linguistic even though they are communicated through language....I also believe it is important to show how much the depressed person, who experiences a pain that often remains silent, is secretly emotional and cunningly impassioned."[85] Note here the special difficulty involved in "recognizing the stranger's voice"—in discerning or penetrating the pain of the depressed woman, who is "secretly emotional and perhaps, cunningly impassioned." The difficulty, of course, is how to gain access to the woman's pain through speech since this is what she has already rejected.[86] As this interview concluded, Kristeva made reference to both her female students and herself, stating, "Today what upsets us and frightens us is not so much sex but the threat of permanent pain, of the potential cadaver that we have become. Who among us wants to confront this directly? Depression remains a secret force, perhaps even a *form of modern sacredness*."[87] We need to look at how Kristeva defines this "form of modern sacredness" before moving on to possibilities of addressing it.

While Kristeva locates women in a space rather than time, she locates depression and the speech of the depressed in time, comparing it to the way Kant talked about nostalgic persons.[88] She notes that melancholy people whose speech is alien or vanishing altogether live with a skewed sense of time. In what manner does time become skewed? Kristeva suggests that time stops so much so that "a *moment* blocks the horizon of depressive temporality....Riveted to the past, regressing to the paradise or inferno of an unsurpassable experience, melancholy persons manifest a strange memory: everything has gone by...no revolution is possible, there is no future."[89] There isn't even a present because melancholy people are "riveted to a past" which is the center of grief. What is the object of their grief? Kristeva explains:

> When I say that the object of my grief is less the village, the mother, or the lover that I miss here and now then the blurred representation that I keep and put together in the darkroom of what thus becomes my psychic tomb, this at once locates my ill-being in the imagination. A dweller in *truncated time*, the depressed person is necessarily a dweller in the *imaginary realm*. Such a linguistic and temporal phenomenology discloses, as I have often emphasized, an unfulfilled mourning for the maternal object.[90]

In the two previous citations one can see why Kristeva is criticized for blurring the boundary between depression and melancholia, but one can also observe why she insists on using both terms interchangeably, at times emphasizing their similarities, at other times the distinctions between them. Thus, for this project, her "melancholic-depressive composite" will remain the focus, and I will not attempt to differentiate between melancholia and depression. I will continue, however, to focus on women who struggle with depression, and this means that I will be concerned with the third type of melancholia as a solution to or resolution of the first two types set forth by Kristeva.

A recovery of the maternal tongue, or at the very least, an identification of what Kristeva calls "tonal modulations" in the speech of the depressed, will help the analyst or in this case, the pastoral counselor to connect language and affect. In other words, the "music of the mother's voice" is hidden in the speech of the depressed person since she has not given up the maternal object. Thus, "*language—considered empty up to this point because cut off from affective and vocal inscriptions, is revitalized and may become a space of desire, that is of meaning for the subject.*"[91] Or as Anna Smith notes, "The precondition for meaning lies in the semiotic working through language as the mother-tongue, and not in the exterior world of objects, concepts or revelationary truths."[92] Meaning in language for women results from their "struggle against the sun" which is ultimately a struggle against a living death. If they are unsuccessful in that struggle then, "[m]elancholia...ends up in asymbolia, in loss of meaning: if I am no longer capable of translating or metaphorizing, I become silent and I die."[93]

Conclusion

We have seen that the feminine in Western Christianity has been reduced to the maternal in such a way that women are consigned to dwell in a land of silence outside linear time. Choices for women within this culture are limited to extremes of virginity, martyrdom or a motherhood which denies jouissance. This leads to either an ecstatic or melancholic affect—sometimes both. In any case, the feminine is still equated with the abject and waste which fosters estrangement from others and leads to a condition of self-estrangement. Women reside as foreigners within Western Christianity estranged from others but more importantly from themselves. Suffering and self-sacrifice are synonymous with woman in a Western Christian economy. Women continue to be viewed as "sick" simply because they belong to "the other race." One could probably sustain the argument, following Kristeva's logic, that all women suffer at least moderately from the second type of melancholia—a neurotic depression. That, however, is beyond the scope of this project.

The difficulty of helping women who struggle with depression in a Western Christian context is all too clear. Without subscribing to the "Law of the father" (i.e., paternal discourse), women have no access to knowledge and/or power. Their silence, which can be viewed as a position of strength in that they reject a discourse that doesn't describe their experience, adds to the difficulty for those who want to assist them. These women, Kristeva says, inhabit an imaginary realm. The challenge is to help them give voice to their experience *in* time.

The third type of melancholia identified by Kristeva will be presented in the next chapter as a solution to or, perhaps, a resolution of the first two types insofar as it is "a source of harmony that goes beyond despair." This type of melancholia gives birth to beauty in that it "emerges as the admirable face of loss, transforming it in order to make it live."[94] As the maternal lives, so too, does the woman. In the next chapter we will see how Kristeva interprets "Renaissance Madonnas" to prepare her own canvas for a portrayal of maternal discourse.

Notes

1. Julia Kristeva, *Desire in Language: A Semiotic Approach to Literature and Art*, ed. Leon S. Roudiez (New York: Columbia University Press, 1980), 17. See also footnote 98 in chapter one. Kristeva writes about identity development using the French word, *procès*, which carries a legal connotation of a "questionable identity." The term also suggests that the developing subject is unsettled in the process of moving forward and is, therefore, "unsettled."
2. Guberman, *Interviews*; see for example, an interview conducted by Elaine Boucquey where Kristeva discusses the "woman effect," 103–112. What does Kristeva mean by "Law of the Father?" This is her point of departure from both Freud and Lacan with regard to psychoanalytic and linguistic theory. As Kelly Oliver notes, "For Kristeva this body that sets up and harbors the Symbolic (at the same time that it threatens it) is the maternal body. The maternal body *prefigures* the Law of the Father and the onset of the Symbolic. What Kristeva calls the 'maternal function' contains both a negation and an identification that precede Lacan's mirror stage. This is to say that both the negation and the identification that are essential to human subjectivity are already operating within the maternal function prior to the subject's entrance into language....In traditional Freudian and Lacanian psychoanalysis it is the paternal function that initiates the negation and

identification that finally propels the infant into both language and subjectivity." *Reading Kristeva: Unraveling the Double-bind* (Indianapolis: Indiana University Press, 1993), 3.

3. Julia Kristeva, *Black Sun: Depression and Melancholia*, trans. Leon S. Roudiez (New York: Columbia University Press, 1989), 28–29. "Specular identification" is a term borrowed from Lacan and describes a "mirror identification."
4. Diane Jonte-Pace, "Situating Kristeva Differently," in *Body/Text in Julia Kristeva: Religion, Women, and Psychoanalysis*, ed. David Crownfield (Albany: State University of New York Press, 1992), 20–22. Jonte-Pace comments on the passage cited in the previous footnote and the gendering of absence and death as feminine in psychoanalytic theory concluding that the "*religious and metaphysical language of presence and absence in western culture is/has become the language of gender*....The gendering of absence, or more specifically the feminizing of absence as lack, is what links religion to women....Yet the sameness of men and women is denied in a discourse of difference focusing on woman as absence, a discourse that conflates woman with death and man with life."
5. Kristeva, "Stabat Mater," *Tales of Love*, 242.
6. Ibid., 236.
7. Ibid.
8. A flagrant Biblical example of the reduction and "consecration" of woman as mother is 1 Timothy 2:9–15 (*NEB*) which ends "it was the woman who, yielding to deception, fell into sin. Yet she will be saved through motherhood—if only women continue in faith, love, and holiness, with a sober mind." In *The Power to Speak: Feminism, Language, God* (New York: Crossroad, 1991), Rebecca S. Chopp raises concerns similar to Kristeva's about the place of women in Christian discourse. She asks "why it is so difficult to say, 'O God our Mother,' and why it is so startling to uncover scriptural images suggestive of God as a woman. To begin, in this way, is to move to the issues of the social-symbolic ordering, to suggest that language has, not only images, but a certain economy, that it itself is ordered symbolically, and that God the Father is more than a metaphor that can be changed at will. No matter what the images or metaphors are or can be, there is a deep symbolic economy in culture that separates, as it divides the name of the Father and the order it represents with what is configured as 'woman' and the chaos she represents" (111). Much of Kristeva's writing on the conflation or reduction of the feminine to motherhood is influenced by Marina Warner's *Alone of All Her Sex: The Myth and the Cult of the Virgin Mary* (London: Weidnefeld and Nicolson, 1976). Kristeva's argument presupposes much of the work done by Warner, especially in "Stabat Mater" which is a focus of the next chapter. With regard to feminine identity, the following is illustrative of Warner's argument: "the fertility ascribed to her reinforces the mythology that motherhood is the central point of a woman's life, where all the streams of her nature converge and prosper....Therefore, although the Virgin's fruitfulness inspires the gayest and most joyful side of her cult, affirming rather than denying the world...it does not transform her into a divinity who restores the equilibrium between the sexes, or looses women from bonds of tedious biological teleology"(284). Warner argues that the myth of a virginal mother interlocks with a cultural and theological ideology of motherhood in which contemporary psychology (especially Jungian) colludes (335–36).
9. Kristeva, "Stabat Mater," 236.

10. Julia Kristeva, *About Chinese Women*, trans. Anita Barrows , reprint ed. (New York: Marion Boyars, 1993), 14. In a prefatory note to the book, Kristeva acknowledges that this work takes the form of a journal written in haste as she returned from her trip to China. The work is divided into two major sections; the first describes her own location as a Western female writer and the second gives an overview of Chinese women including their early matriarchal history. Sexual difference concerns her throughout the musings of her "journal" but it is the first portion with which we are concerned in this study.
11. Kristeva, "Women's Time," 193.
12. Jacques Lacan, "Dieu et la jouissance de la femme," in *Encore* (Paris: Seuil, 1975), 68 as cited by Julia Kristeva, "Women's Time," in *The Kristeva Reader*, ed. Toril Moi (New York: Columbia University Press, 1986), 204. (Title of Lacan's article translated is "God and the Jouissance of Woman.) "Women's Time" is also published in a collection of essays entitled *New Maladies of the Soul*, trans. Ross Guberman (New York: Columbia University Press, 1995), 201–224.
13. Kristeva, *About Chinese Women*, 17, my emphasis.
14. Ibid., 19.
15. Ibid., 21.
16. Ibid., 22.
17. Ibid., 25.
18. *Jouissance* is a technical term in Kristeva's works and remains untranslated in order to preserve a sense of its intended meaning which differs from Lacan's use of the term. Throughout Kristeva's writing it represents a total joy or ecstasy but there is also an implication of "presence of meaning" (i.e., *j'ouïs sens* or "I heard meaning"). See, Kristeva, *Desire in Language*, 16. For a more detailed explanation, see footnote 31 in the introduction.
19. Kristeva, *About Chinese Women*, 26. Here Kristeva makes reference to Ernst Jones' theory of female sexuality in which there is a denial of sexual difference. Her underlying assumption is that the ideal ascribed to by women within Christianity is the ideal of a virgin maternal.
20. Ibid., 27.
21. Ibid.
22. Ibid., 25.
23. I will return to this alternative and its significance for women struggling with depression in the next chapter.
24. Kristeva, *About Chinese Women*, 25
25. Ibid., 27–28.
26. Kristeva, *Black Sun*, 53. This passage recalls the manner in which William James described "sick soul" religion in *Varieties of Religious Experience: A Study in Human Nature*, reprint (New York: Penguin Books, 1983), 160–61. Kristeva's reference to speech as an "alien skin" is reminiscent of the "greenish skin" that James associated with his own depression and "sick soul" religion.
27. Reineke, *Sacrificed Lives*, 91–92.

28. Ewa Ziarek, "Kristeva and Levinas: Mourning, Ethics, and the Feminine," in *Ethics, Politics, and Difference in Julia Kristeva's Writing*, ed. Kelly Oliver (New York: Routledge, 1993), 72–73.
29. Ibid., 73. I will return to this thought in the fifth chapter when I discuss how Kristeva's work might inform those who offer pastoral care and counseling to women struggling with symptoms of depression. Perhaps, they might better be understood as "strangers" who critique the dominant social order by refusing to master its discourse because it belongs to the paternal symbolic order.
30. Ibid., 73–74.
31. Diane Jonte-Pace, "Situating Kristeva Differently," in *Body/Text in Julia Kristeva: Religion, Women and Psychoanalysis*, ed. David Crownfield (Albany: State University of New York, 1992), 13.
32. Ibid., 14.
33. Kristeva, *About Chinese Women*, 32.
34. Ibid., 30. Lisa Lowe's article, "*Des Chinoises*: Orientalism, Psychoanalysis, and Feminine Writing," in *Ethics, Politics, and Difference in Julia Kristeva's Writing*, ed. Kelly Oliver (New York: Routledge, 1993): 150–63 supports my reading of Kristeva at this point. See especially, pages 152–53.
35. More will be said about this in the next chapter.
36. Jonte-Pace, "Situating Kristeva Differently," 13–15. Like Reineke (see footnote 19 in Chapter 2), Jonte-Pace focuses on the work of women as death work and locates the essence of feminine identity in "difference." This means that absence is feminine; when understood this way it "contributes to a deeply embedded personal and cultural misogyny. The entanglement of the fear of woman and the fear of death mitigates against the possibility of transcending misogyny" (15). While I believe Kristeva offers a possibility of transcending misogyny, Jonte-Pace's concern is valid. The gendering of absence as feminine has oppressed women.
37. Kristeva, "Women's Time," *The Kristeva Reader*, 196.
38. Kristeva, *About Chinese Women*, 34.
39. Ibid., 35.
40. Kristeva, "Women's Time," 190.
41. Kelly Oliver, *Reading Kristeva: Unraveling the Double-Bind* (Indianapolis: Indiana University Press, 1993). See especially, her discussion of the double-bind as it relates to "marginal women," 107–13.
42. Kristeva, *About Chinese Women*, 36.
43. Ibid., 36–37.
44. An image of this Italian Renaissance painting may be viewed at Museum of Fine Arts, Boston, http://www.mfa.org as accession number 61.1200, last viewed 02/03/2010.
45. Kristeva, *About Chinese Women*, 36.
46. Ibid.
47. Ibid. 37. Kristeva cites dominance, the superego, and the endorsed communicative word among those values which are masculine.
48. Ibid.
49. Ibid., 38.

50. Ibid. See also, Kelly Oliver, *Reading Kristeva,* 109. Her reading of Kristeva here supports my interpretation.
51. Kristeva, "Women's Time," 191.
52. Ibid. Kristeva first introduces the term *chora* in *Revolution in Poetic Language,* trans. Margaret Waller (New York: Columbia University Press, 1984), 25–28 indicating that she borrows the term but not its particular meaning from Plato. For Kristeva, the semiotic *chora* describes the maternal space of mother-child symbiosis "where a subject is both generated and negated." As Kelly Oliver notes this maternal space is a space of need for the child which precedes desire. See *Reading Kristeva,* 35. Here Kristeva is simply describing that time before speech begins. In "From One Identity to An Other," *Desire in Language,* Kristeva refers to the semiotic *chora* as a maternal receptacle (133).
53. Mary Bittner Wiseman, "Renaissance Paintings and Psychoanalysis: Julia Kristeva and the Function of the Mother," in *Ethics, Politics, and Difference in Julia Kristeva's Writing,* ed. Kelly Oliver (New York: Routledge, 1993), 97. Wiseman's insights in her discussion of Kristeva's article on Bellini's Madonnas are germane to this discussion about "woman-mother" being identified with a space: "Fundamental to classical psychoanalysis is the principle that the mother is always already feminine and her infant masculine and its corollary that a girl becomes a woman by becoming (wanting to become) a mother. Kristeva unties this Freudian knot by freeing the feminine from the maternal and characterizing the mother not as *object* of the child's desire but as a *function,* her body the field on which the genetic code of the species and of the biological individual is written. The woman mother is not the *subject* of motherhood." In an earlier essay, "Stabat Mater," Kristeva does, however, focus on mother as subject.
54. Kristeva, "Motherhood According to Giovanni Bellini," *Desire in Language,* 237, my emphasis. It is important to note that much of what Kristeva has written concerning motherhood was inspired by her own pregnancy and written during the period of time when her son was born.
55. Toril Moi, ed., *The Kristeva Reader,* 188.
56. Kristeva, "Women's Time," 192.
57. Ibid. Another way to interpret the unavoidable contradiction that concerns Kristeva is the pressure women face to conform either to a strand of feminism which negates the true self or the patrilinear culture which requires a woman to subvert her feminine self in favor of an identity, time and history which is constraining. Again, the issue at stake is the absence of a language which really represents the particularity and individuality of each woman. "Woman" is not a collective but rather an infinity of individuals.
58. Ibid.
59. Julia Kristeva, "Women's Time," *New Maladies of the Soul,* trans. Ross Guberman (New York: Columbia University Press, 1995), 206. This is a revision of the essay which appears in *The Kristeva Reader* which states more clearly than the original Kristeva's association of "women's time" with the discourse of religion. Tina Chanter's article, "Female Temporality and the Future of Feminism," in *Abjection, Melancholia and Love: The Work of Julia Kristeva,* eds. John Fletcher and Andrew Benjamin (New York: Routledge, 1990), 68, supports the reading of "women's time" offered here but she is unconcerned with the association between the feminine and the religious.

60. Kristeva, "Women's Time," in *The Kristeva Reader*, 208.
61. Ibid., 210. The "adventure" to which Kristeva refers here is a radical process of "*interiorization of the founding separation of the socio-symbolic contract*, as an introduction of its cutting edge into the very interior of every identity whether subjective, sexual, ideological, or so forth" (emphasis Kristeva's). Kristeva is hopeful that in the future societies will no longer need an actual sacrificial scapegoat or victim but rather that each individual—both male and female—will be able to take an inward journey to recognize the reality that a potential victim and executioner exists within each. This process will result, she hopes, as a result of the tension between women's time or monumental time and linear time (paternal or historical time). I will return to this thought at the end of the chapter when I discuss her proposal for a third generation feminism.
62. See, for example, Toril Moi, ed., *The Kristeva Reader*, 138–39. Moi discusses the importance of the double-bind Kristeva identifies. Jonte-Pace's primary focus in "Situating Kristeva Differently" is not the double-bind or the restoration of a maternal discourse, though she does discuss the homology between women, religion, absence and death. Lowe's article, "Des Chinoises," is more concerned with feminine writing but examines the repression of femininity in the Western world.
63. Kristeva, *About Chinese Women*, 39, my emphasis.
64. Kristeva, *Black Sun*, 29.
65. Kristeva, *About Chinese Women*, 40.
66. Ibid., 40–41.
67. IIbid. 41.
68. Ibid.
69. Ibid.
70. Ibid.
71. The translation of the first stanza from the 1854 publication "*El Desdichado*," in *Les Filles du feu* is provided by Kristeva as follows: I am saturnine—and bereft—disconsolate,/ The Prince of Aquitaine whose tower has crumbled;/ My lone star is dead—and my bespangled lute/ Bears the *Black Sun* of *Melancholia*. See, *Black Sun* (141) for the entire poem and the original French text.
72. Kristeva, *Black Sun*, 150.
73. Ibid., 151.
74. Ibid., 152.
75. Ibid., 151.
76. Anna Smith, *Julia Kristeva: Readings of Exile and Estrangement*, 38.
77. Julia Kristeva, *This Incredible Need to Believe*, trans. Beverly Bie Brahic (New York: Columbia University Press, 2009).
78. Kristeva, *Black Sun*, 151.
79. Ibid., 41.
80. Ibid., 43.
81. Ibid., 43–44.
82. John Lechte, "Art, Love, and Melancholy in the Work of Julia Kristeva," in *Abjection, Melancholia, and Love: The Work of Julia Kristeva*, ed. John Fletcher and Andrew Benjamin (New York: Routledge,1990), 35.

83. Guberman, ed., *Interviews*, 79.
84. Ibid., 80.
85. Ibid.
86. Ibid., 81. In the same interview cited above Kristeva acknowledges that female depression is more common than male depression and "in some respects more difficult to treat because a woman's attachment to her mother is often insurmountable." I will begin to take up her solution to the difficulty in the next chapter.
87. Ibid., 84, my emphasis.
88. Kristeva, *Black Sun*, 60. She states: "Kant asserted that nostalgic persons did not desire the place of their youth but their youth itself; their desire is a search for the *time* and not for the *thing* to be recovered." Immanuel Kant, *Anthropologie in pragmatischer Hinsicht* as quoted by Jean Starobinski in "Le Concept de nostalgie," *Diogène* (1966), 54: 92–115, as cited by Kristeva.
89. Ibid.
90. Ibid., 61.
91. Ibid., 57, her emphasis. Kristeva's emphasis on the importance of the mother's voice and musical or tonal inflection is also evident in Erik Erikson's analysis of the young Martin Luther: "I will state, as a clinician's judgment, that nobody could speak and sing as Luther later did if his *mother's voice had not sung to him of some heaven*; that nobody could be as torn between his masculine and his feminine sides, nor have such a range of both who did not at one time feel that he was like his mother but also, that nobody would discuss women and marriage in the way he often did who had not been deeply disappointed by his mother–and had become loath to succumb the way she did to the father, to fate. And if the soul is man's most bisexual part, then we will be prepared to find in Luther both some horror of mystic succumbing and some spiritual search for it, and to recognize in this alternative some emotional and spiritual derivatives of little Martin's '*prehistoric' relation to his mother* " (my emphasis). Erik Erikson, *Young Man Luther: A Study in Psychoanalysis and History* (New York: W. W. Norton, 1993 reissue), 72–3. I suggest that the "prehistoric relation to his mother" is at the very least analogous to the mourned lost maternal object Kristeva writes about. Kristeva returns to this issue in a more recent publication, *The Sense and Non-sense of Revolt: The Powers and Limits of Psychoanalysis*, trans. Jeanine Herman (New York: Columbia University Press, 2000). See especially Chapters 1, 2 and 5.
92. Smith, *Julia Kristeva: Readings of Exile and Estrangement*, 101. Smith is discussing Kristeva's dissertation, *Revolution in Poetic Language;* the emphasis of this discussion centers on the rhythm or metricality of language as it is associated with the maternal tongue which ultimately is required for language to have meaning.
93. Kristeva, *Black Sun*, 42.
94. Ibid., 99.

CHAPTER FOUR

The Splitting of the Woman-Mother in Western Christianity: The Need for a Maternal Discourse

Who, on Christ's dear mother gazing, Pierced by anguish so amazing, Born of woman, would not weep?

—Stabat Mater

In the last chapter we noted how the association of women with the abject leads to their identification with a space as opposed to a time. This association with the abject also leads to a condition of self-estrangement experienced as depression or melancholia. Western Christianity leaves women with few choices for claiming their difference and giving it a voice.[1] Kristeva views the splitting of the mother or the feminine into a "woman-mother" as the locus of melancholia which intensifies the experience of isolation and silence for the woman-mother since, in effect, she needs to reject a part of herself in order to be able to name herself. Yet, Kristeva maintains that hope is located in the reclamation of a maternal discourse, and leads us to the question raised in the last chapter: "Is there something in that Maternal notion that ignores what a woman might say or want?"[2]

In order to begin to address this question, I will use Kristeva's essay, "Motherhood According to Giovanni Bellini" to show how Kristeva views Bellini's Madonnas as representative of the splitting experienced by women in

Western Christianity. She does so by employing da Vinci's paintings of Madonnas as a foil. At this point, we can anticipate the objection: "But these are *male* artists!" In what manner does Kristeva's discussion of male artists contribute to a discussion of a woman's experience of separation from her mother? How will this help us to understand her experience of depression? Inasmuch as the language of paintings is visual or preverbal, the language of male artists *is* the language of semiotics or what Kristeva has identified as feminine. As she observes, "Bellini penetrates through the being and language of the father to position himself in the *place* where the mother could have been reached."[3] In this sense, by focusing on the male artists' struggle to represent the maternal as "object," we obtain some idea of *how estranged* women are from themselves as woman-mother. In other words, Bellini provides motherhood with a language but "deprives it of a right to a real existence (there is nothing 'feminist' in Bellini's action)."[4]

The "feminist task" of providing a language for motherhood is Kristeva's concern in "Stabat Mater" which serves as a primary text in this chapter. Here, she attempts to render in words what Bellini rendered with images. The realm of motherhood is an "impossible elsewhere." Kristeva continues the themes she introduced in "Women's Time": a woman's time, a woman's space (or place), and the problem of a maternal discourse. In concluding this chapter, I will revisit her essay, "Women's Time," to introduce the possibility of a third generation feminism that represents an attitude rather than a specific era or generation. Her brief essay, "The Wheel of Smiles,"[5] is also a primary text in which she returns to the theme of a counter-Trinity (introduced in "Stabat Mater"). It will serve as a bridge to the fifth chapter where the power of the Word (particularly as love) in Christian and psychoanalytic discourse will be examined. As Kristeva notes with respect to Christianity, "'In the beginning' was the reflection of loving gazes."[6]

The "Woman-Mother" or the Splitting of Motherhood

In order to be able to assist a woman to give voice to her sadness and self-estrangement, one needs to understand her subjectivity as well as her position as a "maternal object." In her essay, "Motherhood According to Giovanni Bellini," Kristeva examines the splitting of motherhood within Western Christianity by reflecting on paintings of Madonnas which exemplify the invisible space that a "woman-mother" occupies. These Madonnas are representations of the woman-mother as "object." She maintains that there are only two discourses (i.e., science and Christian theology) which can account for "becoming-a-mother."[7] Science is flawed since it is unconcerned about the mother as subject; Christian theology, on the other hand, "defines maternity only *as an impossible elsewhere*, a sacred beyond, a vessel of divinity, a spiritual tie with the ineffable godhead, and transcendence's ultimate support—necessarily virginal and committed to assumption."[8] Kristeva's refrain that women are consigned to a place that is no place, the place of the abject,[9] is more than a faint echo here as she discusses Christian theology's definition of motherhood. The difficulty with this theological perspective is that it "establishes a sort of subject at the point where the *subject and its speech split apart, fragment, and vanish*."[10] Is it any wonder then that Christian women often present as depressed with an empty speech since Christian theology consigns their very subjectivity to an "impossible elsewhere" at a point in time when speech vanishes?[11]

Kristeva suggests that we consider the mother as "subject of gestation, in other words the *master* of a process that science...acknowledges it cannot now...take away from her; if we suppose her to be *master* of a process that is prior to the social-symbolic-linguistic contract of the group, then we acknowledge the risk of losing identity at the same time as we ward it off."[12] For Kristeva, the importance of this priority of the Mother is that "the maternal body is the place of a splitting, which, even though hypostatized by Christianity, nonetheless remains a constant factor of social reality."[13] What is at stake here is the function of the mother as woman-subject. She insures reproduction while acting as "more of a *filter* than anyone else—a thoroughfare, a threshold where 'nature' confronts 'culture.' To imagine that there is *someone* in that filter—such is the source of religious mystifications."[14] The woman-mother as a speaking subject then serves not only as a filter for interactions with culture but as the source of a religious attitude. Moreover, if the mother as subject were not "on this threshold, if the mother were not, that is, phallic, then every speaker would be led to conceive of its Being in relation to some void...a permanent threat against, first, its mastery, and ultimately, its stability."[15] The woman-mother is represented as a "no one" in a "no place" or the place of splitting—an impossible imaginary realm. And yet, Kristeva suggests that there has to be a "someone" or a subject in this place of the speaker for the "subject-in-process" to develop appropriately.

The act of "becoming-a-mother" is experienced by the woman-mother as a "reunion with the body of *her* mother."[16] Thus, a reunion occurs with the lost maternal object which was never given up completely occurs. Through this process, the woman-mother "actualizes the homosexual facet of motherhood, through which a woman is simultaneously closer to her instinctual memory, more open to her own psychosis, and consequently, more negatory of the social, symbolic bond."[17] Here again, the woman-mother's relationship to negativity is inescapable. As Wiseman notes, however, this is one point at which Kristeva differentiates herself from Freud and classical psychoanalysis in that she determines there is both a *maternal* and a *paternal* facet to motherhood.[18]

How is this discussion of the facets of motherhood related to the issue, noted earlier, of the maternal tongue and religious discourse as a possible solution to feminine depression? The answer lies in Kristeva's understanding of the woman-mother's relief from this situation:

> *The symbolic paternal facet* relieves feminine aphasia present within the desire to bear the father's child. It is an appeasement that turns into melancholy as soon as the child becomes an object, a gift to others, neither self nor part of the self, an object destined to be a subject, an other. Melancholy readjusts the paranoia that drives to action (often violent) and to discourse (essentially parental, object-oriented, and pragmatic discourse) the feminine, verbal scarcity so prevalent in our culture.[19]

While the symbolic paternal facet of motherhood may relieve the woman-mother's loss of words, it does so only temporarily. The melancholy anguish returns as soon as the child separates from the mother and calls her by name. The woman-mother returns again to mournful silence still clinging to the mother she never agreed to lose. Again, Kristeva's assertion is descriptive of a situation that exists in Western Christian culture: discourse is centered on the Word of the father which leads to a scarcity of feminine discourse. The woman-mother's so-called relief is a state of melancholy but one which opens the window into the soul that Kristeva elsewhere describes as "this psychological space...that is no doubt the hidden side, the invisible and indispensable source of what is Beautiful."[20]

Another window into the "invisible and indispensable source of beauty" that is the maternal body is provided by Western art. The language of art (as opposed to religious or Christian discourse, or even poetic discourse), in Kristeva's estimation, follows a different aspect of "maternal jouissance, the sublimation taking place at the very moment of primal repression within the mother's body, arising perhaps unwittingly out of her marginal position. At the intersection of sign and rhythm, of representation and light, of the symbolic and the semiotic, the artist speaks from a place where she is not, where she knows not."[21] Why is this significant for a discussion of the need for a maternal discourse, especially in Christian discourse? Kristeva states: "The very existence of aesthetic practice makes clear that the *Mother as subject is a delusion,* just as the negation of the so-called poetic dimension of language leads one to believe in the existence of the Mother, and consequently, of transcendence."[22] Thus, the mother is the place where a "subject-in-process" first becomes aware of the "clashes that occur between the biological and social programs of the species."[23] It is the artist, however, who "before all other speakers...bears witness to what the unconscious (through the screen of the mother) records."[24] Moreover, the representation of motherhood in art from "Byzantine iconography to Renaissance humanism" illustrates two emerging attitudes toward the maternal body that prefigure

> two destinies within the very economy of Western representation....On the one hand, there is a tilting toward the body as fetish. On the other, a predominance of luminous, chromatic difference beyond and despite corporeal representation. Florence and Venice. Worship of the figurable, representable man; or integration of the image accomplished in its truth-likeness within the luminous serenity of the *unrepresentable.*[25]

In Kristeva's view, da Vinci represents the former attitude toward the maternal body, i.e., the tilting toward the body or fetish. This is the attitude of "the paternal facet." In contrast, Bellini represents the latter attitude of the maternal facet, whose significance lies in the fact that his brush retains "the traces of a marginal experience, through and across which a maternal body might recognize its own, otherwise inexpressible in our culture."[26] Here, too, the place of the mother is linked with an unconscious truth but it belongs to an "impossible elsewhere" that continues to be inexpressible. Why inexpressible? There is no discourse to represent it.

Though art is not the focus of this project, a complete understanding of how Kristeva envisions motherhood as well as the importance of a maternal discourse is impossible without first examining what she has to say about Bellini, using da Vinci as a back drop. She considers their work a type of narrative.[27] In da Vinci's case,[28] the narrative represents the paternal facet or body fetish especially since he portrays the mother as forbidden, as a "primordial seducer" who serves as "the limit of an archaic, infantile jouissance that must never be reproduced. She established the child's diffident narcissism and cult of the masculine body which he ceaselessly painted, even when a mother figures at the center of the painting."[29] Why is this significant for our discussion? It is the artist alone who makes the maternal figure exist because she is so completely absorbed with her child. Here the maternal space is the object of male desire with no language or experience to name as her own. Even as Kristeva suggests: "As long as there is father, a magisterial Lord, an intimate of Power, Leonardo turns to his symbolic power, eclipsing maternal imprint; he stops the gap in repression and surges towards scientific knowledge rather than investigating through graphic arts the pleasure-anguish within unconscious formations."[30] This would become the dominant form of representation for the next four hundred years. Thus, "[t]he artist, as servant of the maternal phallus, displays this always and everywhere unaccomplished art of reproducing bodies and spaces as graspable, masterable *objects*, within reach of his eye and hand."[31]

Bellini, on the other hand, represents the maternal facet or "luminous yet unrepresentable" space of motherhood. Kristeva insures that the reader is aware of the circumstances of the births of both painters; both men were sons born out of wedlock. The mother in Bellini's paintings is absent and Kristeva wonders if this absence or distance points to "the disavowal of a 'sin' committed beyond the law's purview and of which Giovanni was the result."[32] She encourages us to consider the distance, even outright hostility, which separates the bodies of the infants from their mothers in Bellini's paintings of Madonnas because that distance represents *the maternal space* which "is there, nevertheless—fascinating, attracting, and puzzling. But we have no direct access to it. As if there were a maternal *function* that...was merely ineffable jouissance, beyond discourse, beyond narrative, beyond psychology, beyond lived experience and biography—in short, beyond figuration."[33] In her description of Bellini's depiction of Madonnas[34] one is able to see through Kristeva's window into the "hidden side" of what she deems the soul or source of melancholy beauty:

> Even though the hands clasp the child and bodies sometimes hug each other, the mother is only partially present...head, face, and eyes—flees the painting, is gripped by something other than its object. And the painter as baby can never reach this elsewhere, this inaccessible peace colored with melancholy, neither through the portrayed corporeal contact, nor by the distribution of colored blocks outlining corporeal volumes.[35]

Kristeva conveys in words what Bellini portrayed on his canvas with a brush. The maternal space is unreachable for the child despite the hands clasped or bodies touching in a maternal embrace. Rather Kristeva suggests that it is as if

Bellini "sensed a shattering, a loss of identity, a sweet jubilation where *she* is not; but without 'her'—without eyes or vision—an *infinitesimal division* of color and space rhythmically produce a peculiar, serene joy. To touch the mother would be to possess this presumed jouissance and to make it visible."[36]

The language that Kristeva would use later in *Black Sun* to describe women's depression and melancholia figures prominently in this essay. The woman-mother is "where *she* is not" in Bellini's paintings of Madonnas and her peace is colored by the rhythm of melancholia. Kristeva indicates that touching the mother would be the equivalent of experiencing a "sweet jubilation" or jouissance that can never be reached because the woman-mother is inaccessible. Does this "sweet jubilation" or maternal jouissance which she so poetically describes remain an inaccessible numinous experience for Kristeva? What is one to make of the fact that even her later works continue to pursue sacred themes in relation to the feminine in psychoanalysis? Is it an indication of the continuing inaccessibility of the woman-mother as well as her jouissance? If the return of the lost mother is to occur at all, is it to be experienced in a sacred or religious context?[37]

This representation of motherhood as an "impossible elsewhere" or inaccessible jouissance is important in Kristeva's economy because "Bellini penetrates through the being and language of the father to position himself in the place where the mother could have been reached." [38] In doing so, as Kristeva observes, he portrays "this always-already-past conditional of the maternal function," as a type of incest or "a kind of possession of the mother, which provides motherhood, *that mute border, with a language*."[39] Thus the mother is not portrayed as a "referential object" but the portrait of mother and child evokes an inner experience. The woman-mother previously understood as a silent border, a nonexistent elsewhere, who initiates language development, is provided with a *language*. Yet, we see again, the woman-mother is represented as a mute-border. While the mother-child representation is portrayed as a fetishized image, the luminous background of Bellini's paintings insure that the mother is not seen as "object" but the narrative of the painting discloses an inner, subjective experience. In a sense, the mother is nowhere to be seen but the painter's own inner experience of his mother is portrayed. Thus motherhood is not objectified but an "inner experience" is evoked by Bellini's Madonnas.

How does this assist women who struggle with depression? Somehow the "woman-mother" needs to be able to "touch the mother." As Kristeva concludes, a major goal of analysis is "to reach the threshold of repression by means of the identification with motherhood (be it as heterosexuality or symbolic incest), to reach this threshold where maternal jouissance, alone impassable, is arrayed."[40] Thus in order to "touch the mother," one needs to return to the place where repression first began to occur. Kristeva's study of Bellini's Madonnas assists us in this return to the origins of our repression.

It is beyond the scope of this project to critique Kristeva's "art criticism." The manner in which she traces an attitude toward motherhood in Bellini's paintings of Madonnas does, however, illumine contemporary conversations concerning women and motherhood. In the same essay, she draws a link between Byzantine iconography and Renaissance paintings by offering a brief word study of *ergasterion* (which means workshop) to demonstrate that the "orthodox conception of the Virgin" is that of "privileged *space*, living *area*, *ladder* (of Jacob), or *door* (of the Temple in Ezekiel's vision)—*dwelling*, in short; she is thus seen as a *union*, a *contact without gap, without separation*, and these functions make of her a metaphor for the Holy Ghost."[41] Whether or not one agrees with her interpretation, what is significant for this project is her continual emphasis upon the woman-mother, in this case the Virgin Mary, as a space (the mother's womb, in particular) whose function as mother is primary.

Bellini's early portraits of Madonnas are characterized as "coldly distant and impassive. Contact between mother and child is by the tips of fingers alone....Her contemplative look borders on sadness as if the baby were already crucified."[42] This coupling of the Nativity with the Crucifixion is noteworthy since it is "as if the son's death were supposed to provide a necessarily tragic and human rendition of this *indeterminate passion-anguish-melancholy-joy* giving iridescence to the serenity of the maternal body."[43] Central to an understanding of Kristeva's interpretation of Bellini's Madonnas is her concentration on the separation between mother and child as well as "the split character of the maternal body" which is best exemplified by the *Madonna and Child* in Bergamo.[44] Recall that the mother's body in Kristeva's economy is the place of splitting. Bellini's work progresses from a portrayal of a "cold and sad mother," to a "possessive mother," to a "hostile mother," and finally, to "the luminous space where she surrogates herself."[45] Moreover, in Bellini's progression one may observe how "the sacred, combining retention and instinctual drive, transforms the former distance-pleasure balance into distance-anguish."[46]

It was Bellini's own experience as a father and husband which led to the final transformation of his paintings where one can witness how he came to terms with

> the archaic impact of the maternal body on man...in order somehow to admit the threat that the male feels as much from the possessive maternal body as from his separation from it...and finally, in order, not to demystify the mother, but to find her an increasingly appropriate language, capable of capturing her specific imaginary jouissance.[47]

Notice again, Kristeva's choice of language here: the mystery of motherhood is preserved but the woman-mother acquires "an increasingly appropriate language" through her portrayal on a canvas. In these paintings the woman-mother is portrayed with a characterless gaze and a silent voice, but with an unshakable intimacy as well a definite pleasure.[48] In these paintings, the "volume" of the mother's voice (a somewhat ambiguous term as it can be understood in terms of both depth and sound) is achieved through Bellini's use of color and light. Thus in the final series of Bellini's Madonnas, Kristeva observes that the mother's face is calm, almost as if she is absent from the painting itself, yet dreaming of an experience that resists representation. The infants in this series are painted parallel and close to the bodies of the mothers but appear to be more easily separated from the mother. The canvas is generally divided and flooded with light (distinct from earlier motherhood paintings) but perhaps most important in this final series is the fact that the

> maternal figure increasingly appears as a *module*, a process, present only to justify this cleaved space she is again the ἐργαστήριον (*ergasterion*), privileged space and living area. Moreover, the very human, that is *psychological* passion between adult and child seems to be displaced from woman toward a man....Is not the object-oriented libido always masculine?[49]

Can the woman-mother's experience be signified? Will she be retrieved from the recesses of her impossible elsewhere in order to exhibit a presence? Not simply as represented in a portrait but in reality itself?

Within the confines of portraiture, however, Kristeva believes that the woman-mother's presence makes itself felt in a most surprising place—Bellini's *Venus*.[50] Here, her face is the face of a previous Madonna whose "averted, modest, ecstatic, melancholic, or reticent gaze...projects from the depths of the pupils to see itself, to encounter itself, not in the object-for-others that is the infant, nor even in the viewer...but in the pseudo-object made up by the mirror itself."[51] Now the Venus/Madonna is "[f]ace to face with primary narcissism, restraint persists along with a kind of statement of insurmountable limits: 'This is how it is.' The Virgin has come down from her clothed exile in an elsewhere that racked her."[52] Venus has emerged from the shadows to which the Virgin image had banished her. True, this "uncovered woman" remained split. Yet in his representation of Venus, Bellini added his own unique touch like a man returned from the future insofar as he portrayed this Virgin become Venus with "a luminous coloration surpassing any representation of the nude body. This 'sacred' element had long accompanied the image of his maternal bodies; since it was thus engendered by, but also already detached from, virginal figurations...Bellini...nevertheless encountered and revealed his main preoccupation (jouissance)."[53] Venus, then, is the woman-mother who appears when one steps beyond the threshold of repression, from behind the "looking-glass" into time.

Kristeva's study of Bellini's Madonnas leads her to conclude: "Our long biographical and historical, sacred and figural journey has shown that for Bellini, motherhood is nothing more than such a luminous spatialization, the ultimate language of a jouissance at the far limits of repression, whence bodies, identities, and signs are begotten."[54] It is against the background of her essay on Bellini's Madonnas that Kristeva's own conception of motherhood as woman-mother needs to be understood. This brings us to her well-known essay, "Stabat Mater."

Stabat Mater[55]**—Discourse of Maternal Jouissance**

What are the implications of Kristeva's "Motherhood According to Bellini" for women? Just this: The woman-mother looks back to an impossible elsewhere that reflects on maternal jouissance or looks forward into an impossible elsewhere of the future filled with grief.[56] The accent of the Latin hymn that inspires Kristeva's essay, "Stabat Mater," is upon the mother's grief.[57] In her introduction to "Stabat Mater," Toril Moi reminds us that the opening line of the Latin text literally means, "Stood, the Mother, full of grief." In effect, Kristeva attempts to paint motherhood in words the same way Bellini did with light and color. Just as the body of the woman-mother is a place of splitting, so too, Kristeva "splits" the text into two columns:[58] the left column appears in bold print and represents a somewhat autobiographical account of motherhood while the right column is an analytical text devoted to history and theory surrounding motherhood and the Christian construct of the Virgin

Mary.[59] At times, the left column disappears. The form of this essay is as important as the content insofar as "religious discourse *about* the mother must coexist with a parallel discourse...*by* a mother. This essay's narrative strategies and construction of both its speaking and reading subject(s) are as much part of its meaning as—and inseparable from—its propositional statements or theses."[60]

Kristeva begins her analytic text with a question that seems to counter Freud's famous "What does a woman *want*?" She asks: "What is a woman?" and then suggests that to answer this question would run "the risk of abolishing her difference."[61] Perhaps, then, we first need to ask a more fundamental question: "What is a mother?" In response, Kristeva suggests that the only function for women (other sex) is to become a mother but this is an important function since all of existence is attributed to motherhood (specifically the "privileged space" or womb). Yet upon closer examination "this motherhood is the *fantasy* that is nurtured by the adult, man or woman, of a lost territory; what is more, it involves less an idealized archaic mother than the idealization of the *relationship* that binds us to her, one that cannot be localized—an idealization of primary narcissism."[62] Thus, again, a lost territory or place of absence figures prominently in Kristeva's description of the fantasy that adults hold when it comes to motherhood. Here, however, it is not an idealized maternal object but an idealized relationship that will be the focus of her study. The right column continues with an elaboration of what the "refined symbolic construct" or "maternal" is in Christianity. Of this construct, she writes: "Let us call 'maternal' the ambivalent principle that is bound to the species, on the one hand, and on the other stems from an identity catastrophe that causes the Name to topple over into the unnameable that one imagines as femininity, nonlanguage, or body."[63] The feminine is once again linked by Kristeva to what is unnameable or that which represents an identity catastrophe.

At this point, the left column proceeds to describe, in a personal manner, the experience of becoming a mother. The words literally leap off the page in bold (and sometimes upper case) type:

> FLASH—instant of time or dream without time...Words that are always too distant...folding in unimaginable spaces. Writing them down is an ordeal of discourse, like love....Flash on the unnameable...take a chance with meaning under a veil of words. WORD FLESH....metaphors of the invisible.[64]

It is as if the "metaphors of the invisible" signal the disappearance of the left column for at this point the more personal description ceases for a time (i.e., several pages). The woman-mother, as before, occupies an invisible or unimaginable and unnameable space. The words to paint the picture of motherhood are too distant. Not surprisingly, they belong to an unnameable discourse, but one which is akin to love. A prelude to the "cure" is already present in that the idealized maternal relationship will serve as a basis for the transference relationship which provides the foundation for the speaking cure grounded in love. Thus there is a need to find a discourse for motherhood, one which will recognize the speaking subject as religion once did.[65] What follows echoes, in part, the gospel of John (e.g., the Word became flesh and dwelt among us) as Kristeva continues, "Christ, the Son of man, when all is said and done, is 'human' only through his mother."[66] The woman-mother's body, the space where splitting takes place is still that invisible space where word becomes flesh.

FLASH. With a flash,[67] Kristeva captures the reader's attention and her use of the term brings to mind the term "ontological flash" which Gerhart and Russell offer as "a possible motive for doing metaphoric violence to our worlds of meanings."[68] They suggest that metaphors do not exist but are created; thus, an ontological flash has "the capacity to give a sense of the tension before and after new meaning is created."[69] Similarly, Kristeva employs the very word "flash" to accomplish the metaphorical violence suggested by Gerhart and Russell.[70] It is exactly such violence that she wants to accomplish, challenging our commonplace notions about the place of women in culture. She does so by representing in words—in the left hand column—the very experience (including her own) of motherhood. As Anna Smith observes: "The experience of motherhood...threatens conventional discourse with collapse."[71] Thus the personal voice representing the experience of motherhood challenges the repression discourse about the mother-as-Virgin in the right hand column.

The first move Kristeva makes to subvert maternal discourse is to present a brief historical overview of the "virginal cult" in Christianity. She points to the "translation error" which is responsible for identifying "virgin" with the physiological and psychological condition of virginity (namely, that "virgin" in the infancy narratives simply means that Mary was a virgin prior to the conception of Jesus, thus indicating that he was her first born. The idea that she *remained* a virgin is a later interpretation.) Nevertheless, "[t]he fact remains that western Christianity has organized that 'translation error,' projected its own fantasies into it, and produced one of the most powerful imaginary constructs known in the history of civilizations."[72] This is important since "[i]n the rare instances when the Mother of Jesus appears in the Gospels, she is informed that filial relationship rests not with the flesh but *with the name* or, in other words, that any possible matrilinearism is to be repudiated and the *symbolic link alone is to last.*"[73] Thus primacy is given to the Name and Word of the Father which eclipses the possibility of a maternal discourse from the beginning. Yet Mary's legacy lives on, and its most significant aspect, in Kristeva's view concerns the relationship between Mary and the believer which she describes as "the prototype of a love relationship" insofar as it "followed two fundamental aspects of western love; courtly love and child love, thus fitting the entire range that goes from sublimation to asceticism and masochism."[74] Only after Kristeva introduces the fact that Mary experiences neither sex nor death does the more personal left column reappear. In the ensuing parallelism, the analytic text focuses on the problem of time as well as the nature of human relationships and God-human relationships, while the more personal discourse centers on the personal pain in becoming a mother (analogous to the pain involved in becoming a speaking subject). The reader needs to make a decision about which column to read first and how much before listening to the other voice(s).[75] The bold face type in the left hand column, however, implicitly asks that this column be read first, or if not first, at least be viewed as a "threat" to the conventional discourse of the right hand column.[76]

The written text suggests an atonal or bi-tonal duet of sorts throughout which the voices compete. In the left hand column, the introduction of a possibility of taming the maternal or primary narcissism is inserted before her description of maternal pain, **"the happiness of a faceless head, Narcissuslike touching without eyes, sight dissolving in muscles...peaceful colors. Mamma: anamnesis."**[77] This text like so many of her other depictions of motherhood, suggests an absent mother or at the very least one who is not able to see or respond. The personal discourse proceeds to echo, as if an antiphon mimicking as well as confronting, the historical presentation of the theological debate over Mary's sexless, sinless, deathless (but also joyless) life:

> And yet, when its own joy, my child's returns, its smile washes only my eyes. But the pain, its pain–it comes from inside, never remains apart, other, it inflames me at once, without a second's respite....One does not give birth in pain, one gives birth to pain: the child represents it and henceforth it settles in, it is continuous...a mother is

> always branded by pain, she yields to it. "And a sword will pierce your own soul too...."[78]

The passion that belongs to the woman-mother's space is expressed in the personal discourse that stands over against the analytic discourse in a manner which is much more gripping. The repetition of the word "pain" gives this discourse an emotional power that is missing from the theological discourse.

Here, the images Kristeva uses to describe the birthing process itself are haunting as the topics of life, death, and sexuality (self-consciously repressed in the right hand column) are intertwined in the text. And still the silence of the woman is deafening:

> All those words, now, ever visible things to register the roar of a silence that hurts all over....Yet the eye picked up nothing, the ear remained deaf....Frozen placenta, live limb of a skeleton, monstrous graft of life on myself, a living dead. Life...death...undecidable....Still life. There is him, however, his own flesh, which was mine yesterday. Death, then, how could I yield to it?[79]

Even though the woman-mother inhabits the land of the living dead after giving birth, she does not—cannot—yield to death because she has a child. A part of the woman-mother lives on, no matter what she does. With this comment on death in the context of giving birth, the left column is suspended again while the right column examines the power of the "cult of the Virgin Mary."

The discussion of love and power come together as Kristeva continues her analysis of the virginal cult. She notes that various aspects of "Western love" converge on Mary but in the form of an extreme asceticism as opposed to the type of courtly love which would have been demonstrated for a lady of nobility. Moreover, this Marian cult was responsible for homologizing Mary with Jesus. Nevertheless, Mary and women of nobility

> are the focal point of men's desires and aspirations....This feminine power must have been experienced as denied power, more pleasant to seize because it was both archaic and secondary, a kind of substitute for effective power in the family and the city but no less authoritarian, the underhand double of explicit phallic power.[80]

What is most important about this homology of the Lady and the Virgin is that "the Virgin explicitly became the focus of courtly love, thus gathering the attributes of the desired woman and of the holy mother in a totality as accomplished as it was *inaccessible*."[81] Feminine power is experienced as *denied power* and the woman-mother dwells in an *inaccessible* place. This is the price that the woman-mother is required to pay in exchange for her "elevation" to a status of reverence and devotion. Love reigns, but at the expense of power and accessibility. Thus, the Virgin "became the fulcrum of the humanization of the West in general and of love in particular."[82]

The dialogue of Kristeva's "Stabat Mater" now turns to a discussion of the price of a mother's love as the left column reappears. When the left column or personal voice returns, it begins with a sensual description of nursing the infant. The sensuality of the mother-son relationship is interrupted by a childhood memory of the maternal relationship (presumably Kristeva's own flashback):

> The wakeful tongue quietly remembers another withdrawal, mine....Recovered childhood, dreamed peace restored, in sparks, flash of cells, instants of laughter, smiles in the blackness of dreams, at night, opaque joy that roots me in her bed, my mother's, and projects him, a son, a butterfly soaking up dew from her hand, there, nearby, in the night. Alone: she, I, and he.[83]

The peace is only one that is dreamed about; the "black sun" enters with the blackness, the darkness of dreams. The "flash of cells" recalls the depiction of motherhood from Kristeva's essay on Bellini's Madonnas ("cells fuse, split, and proliferate") so that the splitting of the woman-mother overshadows her experience of jouissance (her joy is opaque). There is looming already a "shroud" of darkness even as there is a partial refrain of "alone of her sex" as well as the mother, "blood-thirsty fury, She is I." Here Kristeva heralds the "counter-Trinity" (i.e., counter to that of Christian theology) that is the focal point in her essay, "The Wheel of Smiles."[84] In the act of giving birth, the woman-mother experiences a closeness with her own mother that she had not previously experienced. This closeness between the woman-mother, her mother and her son is elevated to the level of a mystical experience and offered as a "counterweight" to the Trinity of Christian theology.

At the same time, the analytic text discusses the "famous nativity of Piero della Francesca in London"[85] which depicts a shift in the virginal cult from one of "high spirituality that assimilated the Virgin to Christ" to an "earthly conception of a wholly human mother" which "comes closer to 'lived' feminine experience than the earlier representations did."[86] Whereas before the Virgin held the child gazing lifelessly beyond the canvas, now she is depicted kneeling before her child with her head lowered and this leads Kristeva to conclude that this mother like "every mother is unconsciously aware" that "maternal devotion or even sacrifice is but an insignificant price to pay. *A price that is borne all the more easily since, contrasted with the love that binds a mother to her son, all other "human relationships" burst like blatant shams.*"[87] The analytic text, here, mimics the personal representation of the left hand column in that a woman-mother's immortality is recognized in the fact that she will live in and through her son. For this, she sacrifices her life. It is, however, a sacrifice she is willing to pay because other human relationships—e.g., father to son—are ephemeral in comparison. Hers is a head lowered in grief—for herself, for her mother, for all mothers past, present and future—but, at the same time, she takes immeasurable pride in the fact that a high price was, indeed, paid with a mother's love. This particular representation of the Mother "conveys many essential aspects of maternal psychology"[88] but it "integrates a certain feminine masochism" as it "displays its counterpart in gratification and jouissance."[89] Even in the text there is evidence of the split subject who cannot experience jouissance without a certain sadness or anguish as here the right and left "voices" overlap.

Next, Kristeva addresses the subject of the feminine body related to sexuality. The analytic text reports "[w]e are entitled only to the ear of the virginal body, the tears, and the breast. With the female sexual organ changed into an innocent shell, holder of sound, there arises a possible tendency to eroticize hearing, voice, or even understanding."[90] Thus, feminine sexuality is both denied and displaced. The Virgin is not desexualized, but her sexuality is expressed vocally, aurally, and as spiritualized knowing. Pervading this displacement of her sexuality is an aura of sorrow. What then is the Mother's so-called privilege? Kristeva's answer is that a mother's milk and her tears are privileged signs because they "are the metaphors of nonspeech, of a 'semiotics' that linguistic communication does not account for. The Mother and her attributes, evoking sorrowful humanity, thus become representatives of a 'return of the repressed' in monotheism."[91] She likens milk and tears (i.e., maternal attributes) to Freud's identification of the "father complex" in the history of monotheism, where the murdered father returns to haunt the guilty sons. The mother, also victim of sacrificial death, returns in the form of the one who sorrows for her dying son. In Kristeva's text the "split" is overcome as the two columns begin to converge. Now the anguish of motherhood is evident in both columns.

The left column, written in a "personal voice," had spoken of "milk and tears" prior to the right column. Now it joins the right column in a "chorus" of anguish:

> Absence, inferno, forgetfulness. Rhythm of our loves. A hunger remains, in place of the heart. A spasm that spreads, runs through the blood vessels to the tips of the breasts, to the tips of the fingers. It throbs, pierces the void, erases it, and gradually settles in. My heart: a tremendous pounding wound. A thirst. Anguished, guilty.[92]

The woman-mother experiences absence, a fire, an emptiness "pierced" by overtones of a denied sexuality from which issues guilt and anguish.[93] This is the absence—the abjection—of the feminine. This is the portrait of women in Western religious discourse which gives rise to a struggle with depression for many religious women. The personal voice fades again, **"Nothing reassures, for only the law sets anything down. Who calls such a suffering jouissance? It is the pleasure of the damned."**[94] The "analyst's objective voice" continues the theme for a short time as it discusses Mary's own pain at the foot of the cross which Kristeva claims is unjustifiable "unless it be the desire to experience within her own body the death of a human being, which her feminine fate of being the source of life spares her."[95] This leads Kristeva to wonder if "love, as puzzling as it is ancient, of mourners for corpses relates to the same longing of a woman whom nothing fulfills....And yet, Marian pain is in no way connected with tragic outburst: joy and even a kind of triumph follow upon tears."[96] This, then, is not the railing against death that often characterizes the male response (e.g., Dylan Thomas' "rage, rage, against the dying of the light"), but a quiet, confident internalization of the death of her son, a welcoming of him back to where his life began—in her own body.

From denied sexuality, denied death, pain and anguish Kristeva moves on to discuss belief. Once again the woman-mother's voice reappears as belief in the name of the Father and resurrection (rooted as it is in the mother) is introduced. The "personal voice" claims that "[b]elief in the mother is rooted in fear, fascinated with a weakness—the weakness of language."[97] This recalls a theme Kristeva introduced in *About Chinese Women* where she argues that we exist only in the moment of communication. The weakness in language, then, occurs during the pre-oedipal stage. This is especially poignant for Christians because we make assertions like "in the beginning was the Word"; thus:

> Christians must have found such a postulate sufficiently hard to believe and, for whatever it was worth, they added its [the word's] compensation, its permanent lining: the maternal receptacle, purified as it might be by the virginal fantasy. Archaic maternal love would be an incorporation of my suffering that is unfailing....In that

> sense, any belief, anguished by definition, is upheld by the fascinated fear of language's impotence.[98]

Anguish, sacrifice and archaic maternal love are thus linked permanently with Christian religious beliefs resulting from an abiding but "fascinated fear" that the very language we employ (Word of the Father) to articulate belief is impotent.

Contiguous with the lyrics of the personal voice which represent the anguish of death (though here the left column sounds much more like the right), the analytic voice shifts from a focus on art to music. The various musical settings of the "Stabat Mater" are presented as artistic examples of the manner in which "Man overcomes the unthinkable of death by postulating maternal love in its place...of which divine love is merely a not always convincing derivation, psychologically is perhaps a recall, on the near side of early identifications, of the primal shelter that insured the survival of the newborn."[99] The woman-mother, the maternal space is the space where the potential for religious faith is also born. The only ones who can escape from the "maternal representation...at the place of this subdued anguish called love" are "the saint, the mystic, or the writer," but this is only because they are able to "take apart the fiction of the mother as mainstay of love."[100] Thus, they are able to do no better than identify with love and "*a fire of tongues.*"[101] It is interesting that Kristeva uses an image of Pentecost which represents not the weakness of language but focuses on an ability to communicate in one's native language and be understood. The genre which is best able to communicate the "implementation of that maternal love—a veil over death, in death's very site" is modern art.[102] The distinction being made here, by Kristeva, is that only the modern artist takes full measure of the fact that this maternal love "veils" death, i.e., death hides behind the love. Whose death? Her own (i.e., the woman-mother's). What is inescapable here again, is that losing the maternal object as language is learned (also a weakness of language) brings about a certain anguish forever associated with maternal love, an anguish perhaps also associated with divine love if as Kristeva claims, human awareness of this love is rooted in a mother's love.

Both columns now turn their attention to the woman (as mother). The "personal voice" declares that we live as crucified beings "on that border"—the mother. Thus: "A woman is neither nomadic nor a male body that considers itself earthly only in erotic passion. A mother is a continuous separation, a division of the very flesh. And consequently a division of language."[103] Women live as crucified beings at the border "between pain and pleasure, lack and plenitude, sameness and difference;"[104] in other words, as "strangers to ourselves." The right column continues with a discussion of the mother-child relationship accenting the separation as an abyss which renders the child **"whether *he* or *she*, irremediably an other."**[105] Even though Kristeva's focus throughout the essay is on a mother-son relationship, the experience of motherhood is no different in a mother-daughter relationship. Separation and estrangement are a consequence of language acquisition. Therefore, **"motherhood destines us to a demented jouissance."**[106]

The analyst's right hand column now takes up Freud's work on the archaic mother. Kristeva observes that there is an absence of mothers (and their problems) in Freud's cases which might lead the casual reader "to think that motherhood was a solution to neurosis and, by its very nature, ruled out psychoanalysis as a possible solution."[107] Kristeva examines Freud's answer to his question—"What does a woman want?" and is critical of his response. She maintains that Freud offers only one possible consideration of motherhood (the desire for a child is the transformation of penis envy or anal drive) which amounts to, in her view, "a massive *nothing*, which for those who might care to analyze it, is punctuated with this or that remark on the part of Freud's mother...thus remained for his followers an entire continent to explore, a black one indeed."[108] Implicit here is the fact that motherhood is not a panacea for all of a woman's problems. What Freud *did* say about why a woman might want a child doesn't take us very far in the direction of a solution. One potential solution for "the dark area that motherhood constitutes for a woman" will be born from listening carefully to mothers from the midst of many and varied situations (i.e., "their economic difficulties and, beyond the guilt that a too existentialist feminism handed down, through their discomforts, insomnias, joys, angers, desires, pains, and pleasures").[109] In addition, those who want to help need to attempt to "understand the incredible construct of the Maternal that the West elaborated by means of the Virgin"[110] and the impact it has had on all women.

As the analyst's voice moves away from a brief discussion of Freud, the left column presents a "personal glimpse" of the woman-mother's relationship to her own mother. The anguish is expressed in incisive terms:

> Mummy. Almost no sight—a shadow that darkens, soaks me up, or vanishes amid flashes. Almost no voice in her placid presence. Except, perhaps, and more belatedly, the echo of quarrels: her exasperation, her being fed up, her hatred...the daughter

> could not accept the mother's hatred—it was not meant for her. A hatred without recipient or rather whose recipient was no "I".[111]

The refrain of a woman's place rings in the background: almost no voice, no sight, a shadow that signifies hatred (blood thirsty fury), the daughter "was no 'I'." This points again to the struggles that are peculiar to a woman as "subject-in-process/on trial." Becoming a subject involves speaking and a voice but the language they are required to use is the Law of the Father so there is "almost no voice." At the same time women experience maternal hatred which they then bear toward themselves. To eschew any doubt about this, the personal lament continues, **"[c]omplicity in the unspoken, connivance of the inexpressible...a tone of voice, a gesture....We are in it, set free of our identification papers."**[112] What will avail women of a voice? The "scarring" of Kristeva's text suggests an ontological flash which does metaphorical violence to our world of meanings; that is, the very action accomplished by Kristeva in her text.

If by some chance the woman is able to posit herself as an "I," then

> [e]ither, not wanting to experience her, I ignore her and, "alone of my sex," I turn my back on her in friendly fashion....Or else, outraged by her own stubbornness...I unrelentingly let go at her claim to address me and find respite only in the eternal return of power strokes, bursts of hatred....I do not see her as herself but beyond her I aim at the claim to singularity, the unacceptable ambition to be something other than a child...an echo of the cosmos that unifies us....("There is only One woman") can only impugn it by condemning it as "masculine".113

To be an "I" is to belong to the name of the Father, to be guilty of unacceptable ambition; thus one becomes a traitor to the code of silence of women. There is only one legitimate "I," the Virgin Mother. To be an "I," then, is to risk bearing the brunt of intractable hatred. Yet, the risk of not being an "I" is to slip into an eternal abyss of darkness and silence. In either case, Kristeva does not seem to present appealing options for women. These, however, are the polar opposites that constitute the limited choices women have faced, and all because the Virgin Mary is "alone of Her sex" worthy of praise and adulation.

Is it possible for there to be a woman's discourse, a way out of her darkness and silence? With this question in mind, the personal discourse fades again for several pages. Before the personal lament ends, however, the analyst's voice continues with an examination of the possibilities of the virginal maternal which above all else, is an effective way "of dealing with feminine paranoia." Thus, "The Virgin obstructs the desire for murder or devouring by means of a strong oral cathexis (the breast), valorization of pain (the sob), and incitement to replace the sexed body with the ear of understanding."[114] This accomplishes "the acknowledgment of a longing for uniqueness" but only as "embodied by the Virgin as an inaccessible goal."[115] Kristeva acknowledges that the representation of motherhood as virgin in its ideal is the culmination of Western culture's attempts to "reconcile the social remnants of matrilinearism and the unconscious needs of primary narcissism" with "the requirements of a new society based on exchange and before long on increased production which require the contribution of the superego and rely on the symbolic paternal agency...[but] that clever balanced architecture today appears to be crumbling."[116] The myth is, perhaps, salvageable if some missing elements are added to this discourse of the "virginal maternal": "the war between mother and daughter," "the relation to the other woman," and "the necessity to reformulate representations of love and hatred."[117]

Against this hopeful note, however, the personal voice, making its final entrance, returns and the text now focuses on the love of God. While, in this sense, it resembles the tone of the right column, death has the final word for both columns, though it is articulated by the personal voice. In between, Kristeva describes one more time the plight of the woman-mother (who, unlike the Virgin Mary, is not "alone of her sex"), **"[t]he love of God and for God resides in a gap: the broken space made explicit by sin on the one side, the beyond on the other."**[118] Women, symbolized by the broken space (even sin), the abject, the place of the foreigner, and mothers are **"taken for granted"** even as **"[t]he 'just the same' of motherly peace of mind, more persistent than philosophical doubt, gnaws, on account of its basic disbelief, at the symbolic's allmightiness."**[119] As both voices "let the music die," the analytic voice states Kristeva's hope for the future insofar as it rests upon an ethics dedicated to women, and written by women, "the second sex." This is the "herethics" that *Tales of Love* was written for so that women's experience in "flesh, language, and jouissance" might make a contribution to humanity's ability to "withstand death."[120] A mother's love makes bonds and thoughts more bearable, including the thought of death. The personal voice, however, has the "last say," noting the power of a mother's love to crush and smother while at the same time, and finally, **"the speaking being finds a refuge when his/her symbolic shell cracks and a crest emerges where speech causes biology to show through: I am thinking of the time of illness, of sexual-intellectual-physical passion, of**

death."[121] Thus, the analytic voice–with its note of hopefulness–and the personal voice–with its note of death–continue their struggle to the end, and perhaps, there is a kind of salvation in the fact that neither voice is allowed to silence the other.

Kristeva has been criticized, especially by Edelstein for exhibiting a kind of "maternal elitism" insofar as one's relation to, or transference to each column of the text depends upon *who* as well as what (role specific, for example, a mother or not a mother) one is:

> For those readers not mothers, the discourse *by* the mother may be alien, exotic, spoken by a sort of 'native informant' from the land of mothers. For non-Christian readers, the discourse *about* the Virgin Mother may seem merely a description of a quaint or peripheral phenomenon, not a powerful cultural myth or religious symbol.[122]

This criticism, however, appears to overlook several key aspects of the essay. First, Kristeva is concerned here with the place and/or identity of women in a Western European context which has been influenced by Christianity. In this sense, her text is descriptive and not definitive. The criticism would be more to the point if Kristeva did not in other places consider women from other cultural contexts but she does (e.g., China and India). Moreover, motherhood is to be understood in this essay not solely from a physiological perspective but also as a metaphor for those women who desire to be stable and reproductive in the sense of being generative for society. As Anna Smith has commented concerning her own approach to Kristeva's text she looks within for a "reassuring shelter or mother," and an ability to be able to idealize this mother as well as admire her speech, even replicate her speech through introjection. Thus the experience of reading

> 'Stabat Mater' endorses these expectations: it nourishes and exhorts, but its conceptual strangeness forbids any permanent identification. The discourse of maternity as I read it according to Kristeva swallows the necessity for a paranoid reader ('alone of all her sex') and sustains us instead through a vibrant play with the textures and tongues of language.[123]

In spite of the criticisms that Edelstein herself raises, claiming that Kristeva's essay is Utopian, in the end she finds it compelling, noting that "the mother, the artist, the speaking and reading subjects of 'Stabat Mater' are all positioned at the crossroads" of language and the unconscious.[124] Utopia consists of the manner in which Kristeva views love, maternity and art as "metaphorical, dialogic practices [that] can enable subjects to use, subvert, and renew the sociosymbolic order."[125] But as Edelstein concludes, "one can seek the impossible."[126]

Conclusion—The Need for a Third Generation Feminism

By examining selected texts pertaining to the feminine, women, depression, and melancholia as they relate to religion, I have attempted to trace how identifying women with the abject, the strange and the foreign leads to a place of despair with few options for them to experience health and stability within a Christian or religious discourse that locates them in such a negative space. As Kelly Oliver suggests, "a misdirected abjection is partially responsible for women's oppression."[127] For Kristeva, women exist outside of time in a place that is both unidentifiable and inaccessible—"an impossible elsewhere." What is called for is a maternal discourse that acknowledges women's anguish while it listens for the music that is buried deeply within their souls, "the source of what is beautiful." The "music" is composed of the "textures and tongues of language" that belong to the FLASH which will wreak metaphorical violence to our world of meanings. It is from her place as other, as difference that a woman needs to learn to speak.

Kristeva advocates for a third generation feminism which is unrelated to chronology or a passing of the torch from one generation to the next. Rather, her use of the term "third generation" implies a "signifying space" that represents an attitude or "corporeal and desiring mental space."[128] This means that "the very dichotomy man/woman as an opposition between two rival entities may be understood as belonging to *metaphysics*" and the "de-dramatization of the 'fight to the death' between rival groups and thus between the sexes."[129] She raises up the singularity of each person—whether woman or man—as well as the nature of their relationships from the "desiring mental space" which is represented, at least in part, by a maternal discourse that begins with "Stabat Mater" but cannot end there. Where her maternal discourse leads us is the focus of the next chapter.

Notes

1. In chapter three following Kristeva's argument in *About Chinese Women,* I suggested that women either identify with the "paternal Word" or become subversives but there is precious little language that is both descriptive of their ongoing struggle to be a self (i.e., different from masculine identity) and normative in Christian discourse.
2. Kristeva, "Stabat Mater," *Tales of Love*, 236.

3. Kristeva, "Motherhood According to Giovanni Bellini," 249, my emphasis. The process of female identity formation involves identifying with and yet, separating from one's maternal origins but everything—language, father, law—that is outside of those origins (i.e., the maternal matrix) is foreign and like a foreigner, a woman will experience some self-estrangement. See Anne-Marie Smith, *Julia Kristeva: Speaking the Unspeakable*, 79.
4. Kristeva, "Motherhood According to Giovanni Bellini," 249.
5. Julia Kristeva, "The Wheel of Smiles," *New Maladies of the Soul*, trans. Ross Guberman (New York: Columbia University Press, 1995), 154–58.
6. Ibid., 158.
7. Kristeva, "Motherhood According to Giovanni Bellini," 237.
8. Ibid., my emphasis.
9. Julia Kristeva, *This Incredible Need to Believe*, 28. This theme continues in her recent work as part of her discussion of the radical reformation of human existence currently taking place. The woman-mother is still an abject object against which a speaking being struggles into existence.
10. Kristeva, "Motherhood According to Giovanni Bellini," 237, my emphasis.
11. Kristeva's position on the feminine, women, motherhood, and religion is a very controversial one among feminists. Elizabeth Gross' "The Body of Signification," in *Abjection, Melancholia and Love*, Marilyn Edelstein's "Metaphor, Meta-Narrative, and Mater-Narrative in Kristeva's 'Stabat Mater'," and Janice Doane and Devon Hodges' *From Klein to Kristeva: Psychoanalytic Feminism and the Search for the "Good Enough" Mother* (Ann Arbor: University of Michigan Press, 1992, especially ch. 3) are representative of the those who are critical of Kristeva's position. Many who agree with her have already been cited. I concur, however, with Diane Jonte-Pace who writes "Kristeva brings innovative perspectives and fresh insights to Freudian, Lacanian, and object relational discourses....Neither a critic nor a defender of religion but, in my view, an interpreter of the way religion functions in culture and psyche, Kristeva offers a nuanced reading of religious texts and practices." Diane Jonte-Pace, "Julia Kristeva and the Psychoanalytic Study of Religion: Rethinking Freud's Cultural Texts," in *Religion, Society, and Psychoanalysis: Readings in Contemporary Theory*, ed. Janet Liebman Jacobs and Donald Capps (Boulder: Westview Press, 1997), 248. I suggest that Jonte-Pace's summation of Kristeva's position on religion could be extended to describe her position on motherhood. That is, in the same way that she "offers a nuanced reading of religious texts and practices," she offers a nuanced interpretation of the way mothers function in culture and psyche.
12. Kristeva, "Motherhood According to Giovanni Bellini," 238, her emphasis. The woman-mother is a subject (i.e., a speaking, thinking, and feeling being) but not *the subject* of motherhood. Kristeva is describing a time which is the beginning of the human subject before the appearance of the father, before the child is verbal—a time before birth. To recognize that the woman-mother is a subject rather than an object of the child's desire is to risk "sinking back into the mother" (mother-child symbiosis) or losing our identity even though that separation is necessary for the child to become a "subject-in-process." Moreover, there is no one present within the womb to signify what is actually occurring, thus the womb is a dual and alien space. The first splitting occurs when the cells begin to

divide; the first separation when the umbilical cord is cut. As Wiseman notes in "Renaissance Paintings and Psychoanalysis," "[m]aternity itself is neither masculine nor feminine, and what goes on in the body of the woman mother is mimed by the kind of pictorial representation that results in...the kind of representation of which Bellini was master and with which he initiated the Venetian Renaissance" (97). See also, footnote 52 in chapter three.

13. Kristeva, "Motherhood According to Giovanni Bellini," 238.
14. Ibid.
15. Ibid. Kristeva's theory of the phallic mother builds upon the work of her teacher Lacan. Early in her writing she describes why the woman-mother is the phallus and why separation from her is a form of castration: "Castration puts the finishing touches on the process of separation that posits the subject as signifiable....As the addressee of every demand, the mother occupies the place of alterity. Her replete body, the receptacle and guarantor of demands, takes the place of all narcissistic, hence imaginary, effects and gratifications; she is, in other words, the phallus." In *Revolution in Poetic Language*, 47. See also, Oliver, *Reading Kristeva*, 23.
16. Kristeva, "Motherhood According to Giovanni Bellini," 239.
17. Ibid. This is another example of discourse that is widely criticized by feminists. For example, Doane and Hodges write: "A signifying practice like Kristeva's, a discourse that refuses to discuss the social, political, and economic situation of women (except as symptoms of an archaic relation to a maternal object), can offer little insight into the complex sources of female depression—and little hope for a cure. Further, a psychoanalysis that normalizes the notion of the mother as origin does not engage in the feminist task of destabilizing the familiar categories in which women have been confined" (78–79). While I would not want to say that biology (alone) is destiny, I suggest that Doane and Hodges have overlooked the influence of biology in the development of a female subject. Kristeva should be given credit for taking biology seriously and for making it, at least, her starting point.
18. Wiseman, "Renaissance Paintings and Psychoanalysis," 99. Wiseman writes: "One division made by Kristeva is that of motherhood into two facets, maternal and paternal. Classical psychoanalysis recognizes only the paternal, in which the desire to be a mother is just desire for a child by the father, and the Madonna stands as the realization, in fantasy, of this desire, doomed by the incest taboo to be realized in fantasy only."
19. Kristeva, "Motherhood According to Giovanni Bellini," 239.
20. Kristeva, *The Sense and Non-Sense of Revolt*, 8.
21. Kristeva, "Motherhood According to Bellini," 242.
22. Ibid., my emphasis.
23. Ibid.
24. Ibid.
25. Ibid., 243, my emphasis.
26. Ibid.
27. Wiseman, "Renaissance Paintings and Psychoanalysis," 98. She also highlights the strong contrast that Kristeva draws between da Vinci and Bellini noting that Kristeva "regards the

paintings of Bellini as Freud regards those of Leonardo, namely, as uncanny sublimations of primitive instincts and desires."

28. See da Vinci's *Madonna with the Carnation* at the Web Gallery of Art, http://www.wga.hu, last viewed on 4 February 2010.
29. Kristeva, "Motherhood According to Bellini," 245.
30. Ibid.
31. Ibid., 246.
32. Ibid., 247.
33. Ibid.
34. The specific paintings referenced here are: *Madonna and Child* (1460–69), *Madonna with Two Trees* (1487), and *Madonna and Child* (1487) which may be viewed at the Web Gallery of Art at http://wga.hu, last viewed on 4 February 2010.
35. Kristeva, "Motherhood According to Bellini," 247.
36 Ibid., 247–48.
37. I will return to this idea in the fifth chapter. Numinous here is understood as a religious or mystical experience in which one is confronted by a sense of the holy or in Kristevan fashion by the Other. Jean Graybeal's understanding of Kristeva supports this type of interpretation. She writes: "Kristeva often refers to religious discourse, especially that of the mystics, to illustrate her analysis of the speaking subject and its dynamics. She seems intensely interested in religious language and particularly in those aspects of religious discourse where the drive for order, rationality, and security is *disrupted by an intense and emotional experience of otherness, groundlessness, or interior difference.*" Jean Graybeal, "Joying in the Truth of Self-Division," in *Body/Text in Julia Kristeva: Religion, Women, and Psychoanalysis*, ed., David Crownfield (Albany: State University of New York Press, 1992), 135, my emphasis.
38. Kristeva, "Motherhood According to Bellini," 249.
39. Ibid., my emphasis.
40. Ibid.
41. Ibid., 251.
42. Ibid., 253.
43. Ibid., my emphasis.
44. Ibid., 254; an image of this painting (1480–90) may be viewed at Web Gallery of Art, http://www.wga.hu, last viewed on 4 February 2010.
45. Ibid., 259, 263.
46. Ibid., 259.
47. Ibid., 263.
48. Ibid., 250, 254. It is as if Bellini's Madonnas provided the source for how Kristeva would later describe women as foreigners in *Strangers to Ourselves* (16): "It is not the silence of anger that jostles words at the edge of the idea and the mouth; rather, it is the silence that empties the mind and fills the brain with despondency, like the gaze of sorrowful women coiled up in some nonexistent eternity."
49. Ibid., 264. The literal translation of *ergasterion* is workplace. Clement of Alexandria used the word to represent the womb. See G. W. H. Lampe, ed., *A Patristic Greek Lexicon* (Oxford: Clarendon Press, 1961), 545. Since Kristeva does not cite her reference for this

term it is difficult to discern exactly how she derives its meaning as privileged space. The English translation follows exactly the French original. See Julia Kristeva, "*Maternité selon Giovanni Bellini,*" in *Polylogue, Éditions du Seuil,* 1977, 422.

50. Bellini's *Venus,* as Kristeva identifies it, is also known as *Woman with a Mirror.* An image of this painting may be viewed at the Web Gallery of Art at http://www.wga.hu, last viewed on 4 February 2010.
51. Ibid., 265.
52. Ibid., 266.
53. Ibid.
54. Ibid., 269.
55. The essay was originally published as "*Hérethique de l'amour*" (Herethics of love) in the journal, *Tel Quel* in 1977; the text used in this study was the reprint, "Stabat Mater," published in *Tales of Love* in 1983.
56. Wiseman, "Renaissance Paintings and Psychoanalysis," 102–03.
57 Toril Moi, *The Kristeva Reader,* 160–61. The Latin text of the first stanza is as follows: *Stabat mater dolorosa/ Iuxta crucem lacrimosa/ Dum pendebat filius. Cuius animam gementem, Contristantem et dolentem/ Pertransivit gladius.* The English translation of this stanza is: At the Cross, her station keeping, Stood the mournful mother weeping, Where he hung, the dying Lord; For her soul, of joy bereaved, Bowed with anguish, deeply grieved. Felt the sharp and piercing sword. Moi notes that "Kristeva's study of the Virgin Mother coincides with her own experience of maternity, recorded and reflected in the personal observations which break up the main body of the text....There is, then, an urgent need for a 'post-virginal' discourse on maternity, one which ultimately would provide both women and men with a new ethics: a 'herethics' encompassing both reproduction and death" (160–61).
58. Marilyn Edelstein, "Metaphor, Meta-Narrative, and Mater-Narrative in 'Stabat Mater'," 39. Her reading supports this interpretation: "This text is, like the maternal body, 'the place of a splitting'....The speaking subject may thus reproduce in the reading subject the very tension between sameness and otherness, identification and difference that in Kristeva's analysis, a mother undergoes. With the two columns, we *experience* as well as *read about* the tension between the Logos and those voices always threatening to disrupt it—the voice of woman as other, the voice of the poet, the voice of the body or the unconscious, the voice of the semiotic."
59. Kelly Oliver, *Reading Kristeva,* 53. Concerning the split text Oliver offers these insights: "The split column of 'Stabat Mater' depicts what is left out of the discourse of the Virgin. The split column brings to the surface of the text the mother's sex, two columns joined together out of which the child is born, which is subterranean in the Catholic representation of motherhood...with the two columns and the two kinds of typeface [Kristeva] wanted to give the impression of a scar or wound....Kristeva's identification of the two columns–which suggest the mother's sex–with a scar suggests castration, what she might call in *Black Sun* 'feminine castration.'" Oliver here cites "Julia Kristeva in Conversation with Rosalind Coward," *Desire, ICA Documents,* 1984, 24. In order to preserve the "impression of a scar or wound" when citing the personal discourse of the left column, I will follow Kristeva's example and use bold type.

60. Marilyn Edelstein, "Metaphor, Meta-Narrative, and Mater-Narrative in 'Stabat Mater'," 29.
61. Julia Kristeva, "Stabat Mater," 234.
62. Ibid.
63. Ibid., 235.
64. Ibid., 234–35.
65. Kristeva, *Interviews*, 96. She states: "I want to discuss the speaking subject, focusing on its relationship to the constraints of social unity and to the jouissance that relies on it as long as it can surpass it. Religion was once the privileged vehicle for the speaking subject's expression. In modern capitalism, however, destructuring takes precedence over structure, and excess overrides restraint. As a result, religion has not been able to acknowledge the speaking subject." The reason for this failure in Kristeva's estimation is that religion, for many, no longer provides meaning, love, and security though it once had the power to heal psychic wounds. Kelly Oliver's interpretation supports this reading of Kristeva in *Reading Kristeva*, 124–131.
66. Kristeva, "Stabat Mater," 234.
67. Edelstein, "Metaphor, Meta-Narrative, and Mater-Narrative in 'Stabat Mater'," 35. With regard to Kristeva's use of **FLASH**, Edelstein has this to offer: "This masterful, historico-psychoanalytic text gives birth to another, different text just when it first invokes the terms 'the maternal' and 'maternality.' The first word of the disruptive left column is 'FLASH,' in both French and English. Since the left column generally weaves and folds associatively rather than progressing linearly or chronologically, it's not obvious what 'instant of time' this 'flash' is describing." I suggest, that the ambiguity is deliberate on Kristeva's part since, per her own definition, time in the conventional sense of the word is patrilinear.
68. Gerhart and Russell, *Metaphoric Process*, 120.
69. Ibid. Though their definition is not precise, the following may illuminate further what they intend: "When worlds of meaning are willfully distorted, what is the case was not the case earlier and what was the case no longer is. The metaphorical relationship arises when we *insist* that the relationship between 'already understoods' is analogical. The effect of this insistence is to warp, distort, fold, spindle, and perhaps mutilate our world of meanings. What an outrage! What possible grounds can we have for this violence? We do it because we know that the relationship is true, because we know that the process will work, or at least we claim such knowledge" (113–14).
70. Julia Kristeva, "Stabat Mater," *Tales of Love*, 234, 235, 255. For example, "What is loving, for a woman, the same thing as writing. Laugh. Impossible. Flash on the unnamable, weavings of abstractions to be torn." Or, "The child, whether *he* or *she*, is irremediably an other. To say that there are no sexual relationships constitutes a skimpy assertion when confronting the flash that bedazzles me when I confront the abyss between what was mine and is henceforth but irreparably alien."
71. Anna Smith, *Julia Kristeva: Readings of Exile and Estrangement*, 139.
72. Kristeva, "Stabat Mater," 237.
73. Ibid., my emphasis.
74. Ibid., 238.
75. Edelstein, "Metaphor, Meta-Narrative, and Mater-Narrative in 'Stabat Mater'," 30. Edelstein notes that occasionally the left-hand voice "mimics the right-hand 'voice.'

Perhaps the essay is, like Pergolesi's hymn *Stabat Mater*, a duet as well as a juxtaposition of two solo voices."

76. Alison Ainley, "The Ethics of Sexual Difference," in *Abjection, Melancholia and Love*, eds. John Fletcher and Andrew Benjamin (New York: Routledge, 1990), 58. Ainley writes about the way that the left hand column irrupts into the text supporting the idea that it beseeches us to read it first.
77. Kristeva, "Stabat Mater," 240.
78. Ibid., 241.
79. Ibid., 242–43.
80. Ibid., 245.
81. Ibid., my emphasis.
82. Ibid., 246.
83. Ibid., 247.
84. "The Wheel of Smiles" is a brief study of da Vinci's *The Virgin Mary, St. Anne, and Infant Jesus* (An image of this painting may be viewed at the Web Gallery of Art, http://www.wga.hu, last viewed 4 February 2010). In this essay Kristeva describes the relationships in the painting: "It seems that the petals of a mysterious rose of joy are unfolding, and you are soothed by a kaleidoscope of faces. By means of a circular reflection of gazes exchanged between a mother and her son, a very human story is about to be born beneath your eyes. *She* has a twofold grace, in memory of a past maternal caress. *He* is already engaged in an instinctive and erotic flight toward glory. Modern man lacks the words and images needed to celebrate this imaginary prehistory of the individual" (154–55). And again: "*From a theological perspective*, Leonardo condensed the Immaculate Conception and the Incarnation into the already accepted model of a 'triple Saint Anne'....Between the thirteenth and fifteenth centuries, this theme emerged as a double of and counterweight to the classical Trinity, which is composed of the Father, the Son, and the Holy Spirit. This required that a perspective for the Virgin Mary be created, and that Anne accept Mary's immaculate conception...that both the ternary logic of Christianity and the treatment that it inflicts upon the consecration of a Goddess-mother be enhanced" (156–57).
85. An image of this painting may be viewed at the Web Gallery of Art, http://www.wga.hu, last viewed 4 February 2010.
86. Ibid., 246.
87. Ibid., 247, my emphasis.
88. Ibid.
89. Ibid., 246–47.
90. Ibid., 248.
91. Ibid., 249–50.
92. Ibid., 249.
93. Kelly Oliver, *Reading Kristeva*, 51. Her reading of "Stabat Mater" supports this interpretation: "Man returns the semiotic threat to the maternal body through the cult of the Virgin. The maternal body is allowed joy in only pain. Her body has only ear, milk, and tears....The sexed body is replaced by the 'ear of understanding,' the Virgin Mary of the Catholic Church....Christianity, with its Virgin birth, both unravels and protects the

paternal function....Like sacrifice, the violence of the semiotic returns within the very ritual that attempts to repress it. The maternal semiotic is focused in the symbol of the Virgin and its threat to the Symbolic order is thereby controlled."

94. Kristeva, "Stabat Mater," 250.
95. Ibid., 251.
96. Ibid.
97. Ibid.
98. Ibid., 251–52.
99. Ibid. 252.
100. Ibid., 253.
101. Ibid.
102. Ibid.
103. Ibid., 254.
104. Edelstein, "Metaphor, Meta-Narrative and Mater-Narrative in 'Stabat Mater'," 33.
105. Kristeva, "Stabat Mater," 255.
106. Ibid.
107. Ibid., 254.
108. Ibid., 255.
109. Ibid., 256.
110. Ibid.
111. Ibid.
112. Ibid., 257.
113. Ibid., 258.
114. Ibid., 257.
115. Ibid., 258.
116. Ibid., 259.
117. Ibid., 261.
118. Ibid.
119. Ibid., 262.
120. Ibid., 262–63.
121. Ibid., 263.
122. Edelstein, "Metaphor, Meta-Narrative and Mater-Narrative in 'Stabat Mater'," 39.
123. Anna Smith, *Julia Kristeva: Readings of Exile and Estrangement*, 141.
124. Edelstein, "Metaphor, Meta-Narrative and Mater-Narrative in 'Stabat Mater'," 46.
125. Ibid.
126. Ibid.
127. Kelly Oliver, *Reading Kristeva*, 49.
128. Kristeva, "Women's Time," 209.
129. Ibid.

CHAPTER FIVE

The Power of the Word

The word as minimal textual unit thus turns out to occupy the status of mediator.

–Julia Kristeva, "Word, Dialogue and Novel," *Desire in Language*

Thus far, the portrait painted of the "woman-mother" or more specifically, of women struggling with depression who also dwell within the Christian tradition, is rather cheerless. In Christianity, the metaphors commonly chosen to describe and situate the feminine frequently identify the feminine with the abject, the exile, and the foreigner as a place of oppression. The result of this reality is a form of self-estrangement that contributes to a loss of voice for women and often a subsequent depression, or what Kristeva has defined as a "melancholic-depressive composite." The difficulty identified in previous chapters is that there is a poverty of language to address the needs of contemporary Christian women, especially those who struggle with symptoms of depression. The primary symptoms that Kristeva identifies, as we have seen in chapter three, are a divestment of social bonds and a devitalization of language. This leads to loss of voice and an empty, silent gaze for those women who struggle with depression in an "impossible elsewhere." Christie Cozad Neuger provides a list of symptoms which expands what has been previously presented including: helplessness, hopelessness, sadness, joylessness, eating disturbances, sleep disturbances, self-hatred, guilt, and despair.[1] Moreover, there are different kinds of depression that have different causes, times of duration, and intensity. In fact, there is little widespread agreement among the experts about etiology.[2] As Neuger notes, what we do know is that many women living in the United States will experience depression in their lifetime, perhaps as many as 25 percent.[3]

These symptoms of depression are often exacerbated by the realities of life in a church community. The "realities" of church life which I am most concerned with revolve around the use of language and imagery for God, particularly in pastoral care situations. As Neuger observes in *Counseling Women*,

> language does not just describe cultural reality, but also informs, influences, and to a certain extent determines that reality. How God is named, imagined, and conceptualized significantly affects how we understand ourselves, how we understand our purpose, how we order our social and familial relationships, and how we structure our culture.[4]

Thus if God is identified with male images, men are perceived to be more closely created in the image of God and therefore enjoy higher status and privilege within the structures of a culture that is oriented to believe in this manner. One could argue, as Neuger does, that there is a hierarchy of values in a Western Christian culture that privileges men. Alan Riding noted in a *New York Times* article that by using theorists such as Kristeva and a post-structuralist approach, social groups have been able to identify the source of their oppression in the very language they use.[5] The claim that I am making here is that one source of oppression of women within Christianity is, at least partially, located in the language which has been adopted traditionally to make truth claims about God-human, human-human relationships, and human self-relations. The language used to describe sin or a break in any of these relationships is a primary concern in this project since it is this language which closely identifies the feminine with the abject and the "stranger." The implication then is that women are inherently more flawed and thus more sinful or less valuable. At times these close associations between the feminine and religious code language for sin render women mute. Images for God also need to be considered in this discussion since they contribute to the manner in which social structure is ordered and how power, privilege, and voice are assigned.

Are these the sole causes of depression in women who are struggling with it? No, the causes are many and varied, including (but not limited to): stress, fear of abuse, discrimination—both overt and covert—and violence.[6] Yet, if we are to take seriously the view that language (at least to an extent) determines cultural reality, careful thought needs to be given to the manner in which theological metaphors are chosen. What may be appropriate in one given context may be inappropriate in another. An individual woman's cultural context as well as her personal theological commitments need to be assessed and understood before any theological interpretations of her situation are offered. Sadly, many women have often needed to leave the context of the church in order to heal.[7] Kristeva is critical of American feminists who continue to insist upon a group identity over against the freedom of the individual. She critiques this type of feminism in one of her most recent works as a type of "massifying" of women insofar as the singularity of each woman is sacrificed or denied in order for women to be "compacted" into a "community of women."[8] In this latest work, Kristeva goes so far as to disavow her place as a feminist in favor of an interest in genius or singularity; more will be said about singularity in relation to a "speaking cure" in the final chapter. What interests Kristeva most is "each woman in her intimacy."[9] Moreover, she finds group identities (e.g., feminism, ethnic, sexual, religious) totalitarian; these same group identities eventually lead to the erosion of democracy or a dead end.[10] Kristeva's assertion informs and shapes my own work in this project. The aim of this project is to assist those who guide and counsel women in the church to honor "each woman in her intimacy or singularity" by helping her think and heal in a language which is congruent with her experience. This, I will argue, is congruent with honoring one's identity as a baptized child of God.

Kristeva is interested in the following questions: "How is each woman an individual?" "What can each woman contribute to other women or to humanity?" She wants her readers to be able to ask as well as answer the question: "How am I special?"[11] I, too, am absorbed by these questions and would like to see each woman in her particularity acquire the language that will help her answer these questions affirmatively. My concern is that when these questions are posed to women, the response is often a deafening silence resulting from their experiences with abjection and isolation. If women are going to be assisted in their journey from a silence that represents depression to a speech and subjectivity that is healthy, more attention needs to be given to the manner in which religious language is practiced in all aspects of ministry but particularly, in the area of pastoral care. Dutch pastoral theologian Riet Bons-Storm has expressed similar concern about the absence of a language appropriate for the expression of a woman's feelings in her book, *The Incredible Woman,* noting that women have difficulty voicing their feelings to their pastors (especially male pastors) because their feelings are confused, or vague and frequently they are unable to answer the question asked: "Now, what's really the matter with you?"[12] Bons-Storm also observes that all too often, women are not taken seriously by their pastor and that the pastor's empathy does not mirror their real feelings because their stories seem "too weird, too fantastic or too mad."[13]

At the heart of the contemporary psychic malaise that alarms Kristeva are the vanishing spaces of communication (i.e., family, grandmother, the church) which lead to "new maladies of the soul" or the difficulty individuals experience articulating their problems in words and images.[14] Kristeva's own work has been dedicated to the three things in life she recognizes as worth doing (these tasks serve the purpose of creating space for communication): thinking, healing and writing. The second activity is one that she suggests is more readily identifiable with women.[15] It is unclear if this is because she believes women are more skilled at facilitating healing or if it results from their deeper need to find healing. While, for Kristeva personally, the pursuit of all three of these tasks leads to a sense of resolution or happiness, I will focus on the issue of healing. I will do so by returning to a juxtaposition of Kristeva and McFague in this chapter but will conclude by juxtaposing Kristeva's understanding of what it means to offer "par-don" and to be "for-giving" with a variety of theorists in the final chapter. In this chapter I will be concentrating on Kristeva's interest in Christian love, forgiveness and the Word (even the Word of God) and McFague's maternal model of God. While it may appear that these two very different theorists' works are on convergent paths, I would suggest that they are rather on parallel paths and their apparent affinity is a result of the manner in which I have chosen to juxtapose them.[16] The discussion that follows will examine what Kristeva has written about the power of the Word in various expressions of love and forgiveness that lead to healing. The argument that I am making here is that in a loving relationship with a forgiving other (one who functions as a substitute mother), a depressed woman will find her voice by befriending at the very least her maternal images if not her actual mother. I will not provide a "how-to" guide for counseling Christian women who struggle with depression. Rather, I will explore a broader theological rationale for changing religious discourse, especially in pastoral theology, in light of Kristeva's psychoanalytic critique. *In the Beginning Was Love: Psychoanalysis and Faith*, *Black Sun*, selected essays from *Tales of Love*, as well as selected essays from *New Maladies of the Soul*, and *This Incredible Need to Believe* will be my primary texts.

The Word as Love

Agape: Language of Unconditional Love

Kristeva's *Tales of Love*, which is dedicated to love and the language used to express loving desire, begins with a description of this language as "impossible, inadequate, immediately allusive when one would like it to be most straightforward; it is a flight of metaphors."[17] And yet, it is the very experience of love where "corporeal passion and idealization intersect" that, in her view, is the indisputably "privileged experience for the blossoming of metaphor."[18] Metaphorical language needs to be at the center of the privileged experience of a restorative relationship—a space of unconditional love where the relationship between language and affect is restored, thus giving language new meaning. The privileged space and/or experience which she deems ideal, might best be understood as a transitional space that consists of the "mobilization of two people's minds and bodies by the sole agency of the words that pass between them."[19] Winnicott described this transitional space as

> this important area of *experience* [play] in the potential space between the individual and the environment, that which initially both joins and separates the baby and the mother when the mother's love, displayed or made manifest as human reliability, does in fact give the baby a sense of trust or of confidence in the environmental factor....The potential space between baby and mother, between child and family, between individual and society or the world, depends on experiences which leads to trust. It can be looked upon as sacred to the individual in that it is here that the individual experiences creative living.[20]

What is created in the transitional space between counselor and counselee (or pastor and parishioner) might be deemed the capacity to "play" with words, thus restoring a sense of trust as well as experiences of creative living. Indeed Kristeva emphasizes that analysis (if it ever comes to an end) ceases when "a certain playfulness of spirit returns: 'I am someone else, I cannot say who. There are things that cannot be said, and I am entitled to *play around with them so that I can understand them better'*.... Knowing this, I can also *play for real*, for keeps, at forming bonds: creating communities, helping others, loving, losing."[21] New language is born of this privileged space which offers an opportunity to work through sadness and find new meaning.

In a more recent work Kristeva asks, "[i]sn't a good analyst one who welcomes us with benevolence, with indulgence, without scores to settle, calmly, in a lowly dwelling...giving us access to our own 'lowly dwelling'?"[22] If one accepts, as I do, Neuger's assertion that the church has unquestionably colluded with patriarchy, then one can claim that we have failed to provide, traditionally, the sort of neutral and benevolent holding environment Kristeva deems ideal for providing a "speaking cure." It is rather "want of love that sends the subject into analysis, which proceeds by first restoring confidence in, and capacity for, love through the transference."[23] One could say then, that the woman who struggles with depression also wants for love—especially self-love as well as her mother's love—and her situation is exacerbated in a church context where a repetitive refrain is "God is love";[24] exacerbated because that love seems to exist for everyone but the woman seeking help inasmuch as she is suspicious that the language—"God is love"—is just that, i.e., *words* unsupported by her *experience*. In fact, Bons-Storm presents the stories of six women which support this conclusion. In one of these narratives we hear from "Lucy" that in "church everybody has nice kids. Church is just not the place for people like me. They talk too much about love."[25] From "Sylvia" we hear the following: "'I could not tell my problems to anyone, because I did not have the words.'"[26] And again, from "Lucy," "'I do not go to church anymore because they talk in very difficult language. I just do not understand. And they talk all about God's love but I do not feel that in my life.'"[27]

A woman struggling with depression experiences an absence of loving objects—not even the notion of a loving God who desires her is enough to move her toward an Other; thus, her self-estrangement intensifies as her sense of self diminishes. She is unable to participate in a loving relationship which is initiated by an "Other who turns...suffering into an offering and a welcome."[28] The woman struggling with depression is neither able to accept this welcome nor able to "offer" her suffering to another through language. That Kristeva views this concept of "offering" as central to the therapeutic task is evident in her preface to *In the Beginning Was Love*: "Every question, no matter how intellectual its content, reflects suffering. In our subject may lurk the suffering of religion as well as of rationalism, along with more strictly personal discomforts and anxieties. Let us try simply to be receptive to this suffering, and if possible to open our ears to meaning of another kind."[29] The subject that Kristeva refers to here is the "subject-in-process/on-trial" and the "meaning of another kind" may be interpreted as meaning that relieves suffering as well as strengthens identity or the subject's ability to speak. It isn't simply religion but rationalism which may contribute to the suffering.

Why is restoration of loving desire so important? It is important because it is born out of God's desiring us first insofar as we are created in God's image.[30]

In her essay on Bernard, Kristeva notes that while he recognizes that the desire for God is different from all other human desires it is rooted nevertheless in "the initial human desire" (psychological desire) or "voraciousness."[31] Restoring this desire, then, is a reconciliation of sorts between God and self or within the self, even as Donald Capps asserts: "We are, then, desiring beings, and it is in our desiring that we share a likeness to God, for it was God's nature to desire us even before we desired God."[32] When the capacity for loving desire is restored, we are, in other words, reconnected with God and our true self—the one created in God's image. How are we to go about this process of restoration with a woman for whom language has lost its meaning and for whom religion may be a type of suffering?[33]

Agape: Love of Self or Selfish Love?

We need to recall that we are speaking of women who struggle with depression or who might be described by Kristeva as "melancholic-depressive" or as an "Alice-in-distressland." A woman suffering in this manner is not able to look in mirrors because

> [h]er image and that of others arouse within her wounded narcissism, violence, and the desire to kill—from which she protects herself by going through the looking glass and settling down in that other world where, by limitlessly spreading her constrained sorrow, she regains a hallucinated completedness....Through her fuzzy tear-misted gaze that sees neither you nor herself, she savors the bitter sweetness of being forsaken by so many absent ones.[34]

This is significant because not only does the woman refrain from speaking but she believes she can neither see nor be seen.[35] Thus, her silence, and her lack of sight (even insight) are the mechanisms she uses to protect herself against the absence of recognition. The absence of recognition, at least in Kristeva's construction of depression, precedes loss of sight and voice. Before the woman who is "beyond the looking glass" is able to speak a word, recognition needs to take place; she needs to be on the receiving end of a loving gaze.[36] If, however, she lacks sight (or insight), how will this woman know she is being recognized by an other? Kristeva would arguably say that the beginning of insight is initiated by the telling or retelling of a love story which may need to focus on the significance of a name.

What kind of love story? One that is based on transference: "As long as we remain children (and who has completely escaped from childhood?), we need transference—a synonym for love and faith....Analytic discourse speaks of a humanity that is willing to lose in order to know itself as pure loss and thus pay its debts to the Almighty; it aims for tenuous, temporary ties and relationships."[37] Here Kristeva suggests that there is a relationship between the language of faith (or religion) and the language of psychoanalysis. It is difficult to remain oblivious to the echoes of the language of the synoptic gospels (e.g., Matthew 10:39). In Christianity, Kristeva views the God-human relationship as a human experience of direct and immediate transference to a loving, protecting agency that is analogous to the transference relationship of psychoanalysis. In the former case, God is love and gives a gift of love generously and graciously to the believer which enables the believer to love herself. In the latter case, there is the gift of self that the counselor gives to the woman seeking help which then encourages her to "offer" her suffering as gift.[38] The "gift" which the counselor offers is a willingness to listen. In order for this mutual gift exchange to occur, however, the woman seeking help must be believed and taken seriously, but as Bons-Storm has observed, this is often not the case. She contends that when women do take the risk of telling their stories they are often heard as false or exaggerated stories. Instead of their stories being heard as the truth about disturbing situations

> *the women are labeled as psychologically 'disturbed.'* Women's stories about their confusion, anger, and depression are frequently seen as manifestations of the unbalanced and irrational way they deal with reality. The supposed irrationality of women has to be treated in order to make women 'well adjusted' again, and that means women should play the roles that are prescribed in the sociocultural narrative, when they are placed under the wing of rational men.[39]

It is this very behavior on the part of ministers, in particular, which often drives women to go "behind the looking glass" frozen in time with no desire and little ability to speak up. It is only when women are taken seriously and their stories are heard as truth about disturbing situations that they may be willing and able to lose themselves in the transference relationship. If a woman is believed and taken seriously, she begins the journey toward reclaiming her true self. How does Kristeva describe this process?

Love happens; transference takes place, at least in part, when illusion is restored to "its full therapeutic and epistemological value. Does this mean restoring value to religion as well? Not altogether."[40] While Kristeva isn't ready to fully embrace religion or Christian faith for herself, she does leave room for the possibility that a "love story" told in faith has value. Elsewhere she writes about the importance of imagination for the discourse of transference, of love, and even faith, suggesting that the current "crisis of psychic space" results from "death of God" discourse.[41] What psychoanalysis can do to remedy the absence of illusion is to assert "the permanence of love as builder of spoken spaces...it shows that the transferential or amatory principle is indispensable for a body to be living rather than being a corpse under care."[42] John Lechte's interpretation of Kristeva's writings on "love" supports my own interpretation. He suggests that it would be preferable for an analyst to refuse "to be swayed by such an illusion" (in our situation, the illusion is faith) and instead conduct a rigorous investigation of "love's illusion." Yet he concludes that "Kristeva's response to such questions is to argue, that on the contrary, it is not the concept, or indeed reality of love which is found wanting, but the rationalistic, scientific framework presuming to judge it, a framework unquestionably without love."[43]

The final crisis isn't the dissolution of language but the abolition of psychic space, an abolition to which Western Christian culture has, in its own way, contributed. As Donald Capps contends: "What was a display of healthy narcissism is redefined as an expression of self-centeredness, and the Christian faith is used to legitimate the renunciation of our desire to be mirrored. *This is tragic, for mirroring is at the very heart of the Christian gospel.*"[44] The beginning of the "love story" may occur in the naming or "renaming" that signifies mutual recognition but the heart of the story takes place with the restoration of self-love.

What does Kristeva say about the restoration of self-love? She addresses very directly the tragic concern raised by Capps. "Christian love," she writes, "is an idea that changes my body into a worshiped name."[45] (Her reference here is to Galatians 2:20 and baptism; that is, we are baptized "in the name of the Father, the Son and the Holy Spirit," thus, we die and rise to new life in Christ becoming part of the body of Christ.) She describes the ritual of baptism as the "path through which the body-Self has access to the Name of the Other who loves me and makes of me a Subject who is immersed (baptized) in the Name of the Other."[46] Why is this important for Kristeva, the psychoanalyst? Because this love is "[a] triumph of idealization through a sublimatory elaboration of suffering and of the destruction of the body proper, agape marks, for that very reason, the end of sacrifice."[47] What is most important for Kristeva, however, is the restoration of love of self:

> The Self becomes a center of reference (the others will be loved *as* the believer loves himself) and consequently *removing guilt from the love of self does not constitute narcissism or sinful egoism* but can assert, at least under certain circumstances, that it is worthy of God's love. Furthermore, the love of Self is the prototype of any other love, to the extent that theologians have wondered which of the two is primary.[48]

Kristeva is somewhat puzzled that theologians would need to speculate about which love (i.e., self or other) is primary. A "subject-in-process" needs the recognition of her mother's gaze and the voice which calls her by name in order to develop a healthy self; love of self precedes any love for an other. It does so because, as noted earlier in this chapter, self-love or basic desire is born out of God's first loving and desiring us. It is, moreover, Christian love which "builds psychic space as the complex space of a subject."[49] In other words, it is God's love for us which founds our ability to love ourselves and then move toward an other and in so doing, we become adequate social beings who move past the passive, pre-objectal stage of Narcissus.[50]

Agape: Loving Desire and the Therapeutic Task

If there remains any doubt about the import of loving desire in the therapeutic task, Kristeva returns to this notion in a later article which focuses on depression in children who are unable to or who refrain from speaking. The therapist has a two-fold task: first, she must be one "who fosters desire," and second, she must be a "*speech therapist* who maps out an individual program."[51] Furthermore, Kristeva compares this therapeutic task to the maternal function stating that "[i]deally, mothers give us meaning."[52] Mothers, on the one hand, move their children along the path toward language, but what therapists do, on the other hand is "recognize and often anticipate the meaning of that which remains unsaid."[53] It is this ability to anticipate and understand "walled-up affects and blocked identifications" that "enables us to allow suffering to rise up from its tomb" in order that "the signfier of everyday communication—can cease to be a lifeless and foreign membrane for the child."[54] Though the focus of Kristeva's concern here is a child, the same can be said for the adult woman whose "suffering needs to rise up from the tomb" and for whom language has become lifeless. What is the aim of the "love story" which enfolds the therapeutic task for Kristeva?

The aim is to make life in the "here and now" more hopeful, more desirable. The therapist, the pastor, or the pastoral counselor become for the one who suffers "the other in language." It is in the space of the "here and now" where listening and then speaking or interpreting take place. This "makes the other less hellish ('Hell,' said Sartre, 'is other people'). The result is *not to prepare that other for some sort of transcendental existence but rather to open up as yet undefined possibilities in this world*."[55] Kristeva stops short of speaking about salvation here but it is clear from this statement that salvation is a divine work which is beyond the scope of any therapeutic relationship. What takes places in a counseling relationship is a special kind of listening, a maternal style of listening which is followed by distinct discourse that leads the way to still undefined possibilities in the here and now: "A word of love is often a more effective, profound, and durable treatment than electroshock therapy or psychotropic drugs; sometimes it is the only treatment for a condition that is no doubt a consequence not only of our biological nature but also, and *at the same time*, of an inopportune or ill-intentioned word."[56] The manner in which Kristeva frequently describes the therapeutic task (often using religious metaphors to represent the analytic process) has led one of her interpreters to assert that this "could provide a new occasion to affirm a theology of the Word, not as disembodied Logos, but as flesh to be celebrated."[57] How then, does our understanding of the Word as love change when female metaphors for God are chosen, especially if we affirm an embodied Word?

Agape: Will Maternal Metaphors Blossom?

I return here to the issue raised in the first chapter—the significance of metaphors in model-building in theology. What are the potential benefits derived from speaking about God as mother? Sallie McFague suggests that divine love is understood as agape; divine love then leads to divine activity in the world which is continually creating—especially, relationships. This kind of love seeks justice in the realm of human relationships. One might want to ask: How is this any different from a discussion of the divine love of a father-God? McFague offers the following distinctions: (1) traditionally, in a patriarchal language system, agape has been characterized as an unmotivated and totally disinterested love while a maternal love is interested, and; (2) the male metaphor emphasizes redemption of sins while the female metaphor emphasizes creation.[58] This is reminiscent of Kristeva's discussion of the maternal as a privileged space (the womb is a place of creation). Agapic love defined from this perspective using a maternal image for God is not detached and disinterested; rather it is connected and inclusive, suggesting a model of God who wants all her children to flourish.[59]

It is important to note that McFague emphasizes that a maternal God is not the same thing as a gender stereotyped feminine God. Why? Because "feminine" in this sense would suggest a passive God who is tender and nurturing while the masculine God is powerful because he "creates, redeems, and administers justice."[60] In that all of us—women and men—have our first home in the womb, McFague suggests that there is no better imagery for "expressing the most basic reality of existence: that we live and move and have our being in God."[61] A maternal God is both creator and judge but in a way that is distinctive from the father-God which has defined much of traditional theology:

> [F]or in the picture of God as artist, God is angry because his good, pleasing creation is spoiled by what upsets its balance and harmony, or because what he molded rebels against the intended design, whereas in the picture of God as mother, God is angry because what comes from her being and belongs to her lacks the food and other necessities to grow and flourish. The mother-God as creator is necessarily judge, at the very basic level of condemning as the primary (though not the only) sin the inequitable distribution of basic necessities for the continuation of life in its many forms.[62]

In the former case, God objects to rebellion against a superior; in the latter, God objects to those who refuse to recognize their interdependence and thus, obstruct the goal of maximum fulfillment for all.

McFague's discussion of the distinctiveness of language that describes God in maternal terms leads her to a conclusion that supports the view of agape already presented. McFague, like Kristeva and Capps, asserts the merit of self-love as a basic affirmation of one's existence without which love for an other is impossible. The context of the created world in McFague's economy is the body of the mother-God. Thus, "[l]oving others 'as yourself' means—whatever else it may also mean—willing for others the existence, the right to birth, nurture, and fulfillment, that one wills for oneself."[63] In a word, this is a wish for life. This is not an image for God which is meant to resolve all difficulties, for it can, in fact, create some. One such example is a mother who suffocates or infantilizes her children thus enacting violence rather than attending to nurture and justice. Fathers are also capable of this sort of violence and it has not precluded the adoption of male images for God. Perceived weaknesses are not, however, justifiable reasons to abandon a maternal model for God because "we can model God the creator as the one in whom we live and move and have our being and as the one who judges those who thwart the well-being and fulfillment of her body, our world."[64]

Could it be that part of our resistance to using maternal metaphors for God arises out of the sort of observation made by Bons-Storm on the basis of her own experience? That is, "whatever one's male colleague says, people assume it is spoken as the perspective of a human being. Whatever a woman says will be heard as being said as the perspective of a woman."[65] Male metaphors for God have traditionally been deemed representative of human experience while female metaphors represent, at best, woman's experience only and this experience, in a patriarchal ordering of the world, is subordinate. To this end, however, Bons-Storm offers a caveat to the discussion of the motherhood of God noting that the "patriarchal 'motherhood mystique'" needs to be dispelled otherwise we are left with a maternal image of God that "is damaging for the selfhood of women if nursing and caring is associated with women, while leadership and stewardship continue to be associated with men."[66] Thus, maternal images or metaphors for God need to be ones which, on the one hand, do not eclipse agapic love; and on the other hand, are strong, active metaphors which give women equal access to power. Maternal metaphors for God ought not to reinforce a patriarchal discourse about God which renders women exiles within a language that is supposed to offer redemption and liberation. How then does one come to the assistance of a woman struggling with depression without presuming to speak for her?[67] How do we speak of a loving God using maternal metaphors with a woman who has yet to experience the kind of love which empowers her to acquire language that communicates her story? Kristeva suggests that, in addition to love, the analytic task involves tact, which she defines as the ability to "hear true, along with forgiveness."[68]

The Word as Forgiveness

Forgiveness: "Hearing True Into Speech"

In order to appreciate why Kristeva sees forgiveness as integral to the amelioration of melancholia (and depression), I will revisit her understanding of this condition which she defines in yet another way as "an abyssal suffering that does not succeed in signifying itself and, having lost meaning, loses life."[69] This definition is significant because it is precisely that lost meaning which the analyst, "with utmost empathy," looks for in the analysand's "weird affect," i.e., her "devitalized, vulgarized words—words from which any appeal to the other has disappeared."[70] The therapist needs to employ tact in order to "hear true" or "hear into speech" the affect of the woman struggling with depression. It is noteworthy that "tact" is derivative from the French and Latin words "touch," thus carrying the meaning of a delicate or intuitive perception "of the proper thing to say or do to avoid giving offense; sensitive skill in dealing with people."[71] Tact in the therapeutic relationship is more than a social grace; it is a delicate perception of another's affect. This "hearing true" with tact recalls what Bons-Storm maintains is necessary if women, in particular, are going to be assisted by a pastor or pastoral counselor—they need to be taken seriously and listened to carefully.

To the task of "hearing true," Kristeva adds forgiveness to the therapeutic mix. Critics might be tempted to state in a somewhat hostile fashion "but if a woman has been the victim of abuse or been in anyway shunned and neglected by her church community (which most likely does not understand her situation) in her hour of direst need, then she should be offering forgiveness instead of seeking it and even that is debatable."[72] Moreover, it is exactly this sort of discourse which often sends women away from the church to seek help. To interpret forgiveness in this manner would be a misunderstanding of what Kristeva intends but in keeping with what she describes as "any modern imprecation against Christianity" because it understands forgiveness as "connivance with degradation, moral softening, and refusal of power."[73] We know that in her earliest writings (e.g., *About Chinese Women*) Kristeva is emphatic that women need to have equal access to knowledge and power. While Kristeva acknowledges that these aspects (refusing power, etc.) of forgiveness exist within a decadent Christianity, she emphasizes that forgiveness has a more solemn aspect.

Forgiveness: Defining Possibilities in This World

Forgiveness is "giving in addition, banking on what is there in order to revive, to give the depressed patient (that stranger withdrawn into his wound) a new start, and give him the possibility of a new encounter."[74] Clearly it is the psychological process of forgiveness which interests Kristeva, but her proposed definition touches upon some of the very same aspects Tillich deems necessary in the theological process: "Truth is what reconciles, and reconciles not only in terms of restitution but in terms of creative reunion or growth."[75]

Kristeva returns to the idea of tact as a "for-giving" attitude in a later article emphasizing that it is "a gift of understanding and judgment that I give to the other. I deprive myself of my own understanding and judgment, and I detach myself from my affect and my silence, whose painful and blissful plenitude poses a problem for me. And I do not cease to ask questions."[76] It isn't necessarily the case that the woman seeking help wants forgiveness (refusal of power) or wants to forgive her perpetrator (conspire with her degradation) but she comes in want of love and yearns for someone to "give for her."

Forgiveness is Kristeva's answer to the abject. That is, "the *solemnity* of forgiveness—as it functions in theological tradition and as it is rehabilitated in aesthetic experience, which identifies with abjection in order to traverse it, name it, expend it—is inherent in the economy of psychic rebirth."[77] Kristeva provides an extended study of the theme of forgiveness in the works of Dostoyevsky in order to illustrate how forgiveness is rehabilitated in aesthetic practice (in this case art as writing) and then draws parallels with analytic and religious practice. What then, is the object of forgiveness?

Kristeva answers: "Insults, of course, any moral and physical wound, and eventually death."[78] In other words, the object of forgiveness is those actions which comprise human hurts. Absolute evil belongs to the category of death and in the final analysis, absolute evil warrants forgiveness on a divine scale. Within Christianity, even though it is God alone who can forgive, Kristeva notes that the pardoning of crimes and release from punishment, even though a divine work, is "*first* the work of men," citing Matthew 6:14–15 as supporting evidence of her claim.[79] She muses about Dostoyevsky's own experience as a condemned man who was pardoned at the last moment before his death and its influence on his vision of the beautiful and the just which necessarily included forgiveness. Her musings lead her to conclude that

> there remains the often unquenched melancholy anguish of the subject who has already died once, even though miraculously resurrected....The writer's imagination is then beset with an alternation between the *unsurpassability of suffering and the flash of forgiveness*, and their eternal return articulates the whole of his work.[80]

Dostoyevsky undoubtedly imagined his death many times prior to his pardon, the "miraculous resurrection." What is striking in the passage from *Black Sun* is the language that recalls the "flash" of "Stabat Mater" as well as the violence that metaphor wreaks on human experience. The change or transformation, the definition of new possibilities in this world, particularly in a therapeutic relationship come through the "flash of forgiveness" that Kristeva describes in relation to Dostoyevsky's experience. Anna Smith also makes note of the manner in which Kristeva describes forgiveness as a "flash" experience suggesting that it "leads to reconciliation with a Figure or Power that has become distant. Such tones are indeed reminiscent of the Apostle Paul's experience on the road to Damascus whose intensity left him blinded but repentant. The time of forgiveness is literally the mercy of the journey that contains a transcendent quality."[81] The so-called flash of forgiveness, I suggest, is best used to describe what happens when a person experiences an awareness of divine forgiveness. Forgiveness in interpersonal relationships (even intrapsychically), on the other hand, is best described by a process or journey metaphor which I will revisit in the final chapter. Forgiveness is a voyage or a journey that the stranger, the exile or the foreigner, takes in order to become reacquainted with herself and with speech. Forgiveness is what initiates the rebuilding or recreation of a "personality within a new relation for an other."[82] How is this so?

Forgiveness: "The Third Way"

In her study of *Crime and Punishment*, Kristeva leads us to the conclusion that forgiveness is the "third way" between dejection and murder. Sadness (melancholia or depression) is inverted into crime when the projection of self-hatred onto another is acted on as a defensive reaction against depression. In other words, "murdering the other protects against suicide. Raskolnikov's 'theory' and criminal act demonstrate that logic perfectly."[83] Forgiveness, however, "arises in the wake of erotic enlightenment and appears not as an idealizing movement repressing sexual passion, but as its working through."[84] Though she finds this illustration in *Crime and Punishment*, its analogy to the analytic process is unmistakable. She proceeds to describe what happens when the prostitute, Sonia, follows the melancholy student Raskolnikov to Siberia: "Reconciliation with a *loving mother*, though she might be unfaithful or even a prostitute...thus appears as a condition for reconciliation with one's self."[85] Some may want to raise an objection: "But Dostoyevsky is writing about a *male* student. What does this example have to do with women?"

It is no less significant for women. Why? Because the "loving mother" or analyst, the pastoral counselor or pastor—whether male or female—is engaged in a therapeutic task of "for-giving" with the one seeking help which initiates a reconciliation of the self. As we noted in chapter three, a woman's experience of the maternal object is more immediate and she may, therefore, be more overwhelmed during the separation from the maternal object; the "for-giving" that Kristeva describes as a "more-than-maternal" task of therapy offers the hope of reconciliation with both self and a loving mother. The loving, forgiving mother (a functional mother, not an actual one) is idealized (especially in the act of writing), thus violence (defensive reaction against depression) is spoken instead of being acted upon.[86] This is Kristeva's solution to a woman's location in a religious discourse that defines her as strange and/or abject. Moreover, from a strictly Lacanian or Freudian perspective the "analyst must represent or stand in for" the imaginary father of individual pre-history.[87] Here, however, the analyst's role is "more-than-maternal" and it is a loving mother who "hears true into speech" the possibility of new life in the here and now because language is revitalized and meaning is restored.[88]

Forgiveness: A Timelessness Which Restores Meaning

Forgiveness, asserts Kristeva, is ahistorical because "[i]t breaks the concatenation of causes and effects, crimes and punishment, it stays the time of actions."[89] (Recall from chapter three that women exist outside linear or historical time.) Why is this important? Because it is a loving mother who bestows forgiveness, thus limiting the duration of the "crime": "A limitation that knows the crime and does not forget it but, without being blinded as to its horror, banks on a new departure, on a *renewal of the individual*."[90] This is possible in the context of a therapeutic relationship because of the restorative or regenerative potential that arises from transference love. Thus time stops at two levels of subjectivity: (1) "the *unconscious level*, which stops time through desire and death"; and, (2) "the *love level*, which stays the former unconscious and the former history and begins a rebuilding of the personality within a new relation for an other. *My unconscious is reinscribable beyond the gift that an other presents me by not judging my actions*."[91] Here one can witness the marks of Freud's *eros* and *thanatos* upon Kristeva's theory. In essence she subscribes to his view that the life (or sexual) instincts arrest the organism's progress toward death. What is new is the manner in which she associates this process, especially for women, with a "for-giving" relationship in which love triumphs over their experience of the abject. This is the hallmark of the therapeutic task—"an other who does not judge but hears my truth in the availability of love, and for that very reason allows me to be reborn."[92] Does forgiveness actually cleanse actions? No, she asserts, rather forgiveness "raises the unconscious from beneath the actions and has it meet a loving other."[93] Kristeva terms forgiveness the "luminous stage of dark, unconscious timelessness" which makes possible the renewal of self *and other*.[94] In each new therapeutic relationship the pastoral counselor must also expect to have her truth transformed. How then is meaning restored?

Kristeva maintains that there is no beauty external to forgiveness because forgiveness "remembers abjection and filters it through the destabilized, musicalized, resensualized signs of loving discourse."[95] A woman, in this case one struggling with depression, is not asked to forget her experience or disavow her meaning; rather her meaning is given shape and form through a forgiving relationship which "at the outset constitutes a will, postulate, or scheme: *meaning exists*."[96] It is through this experience of being both able to forgive and accept forgiveness that an individual struggling with depression is now also capable of identifying with a loving father. Thus, for a woman who has previously been unable or unwilling to identify with the language of the father, there is a new possibility for symbolic law and an accession to knowledge and power. Paternal discourse, as we saw in chapter three, is the discourse of history and the means by which a subject-in-process/on trial enters into linear time. The capability to identify with a loving father (even if only the imaginary father of individual pre-history) also has implications for the restoration of imagination as well as the quest for new metaphors in religious discourse. Maternal metaphors need not replace paternal metaphors but the metaphors chosen in a therapeutic relationship need to include gendered experience in a manner which is respectful of human experience. It is Kristeva's own experience with writing as an aesthetic practice which will assist us to see how forgiveness becomes a vehicle for helping the "stranger" (a woman struggling with depression here) to reacquaint herself with affect and language.

Forgiveness: Aesthetic Experience[97]

The aesthetic experience Kristeva examines is writing (not a coincidence since she writes prolifically!) and forgiveness as it is portrayed in Dostoyevsky's *Crime and Punishment* as we have already seen above. All forgiveness is serious but the level of seriousness in this association of forgiveness intensifies in some measure because writing itself is a transference experience that is solitary. The story is written, not spoken and the listener as such is a reader. The forgiveness of "analytic listening...neither judges nor calculates but attempts to untangle and reconstruct."[98] For Kristeva it is the act of writing as an aesthetic experience which permits her to unfold her own unforgettable violence and despair because it provides a separate space with which to deal with "powers of horror" that stand in need of forgiveness.

How is this so? Kristeva suggests that forgiveness is both a "gesture of assertion," an act of the will and "an inscription of meaning" because it includes or incorporates "erosion of meaning, melancholia, and abjection" internal to the process; thus it displaces, absorbs or transforms these negations in order to allow the possibility of new meaning and rebirth to occur. Forgiveness is both technique and art. It "insures the life deal of the imagination."[99] In the analytic process, those who forgive as well as those who accept forgiveness are ready to be reconciled themselves through identification with a "loving father, an imaginary father." Here Kristeva intends the "father of prehistory" whose voice facilitates the mourning process in which an infant agrees to lose her mother in order to be able to name her mother–the beginning of the language acquisition process. This analytic process of forgiveness also creates space for reconciliation with the mother as a step in the journey toward healing self-estrangement. The aesthetic experience of forgiveness, a work of art (writing, for Kristeva, but art and music would also be forms of forgiveness as aesthetic experience) is an experience of "naming and composing" that finally enables "affection for the stranger" including the unconscious affect we repress.[100]

Forgiveness: A Suffering With and Affection for the Stranger

Forgiveness is an action of the speaking being (a subject-in-process/on trial) even if the words are written rather than spoken. It is a serious event in which the listener and the narrator participate equally. A story, in a manner of speaking, is confessed and the listener consents to suffer with the narrator as part of her affection for this narrator/stranger.[101] Kristeva observes that this is forgiveness at the human level. Citing Aquinas she notes that mercy (forgiveness) is attributed to God only in its *effect*, not at the level of *affect* because God drives out or releases our miseries (defects).[102] When we respond to God's call to forgive as we have already been forgiven in Christ, our actions do not equal divine mercy but there is an assumption of "a potential identification with that effective and efficient merciful divinity."[103] Divine mercy excludes sadness but human forgiveness collects to itself human sorrows since we are acutely attuned to the types of wounds that create sorrow in the first place. Nevertheless, we do attempt to model human forgiveness after divine mercy in order that: *"Love, all in all, beyond judgment, takes over from sadness, which is nevertheless understood, heard, displayed."*[104] We are able to forgive ourselves when we release our misery, our lack or our wound, to an other who hears us and reassures us that we belong to an ideal order; thus, we are protected against depression.

We are heard into speech by a loving mother whose "for-giving" allows us to reconcile with a loving father. The time of the depression is something that Kristeva has compared to the "zero time" which is also the "essential time" of Sleeping Beauty's deep sleep which amounts to the stagnation of the present—a time in which an individual flounders with difficulties, understands nothing and thus, communicates nothing.[105] The time of depression is analogous to the time of sleep, a certain kind of death. The revival of time comes through a structure of love and forgiving in a relationship that provides assurance of a rebirth. Does this structure of love and forgiveness suggest new metaphors?

Forgiveness: Regression or Reformation?

If one conceptualizes forgiveness as a refusal of power or a conspiring with one's degradation then forgiveness could only be a regression or collusion with the *status quo*. If, however, one conceptualizes forgiveness as a "for-giving" speech event then it necessarily offers possibilities for reformation or the rebuilding of a personality. The structure of the "for-giving" relationship that Kristeva proposes is comparable to McFague's proposal for God as redeemer to be understood as God as lover. One difficulty with this model of God, as noted by some of McFague's critics, is that it suggests the model for the second person of the Trinity may be reduced to eroticism. McFague is undaunted by the criticism and instead asserts: "If the relationship between lovers is arguably the deepest human relationship, then it should be a central metaphor for modeling some aspects of the God-world relationship."[106] She notes that the imagery of Song of Songs "powerfully expresses divine passion for the world as well as extraordinary intimacy between God and the world."[107] Indeed Kristeva also sees the necessity of including eroticism in a model of God's love in her essay on the Song of Songs, "A Holy Madness: She and He." She invites us to consider the fact that there is an erotic element woven throughout Song of Songs which is just as evident as God's absolute—even demanding—presence leading her to conclude that "the Song of Songs is not a foreign element in the Bible—it merely dots the 'I's.' Desire and God have always been there."[108] The

God as lover model is not without its difficulties, including some of the metaphors that arose out of the medieval mystic tradition—especially the bridal metaphors which subordinate women to men. Even so there are positive expressions that have been derived from the God as lover model which include an expression of closeness, concern and longing or desire between God and humans.[109] At the center of a model of God as lover is value. The perception of being valuable or "finding someone else valuable and being found valuable" is, according to McFague, "the most complete affirmation possible."[110]

Again one might want to raise the question: "How is McFague's proposal of God as lover any different from the tradition that precedes it?" Her model turns on the notion that the world is viewed as God's body, thus avoiding individualism, dualism and the idea that this love is otherworldly. Rather, "God as lover is seen to love not spirits individually in a world apart from the one we know, but all creatures, body and spirit, here and now. And we in turn do not love God one by one in vertical relationships of beloved to lover, but as we love the world."[111] Moreover, we need to retain the passion in this model of God as lover because it is more than sexual desire. McFague calls our attention to the passion of Christ, noting that Jesus' suffering was an "agony brought on by great love toward those who need love most: the last and the least."[112] God the lover suffered with and for those who believed themselves to be without value and those who would be disciples are invited to do the same. Here we begin to see an analogy or an affinity between the model of "for-giving" that Kristeva presents as a model of suffering and affection for an other. This model of God as lover implies three kinds of divine activity—eros, saving, and healing.[113] A complete examination of McFague's proposal is beyond the scope of this project; I will limit the discussion to the divine activity of healing since it is in some partial and imperfect way an aim of pastoral care and counseling to facilitate the potential for this kind of healing.

Insofar as salvation is a divine work it is possible to speak of humans only as the recipients of God's grace and favor. Insofar as human actions can contribute to healing activity in the world (in this project we are specifically concerned with the manner in which a pastor can assist depressed women to find their voices) they can be said to be actions undertaken in God's image. Among the characteristics of healing that make it suitable for an image of the work of God as well as humans, are its affirmation of the importance of bodies (undermining any notion of a body/spirit split); its appropriateness for imaging salvation in an ecological and evolutionary context; and, its emphasis on a dual movement of "resistance to disease, disorder, and chaos," and "identification with the sufferers in their pain."[114]

The first trait calls forth the reunification of a disordered world and "undercuts the heavy anthropocentrism of traditional Christian theories of redemption."[115] In this view illness is not understood as a divine punishment for sin but rather the result of an imbalance in the unity of body and soul which may be produced by evil and sin. The second trait or ecological dimension suggests that "the causes of the disorder, and its solution, are internal and involve a redress of imbalances."[116] The health of the entire world is held in an intricate balance; thus, the "role of the healer...will necessarily be somewhat indirect...a helper working to restore right relationships."[117] In this project we seek to help a depressed woman to be reconciled with herself and to make friends with her internalized images of her mother. This may also be construed as a journey toward love and forgiveness which we will discuss in the final chapter. The third dimension has an active phase and a passive one. Resistance is the active phase in which God "works actively to bring well-being to the beloved," by healing divisions and liberating the oppressed. Identification, or the passive phase, focuses on the death of Christ who suffered in solidarity with the beloved. McFague is adamant that the passive phase must be second to the activity of God as the One who resists oppression, otherwise this model of God would represent an "acceptance of the status quo and a romanticization of suffering."[118] Thus, it would be no different than any models which have preceded it. The model of God as lover is analogous to the experience of a therapeutic relationship which Kristeva describes as a "for-giving," especially for a woman struggling with depression, because there is an opportunity for a reunification with a loving mother and thus, with the part of herself which has been denied and repressed. The woman-mother that has been split has an opportunity for reconciliation through language in which her truth is recognized and the meaning of her life is restored and/or rebuilt. Kristeva's process for the speaking subject and McFague's metaphor—God as lover—provide a resolution to self-estrangement and abjection that is a "tale of love." Can this loving, forgiving relationship provide a cure? What kind of Word does a Mother/Lover God speak?

The Word as Cure

The Crisis of the Subject-in-Process Revisited

Kristeva asks: "These days, who still has a soul?"[119] She is concerned with a "reduction of the private life" and the manner in which "women and men—who are stress-ridden and eager to achieve, to spend money, have fun, and die—dispense with the representation of their experience that we call psychic life. Actions and their imminent abandonment have replaced the interpretation of meaning."[120] She is troubled by the thought that a "new humanity" will be content to mediate its anxieties with a pill and a television screen which results in a standardized expression and a normalized discourse that we cannot even claim is our own. Kristeva wonders aloud with her readers about the new patients who may be a product of the stresses of contemporary life asking if "dependence on medicines and refuge in the image [are] merely modern renditions of the narcissistic inadequacies common to all times? Finally, have patients changed or has analytic practice changed, such that analysts have sharpened their interpretations of previously neglected symptoms?"[121] Whatever our individual and collective concerns may be about, the crisis of the contemporary speaking subject who is always in process, is just that—her inability to represent her suffering in words.

Kristeva emphatically states in a manner which almost chides the reader that analysts (therapists, pastoral counselors) "who do not discover a *new malady of the soul* in each of their patients do not fully appreciate the uniqueness of each individual."[122] The uniqueness of each individual is what needs to command our attention no matter how many times we may have encountered the discourse of those who struggle with depression. The first indication that these "silent strangers" can no longer remain silent is realized in their seeking a listening, loving and forgiving other who will help them give rebirth to their identity. The resolution to the crisis will come when desire, grammar, rhetoric and thus, meaning are restored. Each woman needs to be taken seriously in her personhood, her story needs to be heard as truth, and in the context of the therapeutic relationship it is the counselor's responsibility to understand the "tale of love" as though it is the first time she has encountered this situation—for in fact, it is.

Cure: The Possibility of Telling One's Story

At the beginning of the "more-than-maternal" task a woman may turn to her counselor as a "subject-presumed-to-know," but the reality is that the counselor is "nothing more than a questioning and questioned subject."[123] The suffering with and affection for the sufferer comes alive when "I assume that there is a part of me in you, and I expect that it will give me an answer to the question that the other part is formulating."[124] This is a process of interpretation which "*adopts the psychological profile of a question.* I think I know something, but I give up and allow you to speak. You are the one who must know, speak, lie, think."[125]

As noted earlier, this is the point at which clergy, in particular, often fail with the women who seek their support because they disregard the experience of these women as weird or crazy: "It couldn't possibly be true." Pastors and pastoral counselors need to "give up" and allow the women to speak. What they need to "give up" most is their need to defend God and theology. More often than not, ministers, and church members resort to defending their own particular understandings of God at the expense of the one who is seeking healing. But it isn't simply a matter of "giving up"; caring requires listening with an attitude of seriousness that says, "[Y]ou are the one who must know." The woman struggling with depression is in a sense called by name by the counselor (a loving, for-giving mother) and the words (the interpretation) that are spoken issue an invitation to renewal for the one seeking help. This calling by name is reminiscent of the way in which we are called by name and recognized in our singularity through the sacrament of Baptism. Anna Smith reflects on this power of the word more in the context of literature than therapy, but her points are relevant nevertheless: "Language renews the subject and turns crisis into a pretext for innovation. And so to read is also to hear one's name called across space. If I have lost language and language has lost me, the Word solicits me and comforts me. In that soliciting, in that calling, I return from exile into the name."[126] First there is a calling by name and then there is a shared story in which the listener suffers with and has an affection for the sufferer. Perhaps it is the case that "[t]hose who suffer feel closer to their soul."[127] Inasmuch as the Bible is considered by many Christians, including and especially women, to be a shared story of God's relationship with the people of faith and insofar as we are examining the power of the Word to heal, we will look next at what Kristeva has to say about the Bible's unique role in the healing process.

Cure: The Fulfillment of the Word

Kristeva wants to know who is speaking in the Bible and for whom. Why are these questions important for the psychoanalyst? Because they seem to "suggest a subject who is not at all neutral and indifferent like the subject described by modern theories of interpretation, but who maintains a specific relationship of *crisis, trial,* or *process* with his God."[128] Kristeva's metaphor for the developing self (a process that lasts throughout a life-time)—subject-in-process/on-trial—reappears in the text where she speaks with positive regard for the Bible, a sacred text which carves out a new space for the speaking subject. Thus she claims that the "Bible is a text that thrusts its words into my losses. By enabling me to speak about my disappointments, though, it lets me stand in full awareness of them."[129] The Bible does this, she asserts, by giving meaning to the crises of subjectivity that have been discussed at length in this project (e.g., abjection, strangeness, melancholia and the language of the depressed).

Some will surely want to argue that Kristeva is only using the Biblical text as a metaphor for unconscious processes; this would be a misinterpretation, however. Kearns notes that while Kristeva, like other postmodern critics, approaches both religion and theology with a hermeneutics of suspicion, this does not mean she finds no positive value in religion and theology. (I will return to this topic in the final chapter.) To the contrary:

> Religion is...a discourse, in some ways a feminine discourse, which helps to mediate, in a healing way, between the claims of law and flesh, symbolic and semiotic, order and creativity, self and other. And theology, for its part, seeks to explain, often with greater acuity than philosophy or psychoanalysis has yet achieved, how in principle and by what best strategies that healing may take place.[130]

Kristeva is apprehensive about religious and theological discourse because of the apparent blindness to the terrors and abuses that have resulted from those who employ these discourses without being appropriately self-critical. This reflects the criticisms and concerns of Neuger and Bons-Storm discussed previously in this chapter. Kristeva is also troubled by what she sees as a reification of religious discourse which "strives too hard, in the name of its own version of the law and its own strategies of power, to repress or deny our recognition of materiality, language, and death."[131] Here we see McFague's distress over dead metaphors expressed in a slightly different manner. Nevertheless, these apprehensions point to the reasons why many women struggling with depression may have difficulty finding their voice in a Western Christian context. How then can they be helped to find healing within a feminine religious discourse?

Kristeva finds a parallel process of sorts between the journey of a "subject-in-process/on-trial" and the Biblical description of transformation of sacrifice into language inasmuch as "the maternal is a promised land if you are willing to leave it, an object of desire if you are willing to renounce and forbid it; the maternal is delight as well as murder, an inescapable 'abject' whose awareness haunts you, or which may very well be the constitutive double of your own awareness."[132] This is a variation of the thesis of *Powers of Horror* which was discussed in chapter two. Again, we see that language, in this case a sacred text, can help to provide a resolution to the abjection women experience insofar as it functions as a feminine/maternal voice or discourse which provides a space to work through alienation, especially self-alienation. Is this in conflict with the claim that religious discourse can be a source of oppression for those women struggling with depression? No, because the conflict arises only when the discourse becomes reified and when the metaphors no longer connect with women's experience.

The essay, "Reading the Bible," ends with an imperative that we "should read the Bible one more time" in order to interpret it but also to let it carve out a space for our own subjectivity.[133] It is here in a sacred text that we see the fulfillment of Christianity in the "imaginative capability" of Western humanity which is "the ability to transfer meaning to the very place where it was lost in death and/or nonmeaning."[134] I suggest that it is even possible, (perhaps preferable) to understand the Bible as an *ergasterion* or privileged space that encourages rebirth for women struggling with depression. Though sacred texts can become a source of oppression if metaphors and language are not revitalized, sacred texts are themselves a space which provides for rebirth, renewal, and healing through the telling and hearing of a story into truth.

Cure: A Reciprocal Relationship between Friends

Each time a counseling relationship is entered into we encounter "a new malady of the soul" or we have treated with disrespect the other who comes seeking our help. Each time a counselor begins a new relationship she should expect that her truth or reality will be challenged and transformed as a result of this relationship. With regard to friendship, McFague concludes that one cannot choose one's mother, but "friends choose to be together" and that friendship "is the most free of all our relationships."[135] She is, of course, discussing friendship in the context of using "friend" as a model of God (here understood as sanctifier).[136] Friendship is defined "at its most elemental [level as] the bonding of two people by free choice in a reciprocal relationship."[137] There are, of course, relationships described as friendship which are utilitarian or one-sided but these would not be true friendships. The difficulties with constructing a model of God based upon friendship are not overlooked by McFague. She cites the traditional arguments against friendship which include the perceptions that friendship is elitist, individualistic, a peripheral relationship lacking seriousness, preferential, exclusive and based not on love of another but love of self (in other words narcissistic or object abusing in the worst way).[138] Moreover, it is clear who our mothers and lovers are but "being a friend means many different things to different people in different times and places."[139] Is this metaphor strong enough to construct a model of God (again, no one model is ever complete) and does it help to overcome the source of oppression that many women encounter in religious discourse? A brief summary of McFague's formulation of God as friend will enable us to see that this is the case.

This formulation turns on three paradoxes: "in a free relationship, a bonding occurs; in a relationship between two, an inclusive element is implied; in a relationship supposedly for children and angels, adult characteristics are required."[140] In the first paradox McFague observes that freedom is part of the power of friendship but a bond is formed based on trust which if broken is seen as a betrayal or sin against the friend. Thus, "[w]hat appears, then, as the freest of all relationships, with no obligations except to delight, to play, carries a hidden but powerful responsibility of commitment to the other, a commitment to stay true, to stay trustworthy."[141] This is, I suggest, analogous to the commitment made between a pastor and a parishioner, or a counselor and a client. If a woman struggling with depression can trust the counselor who represents a loving, for-giving other that will not betray her, perhaps then she can find solace in a God who will also befriend her.

How can a relationship between two also contain an inclusive element? What is required is a commitment to a common vision. (The question raised is: "Do you see the same truth that I do?") What is required is a similar vision, not similar minds, which allows friends of various numbers and differences to unite around a common cause.[142] Diversity is an essential element of the inclusivity expressed in this paradox.

Finally, being a friend is more than "mere child's play;" it means becoming an adult and moving from a dependent child's status to an interdependence (as opposed to independence). This is the paradox which states that friendships are for children and angels but require adult characteristics. That is, "mature perception and activity in our world demand interrelating not only with other human beings but also with other forms of being, both nonhuman and divine."[143] Thus we are "invited as friends of the Friend of the world to join in that vision and work for its fulfillment."[144] Self-estrangement is overcome through a friendship that is a companioning through suffering. God as Friend is the One who sustains us and who delights in our companionship. This is the God who literally eats bread together with us and offers hospitality to the stranger, the outcast, or the exile. The "stranger" who struggles with depression is welcomed back into the community and her self-estrangement is healed; meaning is restored. The foreigner is recognized and her story is heard as truth. Thus, in my view, the metaphor of God as Friend is strong enough to counter the source of oppression that many women encounter in religious discourse.

Conclusion

"Real female innovation," Kristeva maintains, "will only come about when maternity, female creation and the link between them are better understood. But for that to happen we must stop making feminism into a new religion, undertaking or sect and begin the work of specific and detailed analysis which will take us beyond romantic melodrama and beyond complacency."[145] This project is offered in the spirit of an analysis of a religious discourse that has contributed to women's oppression and subsequent struggles with depression. We have observed that a woman struggling with depression is like an "Alice in distressland" because she can neither speak nor see; she is neither seen nor heard. Lacking sight, she lacks insight, too. The relationship with her counselor is analogous to the privileged space or *ergasterion* discussed in chapter four. Employing the maternal metaphor, the therapeutic relationship is a womb of sorts which provides a safe place to work through suffering with a loving, for-giving other.

The splitting of the feminine into the "woman-mother" as well as women's location in religious discourse as the space of abjection, horror and terror is reconciled when a maternal discourse is brought to fruition. A woman struggling with depression is reunited with the mother (or at least the maternal object which she has internalized) she never agreed to lose and thus, she is reunited with a part of herself that has been estranged. In fact, I would go so far as to suggest that if she is unable to befriend these maternal images she will probably not regain speech in which she is able to state "She" is not "I." Especially in "Stabat Mater," Kristeva asserts, a woman's real joy or jouissance comes with the experience of motherhood, because a woman is reunited with the very body of her own mother through this experience. At times Kristeva writes of the experience as if it were a numinous experience for her. As a result, many feminists are critical of her work. Yet it is this reconciliation with her mother that also fosters a woman's ability to be reconciled with a loving father as she finds meaning in her life and revitalizes language in relationship to an other. This allows a woman, then, to enter into a paternal discourse—the language of history and power. Each woman is unique; there is no Woman that represents all women. In this relationship, as Kristeva sets it forth, a woman is encouraged to embrace her difference, her strangeness or foreignness in order that foreignness will some day cease to exist. This is her place of strength even if it is often a place of silence.

In the end, there may be, as Kristeva notes, a transference relationship between reader and writer.[146] Since it is my intention to critique religious discourse (not to offer a new theology) and expand borders of meaning in pastoral counseling situations using some of Kristeva's metaphors, there may be meanings which arise for the reader which were not intended by the writer. If we think back to the metaphors examined in chapter two, the pilgrim becomes a voyager. On this voyage or journey there is one final destination related to identity and the struggle to become a speaking subject that will be examined. Kristeva endeavors to take her readers beyond the "blind boundaries of meaning"[147] that may be associated with traditional religious language. While traveling on a journey as a foreigner in a strange land through a study of depression we will examine what she says about our "incredible need to believe" as it relates to forgiveness—a core doctrine, belief, process and practice for pastoral theology.

Notes

1. Christie Cozad Neuger, *Counseling Women*, 152.
2. Ibid., 154.
3. Ibid., 157.

4. Ibid., 12.
5. Alan Riding, "Correcting Her Idea of Politically Correct: Feeling Misunderstood, A French Thinker Tries an Individualistic Path," *New York Times*, 14 July 2001, B9.
6. Neuger, *Counseling Women*, 30–31, and chapter six. She provides a review of recent studies on women struggling with depression that demonstrates women suffer at a rate two to six times higher than men, with American women of European descent having the highest rates. One such research study conducted by the American Psychological Association in 1990 indicated that this was a direct result of their experiences as females in our contemporary culture. Though not stated directly by Neuger, the implication is that contemporary culture is toxic, at least for some women.
7. Ibid. 95, 101. Neuger asserts that the church "has been in unquestioning collusion with patriarchy in terms of assuming the normativity (and believability) of males."
8. Kristeva, *This Incredible Need to Believe*, 38–39.
9. Alan Riding, "Correcting Her Idea of Politically Correct," B11.
10. This thought is supported in a much earlier interview (i.e., 1974), "Woman Is Never What We Say," *Julia Kristeva Interviews*, ed. Ross Guberman (New York: Columbia University Press, 1996), 96–97.
11. Riding, "Correcting Her Idea of Politically Correct," B11.
12. Riet Bons-Storm, *The Incredible Woman: Listening to Women's Silences in Pastoral Care and Counseling* (Nashville: Abingdon Press, 1996), 20.
13. Ibid., 19.
14. Riding, "Correcting Her Idea of Politically Correct," B11. The above examples of vanishing spaces—family, grandmother, church—of communication are Kristeva's own and do not represent an exhaustive list. Given her interest in maternal discourse, especially in *Stabat Mater*, the absence of mother in this list is curious. Object relations seem to exist side by side with the Church which has lost its place as a communication space or *ergasterion*—privileged space. In this same article, Kristeva applauds the efforts of reality television shows which provide avenues of expression for feelings about life, sex and friendship which otherwise would remain unarticulated.
15. Ibid. Again, Bons-Storm addresses this issue in terms of what she sees as a sociocultural narrative that declares "women either have more problems, or need more help than men do, or they are more ready to go to a pastor with their problems" (*The Incredible Woman*, 66). She is critical of pastoral care and counseling resources which reinforce this sociocultural narrative and thus, continue to contribute to women's oppression.
16. See the discussion of juxtaposition in the first chapter, 25–26.
17. Kristeva, "In Praise of Love," *Tales of Love*, 1.
18. Julia Kristeva, "A Holy Madness: She and He," *Tales of Love*, 95
19. Kristeva, *In the Beginning Was Love*, 3.
20. D. W. Winnicott, *Playing and Reality* (London: Tavisotck/Routledge, 1971, reprint ed. 1993), 102–3.
21. Kristeva, *In the Beginning Was Love*, 51, my emphasis.
22. Kristeva, "What Revolt Today?" *The Sense and Non-Sense of Revolt*, 16.
23. Kristeva, *In the Beginning Was Love*, 3.

24. Kristeva's essay, "God is Love," *Tales of Love* (139–150) addresses the development of love from Greek *eros*, to Hebrew *ahav*, to New Testament *agapè.* She suggests that over the centuries the Christian tradition has diminished the meaning of this love which is above all an inaugural gift from God that is unmerited. Her critique of the Christian tradition reflects concerns similar to those of Donald Capps which will be discussed shortly, i.e., love of self is often understood as narcissistic rather than being inspired by God. Kristeva traces the meaning of love through the synoptic gospels to Paul, observing that emphasis is placed on the source of love—God—and the human response to God's gift, or faith (140).
25. Bons-Storm, *The Incredible Woman*, 45.
26. Ibid., 61.
27. Ibid.
28. Kristeva, "God is Love," 141.
29. Kristeva, *In the Beginning Was Love*, xiii.
30. Kristeva, "Bernard of Clairvaux: Affect, Desire, Love," *Tales of Love*, 160.
31. Ibid., 159.
32. Donald Capps, *Agents of Hope: A Pastoral Psychology* (Minneapolis: Fortress Press, 1995), 58. He is concerned with the connection between desire and hoping; our primary interest here is the connection between desire and love, especially for God and self.
33. *Interviews*, ed. Ross Guberman, 75. In an interview conducted by Françoise Collin in 1985 (shortly after the French publication of *Histoires d'amour*), Kristeva elaborated on the meaning of suffering religion: "Religion is rooted in our inherent separation. For the Indo-Europeans, 'to have faith' means that I make a pledge and a gift to someone from whom I am separated and whom I expect to pay me back, which presumes that separation is a place of suffering. The analytic contract presumes that someone comes along who is suffering because he is separated. He enters into a new relationship to remedy this prior and traumatic separation and must be able to separate himself in a less painful way." The separation that occurs in a hopefully less painful way is the separation from the therapist when the therapeutic relationship ends.
34. Kristeva, *Black Sun*, 74. Kristeva offers us a case illustration, "Helen," to underscore her point about voice and sight, even as "Helen" says: "As much as I try to imagine her [mother] face, now or at the time of my childhood, I don't see it. I am sitting on someone who holds me, perhaps on her lap, but actually it isn't anybody. A person would have a *face, a voice, a glance, a head.* The fact is that I perceive nothing of the sort, merely a support, that's all, nothing else," my emphasis (75).
35. Donald Capps, *The Depleted Self: Sin in a Narcissistic Age* (Minneapolis: Fortress Press, 1993), 66. He asserts: "Melancholy, then is the result of inadequate or nonexistent mirroring. To become melancholic means to lose one's belief that one is the object of recognition, that one is not only *see-er but also seen,*" my emphasis.
36. Erik Erikson addresses the importance of a ritualization of recognition between mother and infant which begins each day. In *Toys and Reasons* he notes that "the mother calls the infant by a name. This may have been carefully selected and perhaps certified in some name-giving ritual, held to be indispensable by the parents and the community. Yet, whatever procedures have given meaning to the name, that meaning now exerts a certain effect on the way in which the name is repeated during the greeting procedure...the mother

also refers to herself with a special designation. This mutual assignment of a very special meaning is, I think, the ontogenetic source of one pervasive element in human ritualization, which is based on a *mutuality of recognition*, by face and by name" (87, Erikson's emphasis). Voice and sight are necessary in this ritual of recognition. Thus, Erikson's earlier work underscores the point being made by Kristeva and leaves the door open for a "remembrance" of an earlier ritual—baptism. This passage also reflects Isaiah 43:1 ("I have called you by name, you are mine"). *Toys and Reasons: Stages in the Ritualization of Experience* (New York: W. W. Norton, 1977).

37. Kristeva, *In the Beginning Was Love*, 55–56.
38. Ibid., 25.
39. Bons-Storm, *The Incredible Woman*, 72, my emphasis. Bons-Storm building on Nelle Morton calls this process of counseling a "hearing into speech" which "means listening carefully and patiently while someone finds the courage to say what she or he really means" (150).
40. Kristeva, *In the Beginning Was Love*, 21. In *Black Sun*, Kristeva appears to chastise those psychoanalysts who believe they can be efficacious in a vacuum suggesting that they need to pay more attention to the literary and religious representations of a person's struggle with "symbolic collapse." In her view psychoanalysts "owe it to themselves to enrich their practice by paying greater attention to these sublimatory solutions [literary and religious representations of psychic struggles] to our crises, in order to be lucid counterdepressants rather than neutralizing antidepressants" (24–25).
41. Kristeva, "Extraterrestrials Suffering For Want of Love," *Tales of Love*, 381.
42. Ibid., 381–82.
43. John Lechte, *Julia Kristeva* (New York: Routledge, 1990), 170. See also, 167–175.
44. Donald Capps, *The Depleted Self*, 65, my emphasis.
45. Kristeva, "God is Love," *Tales of Love*, 146.
46. Ibid.
47. Ibid. Kelly Oliver's elaboration of this passage is helpful: "As Kristeva describes it, Christian love sounds very much like the psychoanalytic account of the move through the mirror stage into speech. Christian love's 'killing' of the body so that the subject can be born into the 'Name of the Other,' language, echoes the primary transference love that Kristeva describes as the assent to language." *Reading Kristeva*, 28. Moreover, Oliver notes that Kristeva uses "psychoanalytic metaphors in order to analyze religion," and "religious metaphors in order to describe analytic processes." The very fact that Kristeva does this suggests that these two discourses are not always separate and distinct. Thus, the psychoanalyst does provide theological insight here, even when she does not intend to; i.e., love of Self does not constitute sinful narcissistic personalities, rather it is the foundation for all love because it is an inaugural gift from God. Self-effacement or self-abnegation would not be the prototype for love but rather the prototype for sin, especially for women who already struggle with a loss of self. This equation of love with self-sacrifice is addressed by Brita L. Gill-Austern in greater depth in "Love Understood as Self-Sacrifice and Self-Denial: What Does It Do to Women?" *Through the Eyes of Women: Insights for Pastoral Care*, ed., Jeanne Stevenson Moessner (Minneapolis: Fortress Press, 1996): 304–21. For example, she writes: "The Christian understanding of love as self-sacrifice and self-denial

has taken on its power in a tradition that has too often glorified suffering...women have become acculturated to accept abuse, because they come to believe it is their place to suffer" (308).

48. Kristeva, "God is Love,"147, my emphasis.
49. Ibid.
50. Lechte, *Julia Kristeva,* 172.
51. Kristeva, "The Inexpressible Child," *New Maladies of the Soul,* 105, Kristeva's emphasis.
52. Ibid., 109.
53. Ibid.
54. Ibid.
55. Kristeva, *In the Beginning Was Love,* 27, my emphasis. Paul Tillich offers a similar description of pastoral care in "The Theology of Pastoral Care: The Spiritual and Theological Foundations of Pastoral Care," *The Meaning of Health,* 126. He notes that the goal of any and every "care is the fulfillment of human potentialities....The first aim, and in some sense the total aim, toward which we have to work in pastoral care is 'acceptance.'"
56. Ibid., 48–49.
57. Martha J. Reineke, "Life-Sentences: Kristeva and the Limits of Modernity," *Soundings* 71 (Winter 1988): 459.
58. Sallie McFague, *Models of God,* 102–3. McFague notes that "female metaphors for God should be inclusive of but not limited to maternal ones" (99). While I concur, the primary focus of this project is on the need for a maternal discourse that empowers women to find and use their voices; thus in the interest of limiting the scope of this project, the female metaphor chosen for further examination is that of "mother."
59. Ibid., 108.
60. Ibid., 99.
61. Ibid., 106.
62. Ibid., 114.
63. Ibid., 117.
64. Ibid., 116. McFague does not object to male metaphors of God per se; she objects to the sole use of male metaphors at the exclusion of female ones (99). She cites an often overlooked passage from Tillich's third volume of *Systematic Theology* (293–94) to bolster her argument that God is beyond male and female but nevertheless male and female imagery is appropriate (101). By her own admission she does not seek to eliminate a paternal metaphor but rather emphasizes a parental model that includes Father and Mother. McFague notes that "one reason for including maternal language in a tradition where paternal language has prevailed is to underscore what the negative theological tradition has always insisted: God is unlike as well as like our metaphors" (97). While McFague argued in her earlier work, *Metaphorical Theology,* that metaphor is *unsubstituable* as a means of constructing theological models she did not argue that metaphors could not be substituted. See for example, Garrett Green's critique of her work in "The Gender of God and the Theology of Metaphor," *Speaking the Christian God: The Holy Trinity and the Challenge of Feminism,* ed., Alvin F. Kimel (Grand Rapids: Eerdmans, 1992): 44-64. Green's argument suggests that metaphors never die and that

changing religious language brings about a new religion or at the very least distorts the meaning of an existing one. This represents the sort of argument that a theologian or a pastoral theologian can appreciate but it seems to miss the point that the women who dwell in silence with the sorrowful gazes of depression will not be roused from their silence with yet another discourse that reinforces the status quo. I suggest (see chapter one) that Gerhart and Russell's theory of metaphor as a "knowledge-in-process" which emphasizes the way questions change is to the point here. What is of particular importance for women who seek counsel from pastors is how questions change. Will those who represent the Christian tradition cease being defensive about the tradition long enough to listen to the questions and voices of those who have been under-represented? (See Colin Gunton, "Proteus and Procrustes," *Speaking the Christian God*, 65–80 who acknowledges that a "merely defensive and conservative theology has never been true to the eschatological dynamic of the faith" even though he reduces McFague's argument to pantheism 68). Janet Soskice raises just such a question: "Can a feminist call God 'Father'?" in *Speaking the Christian God*, 81–94. She summarizes the feminist position succinctly noting that the "real objection to the rhetoric of patriarchy" is "not just that it subordinates women but that it also gives divine justification to a hierarchical reading of the world invariably conceived in terms of powerful/powerless, superior/inferior, active/passive, male/female" (86). Soskice appeals to Kristeva's *In the Beginning Was Love*—especially to her analysis of the Creed—for an answer to this dilemma which leads her to conclude that the "Other is both maternal and paternal" (94). Here she is in agreement with McFague. Soskice closes her essay by stating that Christianity needs to address a serious challenge concerning core metaphors, narratives and ideologies or it may simply "linger on as a pleasing anachronism distant from the life of the cultures it inhabits" (94). What is at issue in this project is not the authority of Scripture or God's self-revelation; rather the manner in which Christianity has been and continues to be culture accommodating to patriarchy.

65. Bons-Storm, *The Incredible Woman*, 49.
66. Ibid., 129.
67. Kristeva, "Joyce 'The Gracehoper' or Orpheus' Return," *New Maladies of the Soul*, 178. In this article Kristeva offers a partial solution to this question which simultaneously emphasizes the importance of metaphor: "Indeed, transference incites the analyst's words as well as his affect. To guide my speech to the psychic place in which my patient acts out her convulsive crises, for instance, I must participate in her *affective* suffering before rushing into the *language* of signs and giving a name to our shared affect that we had not been able to name," Kristeva's emphasis. She concludes that this participation in affective suffering is a metaphorical experience and metaphor is the *sine qua non* for the advent of the subject.
68. Kristeva, *Black Sun*, 189.
69. Ibid.
70. Ibid.
71. *Webster's New Universal Unabridged Dictionary*, 2nd ed. (1983), s.v. "tact."
72. Neuger, *Counseling Women*, 101. She provides a brief summary of Marie Fortune's work with victims of violence and the church's frequent complicity in asking the "powerless one to forgive the one with all the power" when instead Christian Scriptures state unequivocally

that "forgiveness comes from the one with power to the one without power, as in forgiving a debt."

73. Kristeva, *Black Sun.*, 190.
74. Ibid., 189.
75. Paul Tillich, "Estrangement and Reconciliation," *The Meaning of Health*, 9.
76. Kristeva, "Symbolic Castration: A Question," *New Maladies of the Soul*, 90.
77. Kristeva, *Black Sun*, 190.
78. Ibid., 194.
79. Ibid., 200. She refers to the passage in the Sermon on the Mount which immediately follows the instruction Jesus provides the disciples for how to pray. "For if you forgive others the wrongs they have done, your heavenly Father will also forgive you; but if you do not forgive others, then the wrongs you have done will not be forgiven by your Father." Since Kristeva's concern is primarily human-human relationships I understand her to mean that although forgiveness is ultimately a divine act, in the context of human relationships forgiveness is first and foremost something that happens between individuals.
80. Ibid., 195, my emphasis.
81. Anna Smith, *Readings of Exile and Estrangement*, 80.
82. Kristeva, *Black Sun*, 205.
83. Ibid., 196.
84. Ibid., 199.
85. Ibid., my emphasis.
86. Ibid., 200.
87. Cleo McNelly Kearns, "Art and Religious Discourse in Aquinas and Kristeva," *Body/Text in Julia Kristeva*, ed. David Crownfield (Albany: State University of New York, 1992), 118. This father of individual pre-history is the Third Party in Kristeva's Oedipal triangle. The Third Party is seen only through the eyes of the mother but the sound of this Third Party's voice as well as the mother's response to it, facilitates the separation between mother and child which enables language to develop. Again, the reference is not to an actual father but someone who functions as a Third Party that the infant is only vaguely aware of. See "Freud and Love: Treatment and Its Discontents," *Tales of Love*, 24–29 and *Black Sun*, 23–25, 45–46. This Third Party, as Antoinette Goodwin points out in her article, "Freud and Erikson: Their Contributions to the Psychology of God-Image Formation," *Pastoral Psychology* 47, no. 2 (1998): 97–117, is "the basis for the creation of 'the Ego Ideal,' and is the basis of the first images of God" (97).
88. Lechte, *Julia Kristeva*, 192. Lechte comments on this passage in *Black Sun* concerning Dostoyevsky's writing as an aesthetic practice which produces forgiveness stating: "And it is to a mother (or a substitute for her) to whom the writer (but we are all writers in this sense) turns in order to be forgiven. For it is she who has been killed by signs in the quest for individuality. Forgiveness, then, is fundamentally equivalent to a reconciliation with the mother." Kristeva's analysis of the Creed provides an insight into what "more than maternal" might mean. There is a separation, in this case from God, which is overcome by Christ's death and resurrection which provides for a reunion with the father, whom in the end, Kristeva maintains is a symbolic substitute for the mother. The one who gives counsel to a depressed woman then, is a functional mother or a substitute for one. That is, the

pastor or counselor is someone like the father of individual prehistory who makes speech possible.

89. Kristeva, *Black Sun*, 200.
90. Ibid., 203, my emphasis.
91. Ibid., 205, Kristeva's emphasis.
92. Ibid.
93. Ibid.
94. Ibid., my emphasis.
95. Ibid., 206.
96. Ibid.
97. See Carol L. Schnabl Schweitzer, "'For-giving' and Forgiving: Process and Practice in Pastoral Care," *Pastoral Psychology*, forthcoming.
98. Kristeva, *Black Sun*, 206.
99. Ibid., 207.
100. Ibid., 214.
101. David W. Augsburger, *Helping People Forgive* (Louisville: Westminster John Knox Press, 1996), 11–12. Augsburger writes about the various strands of metaphor that are intertwined to make a composite understanding of forgiveness. In the category of philosophical metaphor one of the elements he focuses on is forgiveness as a "performative utterance" which he describes as follows: "[T]he actual occasion of forgiveness is performed by a recognized verbal formula. 'A performative utterance' offers a (1) conventional procedure (2) with a ritual effect (3) through certain words (4) by certain appropriate persons (5) in certain appropriate and particular circumstances; (6) the procedure is executed by all participants correctly and (7) completely, (8) with congruent and sincere thoughts and feelings (9) resulting in their so conducting themselves subsequently."
102. Thomas Aquinas, *Summa Theologia*, Latin text and English trans. Thomas Gilby, O.P. (New York: McGraw Hill, 1963), vol. 5, question 21, 77 as cited by Kristeva, *Black Sun*, 215.
103. Kristeva, *Black Sun*, 216.
104. Ibid., my emphasis.
105. Julia Kristeva, "The Inexpressible Child," 111.
106. Sallie McFague, *Models of God*, 126.
107. Ibid., 127.
108. Kristeva, "A Holy Madness: She and He," *Tales of Love*, 96.
109. McFague, *Models of God*, 127.
110. Ibid., 128.
111. Ibid., 128–29.
112. Ibid., 129.
113. Ibid.
114. Ibid., 146–148.
115. Ibid., 147.
116. Ibid., 148.
117. Ibid.
118. Ibid. 149.

119. Julia Kristeva, "The Soul and the Image," *New Maladies of the Soul*, 7.
120. Ibid.
121. Ibid., 9.
122. Ibid.
123. Kristeva, "Symbolic Castration: A Question," 89.
124. Ibid., 88.
125. Ibid., 89.
126. Smith, *Readings of Exile and Estrangement*, 13.
127. Marcel Proust, "Les Plaisirs et les jour," Jean Santeuil (Paris: Bibliothèque de La Pléiade, 1971), 6 as cited by Julia Kristeva, "In Times Like These, Who Needs Psychoanalysts?" *New Maladies of the Soul*, 28.
128. Julia Kristeva, "Reading the Bible," *New Maladies of the Soul*, 117.
129. Ibid., 119.
130. Kearns, "Art and Religious Discourse in Aquinas and Kristeva," 112.
131. Ibid., 116.
132. Kristeva, "Reading the Bible," 120.
133. Ibid., 126.
134. Kristeva, *Black Sun*, 103.
135. McFague, *Models of God*, 159.
136. Even one of McFague's unyielding critics has to admit that the metaphor of friend "has a positive relation to the biblical narration of the Jesus history." Gunton, "Proteus and Procrustes," 77.
137. McFague, *Models of God*, 159–60.
138. Ibid., 160–61.
139. Ibid., 161.
140. Ibid., 162.
141. Ibid.
142. Ibid., 163–64.
143. Ibid., 165.
144. Ibid.
145. Julia Kristeva, "A New Type of Intellectual: The Dissident," *The Kristeva Reader*, 298.
146. See for example, Kristeva, "Word, Dialogue and Novel," *The Kristeva Reader*, 36–37. and "How Does One Speak to Literature?" *Desire in Language*, 119.
147. Kristeva, "From One Identity To An Other," *Desire in Language*, 125.

CHAPTER SIX

An Incredible Need to Be Heard and Believed

Whether I belong to a religion, whether I be agnostic or atheist, when I say "I believe," I mean "I hold as true."

—Julia Kristeva, *This Incredible Need to Believe*

Introduction: Speaking Is Believing

A foreigner (or an exile) ceases to be a foreigner when she is able to speak the language of her newly adopted home with fluency. The foreigner is a metaphor for women struggling with depression—women who often seek out their ministers for help. What draws individuals to their ministers to seek help, especially when they struggle with depression, is the belief that a pastoral relationship is a relationship grounded in love or agape as we have seen in the last chapter. In other words, there is a belief or at least a burgeoning need to believe that sends an afflicted person seeking a loving and "for-giving" other who will listen without judgment. Kristeva argues compellingly that what enables us to succeed in our struggles to become speaking subjects is precisely our "prereligious need to believe."[1] She looks to Psalm 116:10 and Paul (2 Corinthians 4:13) to support her thesis that we speak because we believe—even and especially from the midst of our afflictions. This need to believe arises in infancy when a child is able to project herself onto the father of individual prehistory (a loving third party who loves the mother and is loved by the mother) and this is why Kristeva identifies it as a "prereligious" experience (because it is a precognitive experience).

In this final chapter we will examine why a counseling relationship may be construed as a maternal type of relationship that is undergirded by a need to believe. The process is one that is guided by "for-giving" and "par-don" so that a person's desire to know (to ask questions), to love, and even to extend forgiveness may be restored. Kristeva's own experience as a psychoanalyst leaves her convinced that what her clients desire is "a sort of pardon, not in the sense of the effacing of his misery, but in the sense of a psychic and even physical *rebirth*."[2] The misery or the memory of the misery is not erased or lost but is resolved in such a way that rebirth occurs. This conviction contains at least a faint echo of what it means to be baptized insofar as there is a rebirth which occurs in the space of a "for-giving" maternal relationship (recall from our discussions of feminine identity and the woman-mother in chapters three and four that women in Christianity have a vital role in preparing their children for baptism *in the name of the Father*). Thus Kristeva calls the possibility of a new beginning a "par-don [*by-gift*]: to give and give oneself a new time, another self, unforeseen bonds."[3] These unforeseen bonds are potential relationships whose onset is in some way a new beginning in time, much the way baptism is a ritual of initiation. Moreover, she concludes that it is at the intersection of diverse disciplines (such as psychology and religion or theology) that hope for the future rests in our ability to "elucidate that which remains enigmatic."[4] I suggest that this is especially the case when a woman struggling with depression turns to her minister for help; she does so in the belief that this relationship will illumine the source of her pain and restore meaning to her life because a primary foundation of that relationship is agape or love. Some truths may be revealed but the pastoral nature of the relationship means it is more about a search for self and love than it is a search for "Truth." The thoughtful reader may object at this point stating: "I thought that the woman's story needs to be heard into truth." Yes, this is so. But the woman struggling with depression doesn't need the counselor to present to her an Absolute truth (she most especially doesn't need or expect the minister to defend God, tradition or patriarchal language as truth); rather she needs the counselor to affirm her story as truth in a loving, "for-giving" relationship which may be understood as "par-don." Once meaning is restored, the woman struggling with depression is able to re-engage with the "language of the father" in order to regain a sense of agency or power in the world.

A pastoral therapeutic relationship understood in this manner (the intersection of diverse disciplines) extends beyond relationships with individuals struggling with depression to individuals struggling with many other types of afflictions but the focus here will continue to be on those women who struggle with depression. When a specifically Christian theological perspective is added to the dynamics of the therapeutic relationship there is potential to reach what Kristeva calls the sacred as we shall see. My primary text in this last chapter will be Kristeva's *This Incredible Need to Believe* (which consists of lectures and interviews) in conversation with a number of recent works on forgiveness from an interdisciplinary perspective including *Dimensions in Forgiveness, Forgiveness in Context, Forgiveness,* and *Practicing Theology* which is a helpful counterpoint to Kristeva's psychoanalytic perspective on believing.

Believing and the Search for Self

Kristeva suggests that analysis begins with a type of believing insofar as analysts begin the therapeutic relationship by "believing" in the psychic reality of their clients; the reality of the "speaking cure" rests upon the conviction that the interpretations offered are well-founded.[5] How is this type of believing maternal and constituent of a search for self? Aesthetic and religious experiences are both shaped by the precognitive relationship that a mother has with her child—the dependent relationship that exists prior to the child's dawning awareness that there is a third party or father. Thus Kristeva asserts: "'I' am only if a beloved authority acknowledges me."[6] The beloved party is the father of individual prehistory. Thus one may contend here that Kristeva's work actually argues for male metaphors and images of God. What I suggest is that Kristeva does argue compellingly for the existence of both paternal and maternal religious language so that religious language is richly nuanced and reflective of the entirety of human experience. The prereligious need to believe is born out of an infant's increasing awareness of "paternal function" and "maternal passion."[7] Thus once an identification is made with the father of individual prehistory, the "I" continues to seek "the primary constituents of his identity in his incredible need to believe."[8] The search for self is, at least to some degree, a search for connection to the pre-oedipal triangle and this triangle forms the container from which faith cultivates inner experience.[9] One may want to take exception here because thus far, the searching and the need to believe is precognitive but Kristeva suggests that the process of searching for self and the constituents of identity continues beyond this precognitive stage of development; we need to take the need to believe seriously. How seriously? We shall see.

Kristeva asserts that taking the prereligious need to believe seriously would make it possible for us to "confront not only religions' past and present fundamentalist off-course drift but also the dead ends of secularized societies."[10] She is equally critical of both extremes suggesting that in the former case the pathway is paved toward violence (especially religious wars which continue to make headline news) and that in the latter case there is an "automation of the species" or a type of dehumanization taking place. These realities contribute to a global adolescent unrest in secularized societies and interrupt the adolescent's search for self and quest for an idealized "object of desire and/or love."[11] Here it begins to sound as if Kristeva is making a compelling argument for the restoration of belief as essential to the struggle to become a speaking subject and in fact, as we shall note at the conclusion of this chapter, I suggest this is precisely what she does though she disavows faith for herself. (It may be of interest to some readers that in this recent work devoted to matters of belief, Kristeva self-discloses the meaning of her patriarchal name—"of the cross.")[12]

Why is this important for a discussion of women struggling with depression? The capacity of an adolescent to believe that an "Ideal Object exists" is what makes passionate believers of us all as Kristeva states: "Faith implies a passion for the object relation: faith is potentially fundamentalist, like the adolescent."[13] The potential for fundamentalism becomes reality as the belief in an "Ideal Object" (God) is threatened in an ever increasing secularization of society. Thus the opposite side of a passionate search for an "Ideal Object" results in punishment and self-punishment or what Kristeva has called an adolescent "cortege: namely, disappointment-depression-suicide; not to mention, a more regressive and somatic mode, the anorexic syndrome; or even should the political context lend itself, the urge to destroy oneself-with-the-others that I've called the kamikaze syndrome."[14] Thus a failure to take the prereligious need to believe seriously may result in forms of abjection or anti-feminine behavior, on the one hand, exemplified by anorexia which Kristeva describes as a "break with the maternal line, and reveals the battle of the young woman against femininity, but brings about an overinvestment in the pureness-and-hardness of a body"; this eventually leads to the disappearance of the whole body "into a Beyond with strong paternal connotations."[15] On the other hand, a religious fundamentalism may arise where this prereligious need to believe is neglected resulting in a restriction of a woman's access to language and power, and/or violence toward others.

What is it that the adolescent pursues with such relish and fervor? Kristeva concludes that the fanatical belief in adolescence is in the existence of an "absolute partner" or "absolutely satisfying other." Thus when disappointment sets in with the realization that this person or Ideal Other does not exist an adolescent may begin to act out, have explosive speech or become depressive in the guise of boredom. Thus in a quest to know self, the adolescent looks for an absolute other who will at some level mirror back the constituents of identity but when this quest is disappointed the adolescent suffers from what Kristeva identifies as a malady of ideality like Romeo and Juliet. It is at this point—where the disruption occurs—that the analyst or pastoral counselor, in our situation, may be most helpful. In a temporary way, the pastor or pastoral counselor may become an Ideal Other. How does this occur? It is through the counselor's ability or capacity to know, to recognize, even to metabolize or bless the adolescent's fervent need to believe; a need which is no longer prereligious but religious. By naming or sharing in the ideality of the adolescent the counselor "may eliminate resistances and help the adolescent along the path to an analytical process" which includes a "shared pleasure of thinking, questioning and analyzing."[16] When a minister, therapist, or pastoral counselor is able to make these connections through the power of transference, transference love, or agape, the person struggling with a mental affliction or malady of the soul is able to reinvest in the bonds of human relationship. What we have been discussing thus far is related to the libidinal and death drives. What if any affinity is there with an understanding of Christian belief and practice—especially one that concentrates on forgiveness? And, how will this assist us in our journey to aid the women who struggle with depression?

Belief and Practice

A comprehensive examination of "belief" and "practice" is a task beyond the scope of this project. I am indebted to an article by Amy Plantinga Pauw[17] for a succinct as well as helpful understanding of religious beliefs which states "[r]eligious beliefs are interwoven with a larger set of other beliefs and embedded in particular ways of life. They are couched in the language, conceptuality, and history of a particular people and reflect personal and communal experience and desires. Religious beliefs shape and are shaped by religious practices."[18] Or even as Kristeva herself asserts: "I would not speak if I didn't believe; believing in what I say, and persisting in saying it, comes from the capacity to believe in the Other and not at all from existential experience, necessarily disappointing."[19] Kristeva's emphasis, quite naturally is upon the role of language in shaping belief because in the "final analysis" human relationships will leave us disappointed. Pauw gives equal attention to the role of language and human experience rooted in specific historic communities and practices.

The religious practice we are most interested in for the sake of women struggling with depression is forgiveness. Pauw's illustration of the gaps that exist between belief and practice is grounded in her interpretation of the Jonah story as it relates to God's indiscriminate mercy. She concludes that the belief in God's mercy is "rendered more credible by religious practices of mercy."[20] This has positive benefits even for those who take up the position of outsider to the religious community. By extension one may conclude that an individual's or a community's theological beliefs about forgiveness are to some extent shaped by the practice of forgiveness in that community of faith. Their practices grounded in their belief of what is holy and true do have the power to shape or influence those who are outside the community of faith. One may discern an unlikely but nevertheless strong affinity between Pauw, the theologian and Kristeva, the psychoanalyst and avowed atheist, insofar as Kristeva offers an assertion about what is true that resembles Pauw's own position: "Whether I belong to a religion, whether I be agnostic or atheist, when I say 'I believe,' I mean 'I hold as true.'"[21] In Pauw's case what is true shapes religious practice; for Kristeva what is true shapes identity and relationships.

One powerful illustration of how practices may shape beliefs about forgiveness is the Amish response to the school shooting in Nickel Mines, Pennsylvania. Much has been written about their experience of tragedy which occurred in October 2006 with a mixture of admiration as well as skepticism. Admiration arose in the form of media attention and dollars raised for the children who were maimed because the Amish community moved so immediately to extend forgiveness to the perpetrator's family, even sending a delegation to attend his funeral. Skepticism arose from other arenas for precisely the same reason—the immediacy of the forgiveness. Yet even the Amish acknowledge that "forgiveness is hard work that never ends" and for many in Nickel Mines it was easier to forgive an outsider than it is to practice forgiveness in their own community.[22] The Amish community continues to work at this practice but maintains a sense of agency in the midst of tragic losses by extending what appears to be immediate forgiveness. Thus the practice is a process, not a one-time event. This practice (more accurately identified as process) is embedded in their way of life.

Though religious practice does indeed shape religious belief, Pauw admits a caveat—gaps between belief and practice exist insofar as the practice of a belief may provide some shape to the belief but it doesn't ultimately render the belief true (or false). Beliefs are then, what a religious community holds to be true. This leads some like L. Gregory Jones[23] to conclude that the only valid approach to forgiveness is one conceptualized theologically which is different from the conclusion that others (including myself) would draw which is to say that human abilities or capacities to forgive reflect—if only dimly—our participation in creation with God and may, in fact, be expanded when we attend to meanings of forgiveness constructed in psychology.[24] Thus an important and helpful distinction is offered by Fraser Watts—an understanding of forgiveness that is conceptualized in a discipline outside theology does not necessarily suggest that forgiveness occurs apart from God.[25] How then is practice to be understood as it relates to belief?

Craig Dykstra and Dorothy Bass offer the following characterization of Christian practices as "things Christian people do together over time to address fundamental human needs in response to and in the light of God's active presence for the life of the world."[26] These fundamental human needs include conditions "such as embodiment, temporality, relationship, the use of language, and mortality" that are addressed by joining together "concrete human acts" with "substantive convictions about how things really are."[27] Christian practices, according to Bass and Dykstra, deepen our knowledge of God and the world, they are social and historical, and "share in the mysterious dynamic of fall and redemption, sin and grace."[28] Forgiveness has been identified by Bass and Dykstra as one type of Christian practice, but as Fraser Watts contends, forgiveness is not simply something we *do* but rather something we *participate* in.[29] If beliefs, stated simply, are what a Christian community deems truth and their practices are actions that respond to human needs in light of God's activity in the world, then forgiveness may be construed as both a belief and a practice since theologians focus on doctrines like justification, atonement, and redemption which are "terminological guises" for the concept of forgiveness.[30] One may want to raise the question: "What is the relationship between a theological belief about forgiveness and our Christian practices of forgiveness?"

Serene Jones raises this question in a somewhat different fashion by asking: "What is the relation between our salvation and the concrete way we structure our lives?"[31] She focuses on justification (theological guise for forgiveness) and sanctification to illustrate the interrelatedness of belief and practice. The scope of her work would take us in a different direction but an image she borrows from French feminist Luce Irigaray is instructive. Jones discusses the notion of "adornment" likening it to the manner in which we "put on clothes, behaviors, beliefs, and other elements that define who we are."[32] Again, a baptismal image is suggested in that the sacrament is analogous to "putting on a robe." We may "adorn ourselves" or be adorned by culture, language, or our religious community but whatever the "adorning materials" may be, they "determine not only how others perceive us, but also how we perceive and embody our understanding of our own deepest identity in relation to others."[33] Thus the clothing we adorn isn't ornamental but rather "the container of our existence."[34] The container of our existence or adornment of Christian practice identified by Serene Jones is reminiscent of the *ergasterion* that Kristeva identifies as the privileged work space or maternal space of the therapeutic relationship. The process of adornment does in some manner shape identity and is then by nature psychological as well as theological. Jones offers the following observation concerning the interplay of belief and practice: "Practices play a role in writing the unconscious and in ordering the non-conscious ways in which the body 'knows'; and these, in turn, directly inform how we imagine the specifics of the doctrinal landscapes we occupy."[35] Here one may want to draw upon the importance that Kristeva identifies in writing as an aesthetic practice of forgiveness. Identity, practices, and doctrines (or beliefs) are continually being reshaped in the interplay between practice and belief. If then one chooses forgiveness as an adorning material, one may practice forbearance in relationship which results in an expanded capacity to live life abundantly and deepens one's faith; the continual interplay between belief and practice leads to a deeper knowledge of self, God, and world (for this project, the primary focus on knowledge of God and self in relation to the world or creation is contained in a therapeutic relationship and the potential for a "speaking cure"). What makes any practice a faith practice or Christian practice? Jones contends that it is the "intent of the practicing subject."[36]

Serene Jones also attends to the significance that the interplay of belief and practice has for the negotiation of power relations. While it is a minor point raised in her conclusions it is a major point for pastoral theology since *the one who determines* the extent of a "wrong" or an injury is often the one who enjoys the most privilege in a relationship. Thus individuals or communities who have traditionally lived on the margin have had little or no voice when it comes to expressing a desire for justice. They may well be those who are best equipped to forgive—out of necessity—but are the actions of those who perpetrate the injustices ever taken seriously? That is, does the practice of forgiveness ever provide tacit permission to those in need of forgiveness (the ones responsible for wrongdoing or injustice) to continue living in an unrepentant posture? I believe it does and will revisit this notion later. Nevertheless, those who are often expected to forgive have previously been powerless; thus it is incumbent upon those who provide care and counseling to become aware of the ways in which forgiveness, whether it is used as a Christian practice or therapeutic process, has the potential to further exploit those who traditionally have been oppressed. Here again, those in the therapeutic community seem to be more aware of the potential risk involved, which is characterized by psychologist Mary Anne Coate, as "the giving up of omnipotence" insofar as we "become subject to the other" and "we risk rejection for we cannot compel the other to accept our overture."[37] Thus the one who has been hurt may be hurt again if their forgiveness isn't acknowledged or worse yet is rejected. When a previously marginalized or oppressed person refuses to extend forgiveness that individual may suddenly acquire power that she did not enjoy previously but at what expense? The practice of forgiveness in everyday life is more complicated than many theologians would like to admit.

Forgiveness

Forgiveness: A Central Tenet of Christian Faith

Why do we forgive? We forgive, at least in part, because we believe. Thus we hold true the biblical mandate issued by Christ to "forgive seventy times seven." We forgive because we have been taught to pray "forgive us our sins as we forgive those who sin against us." Yet psychologists are wont to remind us that these imperatives create difficulty for us in human-to-human relationships because we are each unique individuals who do not possess equal capacities and abilities to accept and extend forgiveness.[38]

Martin Marty notes that "the concept of divine forgiveness, mediated through humans, is one form of the love that should characterize the full life in the community and beyond."[39] Thus it is an ideal which does not always characterize life in Christian community because this life is also tainted by sin. Here Marty's characterization is congruent with what Gregory Jones proposes insofar as Jones states that

> "forgiveness is not so much a word spoken, and action performed, or a feeling felt as it is an embodied way of life in an ever-deepening friendship with the Triune God and with others...it ought to be focused on the reconciliation of brokenness, the restoration of communion—with God, with one another, and with the whole Creation."[40]

Rather than speak of forgiveness as a doctrine, Marty identifies it as an ethos (a disposition, character or fundamental value) which is analogous to the way in which Serene Jones borrows the image of "adornment" to speak about the interrelatedness of belief and practice. Marty differentiates his position from theologians like Gregory Jones who suggest that divine forgiveness is a model for human forgiveness, by defining it as a "quatritarian organization" of the reality of forgiveness insofar as he distinguishes human expressions from divine expressions of forgiveness as responses to or transmissions of divine activity.[41] Marty's distinction reflects a concern similar to that raised by Watts:

> We humans are not God, and not everything that is characteristic of God is possible or appropriate for human beings. There is a parallel issue about the currently fashionable theological claim to the effect that the pattern of relationality that exists within the persons of the Trinity provides a model for human relationships. That is also a very doubtful proposition, in part because each human being is separate from every other human being in a way that the persons of the Trinity are not separate from one another.[42]

Yet these characterizations of forgiveness do not, as of yet, tell us what it is or what it means. *Webster's New Universal Unabridged Dictionary* defines *forgiveness* as "to give up resentment against or the desire to punish, to cancel a debt, to pardon, to absolve or release, and to exonerate."[43] The Amish understand this as a willingness to forego revenge and make a conscious commitment or decision to forgive but this doesn't preclude lingering feelings or emotions of anger and resentment.[44] Here one may want to reflect on Kristeva's notion of "par-don" as a foundation for a healing relationship. It is a gift given; so too, is forgiveness a gift given which resets the clock in relationships. Time that was once frozen begins to move again. Thus forgiveness is relational but can it occur without repentance? This is a question I will take up later but for now do suggest that forgiveness can occur without repentance especially if "for-giving" (see chapter five for an in-depth discussion of "for-giving") occurs in its place.

The emphasis, thus far, both from a psychological and a theological perspective has been concentrated on forgiveness as it relates to events in the past but Watts calls our attention to the reality that the "forgiveness of the bible is at least as much about a promise for the future."[45] One may infer here, a hope for the future that implies reconciliation or the restoration of relationship and communion with God. This hope is central to Gregory Jones' views on forgiveness as an embodied way of life. It may be the sort of hope contained in the notion that "believers can lean on the communal practice of forgiveness by asking others to forgive the enemies they find themselves incapable of forgiving."[46] Hope for restoration of relationship in the realm of human relationships is an ideal but I would simply offer a caution here that psychologists take a more realistic view of reconciliation in terms of human relationships that occur in penultimate realities—restoration of relationship may not always be possible or appropriate. Examples of forgiving that don't have restored relationship as an intended outcome of the process include (but are not limited to) experiences such as forgiving someone who is deceased or forgiving an "anonymous terrorist."[47]

Watts offers one last distinction which we will revisit later in relation to Kristeva's discussion of the sacred as it is intertwined with Christian notions about suffering.[48] Watts notes that forgiveness "undertaken in conscious obedience to the purposes of God and with the resources of grace that God offers, can be a sign of the presence of God."[49] I take this to mean that a counselor whose self-understanding is oriented to the world in such a way that she believes her ability to be "for-giving" as well as forgiving in a therapeutic process is in obedience to the purposes of God does allow for the possibility that the therapeutic relationship is graced by the presence of the Spirit or at the very least is experienced by therapist and client as a type of sacred moment. Watts also suggests that as we struggle to offer and receive forgiveness we discover God within ourselves. Here, I connect this to my understanding of what it means to be baptized insofar as living into the promises of baptism is a process entwined with God's promises of forgiveness.[50] Watts concludes: "By giving and receiving forgiveness, we extend God's kingdom and make his presence among us a more tangible reality. The practice of forgiveness can, in that sense, be a sacrament of the presence of God."[51]

A counseling relationship that is informed by a Christian belief in forgiveness is in some sense, then, sacramental. In fact, there were occasions in the history of pastoral care when ritualized acts of forgiveness were the whole focus of pastoral care.[52] This point provides a helpful bridge to a psychological understanding of forgiveness as a therapeutic process because it raises the question of whether or not forgiveness that is unconsciously obedient to God's purposes may also be understood as a "sacrament of the presence of God." In other words, if the process of forgiveness conceptualized psychologically and practiced therapeutically is not consciously performed in obedience to God's purposes and promises, does the process still participate or contribute to the realization of God's purposes? I believe it does but just how it does remains to be seen.

Forgiveness: A Therapeutic Process

Psychologists recognize the reality that there are benefits for those who do practice the art of forgiving in situations such as intimate violence but they are more keenly aware than many theologians that forgiving may have negative outcomes especially for the one who is forgiven.[53] Gregory Jones is one such theologian who takes a rather naïve approach to understanding the value of therapeutic process suggesting that it is unfortunate that we are not immunized against therapeutic language but instead have allowed "the grammar of Christian forgiveness" to become "largely co-opted by a therapeutic grammar."[54] Jones contends that forgiveness is a "marginal notion" as a direct result of the growing interest in forgiveness among those in the therapeutic community. Fortunately, there are more moderate voices like Marty and Watts who contend that in fact, our Christian understandings of forgiveness have been clarified, even expanded, as a result of the increased interest from the therapeutic community.[55] Both conclude that Jones distorts the scientific study of forgiveness and creates a false dichotomy between a psychology and theology of forgiveness.

Forgiveness has been studied almost solely in terms of the one who extends forgiveness. Clinicians and social psychologists have been much more attentive to the reality that there are potential negative outcomes of forgiving, perhaps best exemplified by a "troubling scenario: a forgiveness that facilitates the well-being of the forgiver, but at the same time supports the perpetrator's misbehavior."[56] When an expectation for transformation of the perpetrator's behavior is lacking, the expression of forgiveness is incomplete since in some regard justice is also absent. This troubling scenario was, in fact, the fear I heard expressed most frequently by those who struggled to move beyond their experiences of intimate violence. The problem of intimate violence has not diminished since I entered ministry nearly twenty-five years ago but it has become more complex and receives more media attention. What then are the psychological benefits of forgiveness, particularly for one who has been victimized?

The primary benefits include an ability to release a grudge, thus bringing to a conclusion feelings of anger and resentment toward a perpetrator which when sustained "over time can be unpleasant, stressful, and unhealthy."[57] These same feelings often exacerbate depression and inhibit a person's ability to give voice to their fears. Those who are able to forgive also experience an increased capacity for empathy, discern new meanings in the hurtful event, and even discover new purpose in life accompanied by a sense of freedom.[58] Baumeister et al. recognize that forgiveness has an intrapsychic as well as an interpersonal dimension; both those individuals who have been victimized as well as those who perpetrate injustice experience costs and benefits associated with the process of forgiveness. The one victimized releases a debt and in so doing experiences a loss. This loss may be associated with the cost of forgiveness for one who has been victimized. From an intrapsychic perspective these researchers acknowledge that it is "meaningful to speak of forgiving someone who...would have no way of knowing whether he or she has been forgiven."[59] Thus, at least from a psychological or therapeutic perspective, it is possible to extend forgiveness without the remorse or repentance of the offender. The benefits for the one victimized include working through anger and resentment in order to let these feelings go. From an interpersonal dimension there is also a cost for the one who has been victimized because the transgressor does not need to "make it up or pay it back"; in a manner of speaking, the transgressor is "off the hook" or released from a sense of guilt—a benefit for the transgressor—but there is no assurance that the incident will not be reoccurring.[60]

This may be interpreted as a benefit for the transgressor but it also comes at a cost to the transgressor because forgiveness understood this way does not assure a change in misbehavior nor does it assure the possibility of reconciliation which amounts to a relationship loss. In situations of intimate or domestic violence there is ample evidence that forgiveness may have a high cost, especially for the one victimized, since the third phase in a reoccurring cycle is that of remorse on the part of the transgressor or perpetrator. This leaves the one who has taken up the role of forgiver in a vulnerable position subject to repeated incidents of violence. One may want to ask then: "Why forgive?" Those who research forgiveness scientifically can document, at least to some extent, what theologians have believed for centuries: "[T]here was not one instance in which a group experiencing forgiveness education showed a decline in psychological health. In fact, statistically significant improvement in such variables as hope and self-esteem, as well as significant decreases in anxiety and depression, were more the rule than the exception."[61] That is to say, forgiveness as a way of life does make significant and positive contributions to individual well-being as well as life in community. Where does this lead us? We will examine next what Kristeva has to say about the contributions of Christian discourse and Christianity to the ability to be a listening presence in suffering.

For-giving: A Listening in Suffering

In a lecture that Kristeva was invited to give during Lent 2006 at Notre Dame Cathedral in Paris she addressed the subject of suffering with her audience "as they experience it from the starting point of their faith."[62] The analytic relationship, a for-giving relationship for Kristeva is one which she defines as a type of listening in suffering that reaches out to her clients, to the believers in the cathedral and others who suffer in such a way that they feel contact with the listener (analyst), or connected and as a result, their suffering is illuminated. Kristeva has listened tactfully to innumerable stories of incommensurable suffering which leads her to be critical of those who would desire to turn God into "an all powerful painkiller" because this is "already a kind of nihilism."[63] The purpose of listening in suffering is not to eradicate it but rather to help the one seeking a cure to "cross it indefinitely by renewing bonds, languages, creativities, having another relationship with time—a sort of rebirth, of serenity, of joy."[64] It is, I suggest, not coincidental that Kristeva identifies the purpose of listening in suffering as a "crossing" of suffering since somewhat later in her lecture she concludes that the suffering of Christ also known as kenosis reaches beyond the limits of what is religious to what is sacred.[65] But does she really understand suffering from the same perspective as Christians—especially Christian theologians?

If Kristeva doesn't adhere to a Christian notion of suffering she is at least well-acquainted with obvious overlaps as well as differences. The main distinction for Kristeva between psychoanalytic and Christian theological understandings of suffering is that

> for psychoanalysis, psychic suffering, far from being of value, is the result of repression, of resistance to pleasure, of the desire 'not to want to know.' Whereas Christianity begins by valorizing pain, as a necessary path toward the love of the Father: not however, without working it out in the representation of joy, by means of sublimation (music, painting, literature).[66]

The points of overlap or intersection for Kristeva center on "the recognition of suffering as an integral part of the speaking being and the valorization of language as the royal road to traversing it, to its relief."[67] Those who claim not to know suffering, according to Kristeva, live in denial of it. How does this assist us in our efforts to assuage the suffering of those struggling with depression?

Kristeva notes that the Beatitudes (Matthew 5) "extract suffering from its secretiveness and shame" and compares this with the experience a person suffering with depression has when she weeps on the analyst's couch because in that moment she distances herself from the possibility of suicide; thus her suffering is transformed.[68] In fact, Kristeva asserts that Christianity is "the only religion that addresses suffering 'intimately' [*la tutoie*]—that tames it."[69] This leads Kristeva to a conclusion that is reminiscent of language in her essay "Stabat Mater," a conclusion that leaves her "Alone of her sex." Kristeva distances herself from Freud (and many others) when she claims that religion is not merely an illusion and source of neurosis; rather she contends that the "time has come to recognize, without being afraid of 'scaring off' either the faithful or the agnostics, that the history of Christianity is a preparation for humanism. Of course, humanism is in a state of rupture with Christianity."[70] Indeed her interviewer takes note of the fact that at least certain parts of this text could have been written by a Christian to which Kristeva responded that her father would have taken delight in this fact. Why is all of this significant for those who struggle with depression—especially women? Kristeva answers that in the suffering, death, and resurrection of Christ, "Christianity announces its discovery, which is that depression is an indispensable and decisive stage of thought....It tells us also that suffering is the flip side of creative exaltation (in the artist, for example)."[71] Kristeva leaves a door open here to the healing power of Christian discourse and the sacraments, especially a celebration of the Eucharist. Just how she does we will see.

The Speaking Cure

Kristeva suggests an affinity between the practice of psychoanalysis and the accomplishment of faith which is "intelligence moving through love" or the client recognizing her own "particular singularity" which encourages the creativity necessary to draw the analytic relationship to a conclusion.[72] When creativity is awakened or reawakened through a process of the dissolution or sublimation of suffering (perhaps through music, art, or writing) the depression subsides and the client is able to enjoy active intelligence or a "plenitude of loving experience."[73] The aim of the analytic or speaking cure, the healing power of the Word in Christian discourse is to facilitate an investment in the bonds of human relationships, to encourage the reacquisition of language, and to reinvigorate creativity and pleasure. I have suggested throughout this work, following Kristeva's critique of patriarchal religious discourse, that what is needed is a maternal language that recognizes maternal passion and jouissance. Moreover, I have argued that the therapeutic relationship itself resembles a maternal container or *ergasterion.* Kristeva returns to this notion again in her recent work.

Maternal time is according to Kristeva, a time or "*duration with new beginnings.*"[74] She states that the time of motherhood, with the arrival of children in the world, has a quality of the ephemeral; thus it means having both the freedom and the courage to begin again. This is significant because new beginnings or the recognition of one's singularity is what the therapeutic relationship heralds. It is maternal passion's capacity for sublimation which makes possible a child's own creativity.[75] Thus we see how the analyst, the pastor, or the pastoral counselor's own passion and capacity for sublimation encourage the creativity of those who seek to be healed and for-given. What Kristeva identifies here in this later work as a maternal passion that "enacts a transformation of the libido such that sexualization is postponed by tenderness" has elsewhere been identified as transference love (see *Tales of Love*).[76] But it is not simply maternal passion that gives the therapeutic relationship a maternal character. Suffering is relieved in some manner (at least for those who believe *in the name of the Father*) by a celebration of the Eucharist insofar as it "reconciles the believer with the Son-Father tortured to death and, to an even greater extent, gives the body of this suffering Man, which 'I' myself become when I swallow the Other, the attributes of *a good and nurturing mother*."[77] Here too, is a time of new beginnings or rebirth—a time that resembles the temporality of motherhood.

Earlier we noted Kristeva's remark that no other religion addresses suffering as intimately as Christianity. Christianity also encourages sublimation more effectively through the narrative of the death and resurrection of Christ and Christians participate in this each time the Eucharist is celebrated.[78] This process of sublimation "effects contact with what is real"; it is an illumination of the sufferer's experience provided by the one who listens in suffering or the purpose of the "speaking cure."[79] This exchange between one who struggles to speak and one who listens in suffering is also known as the exchange of transference and countertransference or "a modern variation of the act of pardon, let us write *par-don* [by-gift]. The suffering, like the bad [*le mal*], suffered or inflicted, is not effaced, but from now on both are part of my capacity to think and to share, thus to create. A sort of rebirth."[80] Suffering still exists but is able to be endured or "crossed" because it is shared. Even the nonbeliever, Kristeva, sees the wisdom and beauty of the sharing which is

> first of all, between humans and Christ, who, in assuming it [the suffering], confers upon it extraordinary dignity, at the interface of the human and the divine; sharable, next, and consequently, among human beings themselves, who only allow themselves to look for a way to relieve it on the condition that they can look it in the face, give it a name, and interpret it.[81]

It is faced, named, and interpreted in the context of a loving, "for-giving," maternal and privileged space which is the sacred context of a pastoral counseling relationship. Thus an experience of "for-giving" may renew creativity to such an extent that the woman struggling with depression is once again able to speak, to accept and offer forgiveness as well as love because she has experienced love in the safety of maternal passion which makes possible her return to a world structured by paternal function and language. Even if no other human is able to share precisely in her suffering, an other listens in suffering and assures her that Jesus has already shared in her suffering. Rebirth is possible.

Conclusion: A Reprise or Re-presentation, and a Representation

The tensions that exist between Christian doctrine and practice, and therapeutic process and "scientific study" of forgiveness have been a personal passion for the duration of my entire ordained ministry. My original interest in the importance of forgiving as a therapeutic process, as well as a Christian belief, arose out of my own struggles to provide pastoral care in difficult situations. This interest continues today not so much from the perspective of a counselor as it does from the perspective of a teacher and mentor. When the phone rings in my office and I hear the voice of a woman who is in tears, it is almost always a former student, now an ordained minister, who is experiencing some form of "violence" to her soul because the congregation she serves or powerful individuals in the congregation question her authority as a woman in ministry. She struggles to have her story heard as truth; it is an incredible need to be heard and believed that issues forth.

Kristeva has argued passionately for decades that we need a discourse that focuses on the complexity of the vocation of motherhood. I suggest that at the very least she has offered us a beginning and a rebirth of maternal language which honors women in their singularity. When I was a Master of Divinity student in a denominational seminary I refused to call myself a feminist because it meant that I had to surrender any sense of my own unique identity. Kristeva has opened up the door to innumerable potentialities for women through her insistence that there is no Woman but many women. Even women who do not physically give birth carry within themselves the characteristics of the "woman-mother" that we have discussed at length. To be a woman, Kristeva says is "to live for the other, including, and above all, when this is impossible and traumatizing. Far from locking themselves into the obsessional palace of pure thought, thinking for women, cannot be shut off from carnal sensoriality...*eros* for them is not dissociable from *agape*."[82] In some sense, what Kristeva describes as the experience of women fully alive is what it means to engage in the practice of pastoral care and counseling. It is a "par-don" or gift that is given in love. Women, especially those suffering with depression, have an incredible need to be heard and believed. Once their stories are heard as truth, their capacity to begin again and to believe is renewed. The therapeutic relationship when enlivened by maternal passion and discourse becomes a privileged working space that encourages a woman to make peace with the constituents of her identity—a loving mother and father. What then is left to be "represented"?

Kristeva states that the "genius of Christianity promoted a formidable *counterweight to suffering*...that is none other than *its sublimation or its working through* by psychic and verbal activity. 'I,' suffering being because desiring/thinking, loving/loved, am able to *represent* my passion to myself, and this *representation* is my resurrection."[83] We represent our suffering in words to one who listens in suffering and are assured in faith that there is above all a God who listens and speaks to us because our suffering has already been shared by Christ. This is what makes suffering sovereign as well as sacred according to Kristeva. It is also what makes the search for self in the context of pastoral counseling a sacramental endeavor.

Kristeva concludes *This Incredible Need to Believe* with an admonition: "Don't be afraid of Christianity, and together we won't fear religions!"[84] I would offer a similar admonition to those who provide pastoral care and counseling—"Don't be afraid of psychology and together our capacity to be for-giving will expand." My purpose has been to examine a limited number of Kristeva's major texts in conversation with other psychologists and theologians to discern how I might incorporate her insights into a pastoral theology for women struggling with depression. Thus I have devoted most of this project to an intimate conversation with Kristeva not in an effort to correct what others may perceive as her theological short-comings but in order to enhance my own work as a pastoral theologian. Kristeva's insights on "for-giving" and the role of forgiveness have forever transformed the way I conceive of therapeutic relationships. Her passionate argument for a maternal discourse does not displace my own use of male images and metaphors for God; I was, after all, ordained "*in the name of the Father, the Son, and the Holy Spirit*" and continue to carry on my ordination obligations according to these traditional Trinitarian formulations. Kristeva does, I would argue, show us just how impoverished our religious language has become because the maternal passion is absent. This corrective has been transformative for my own work as a pastoral theologian with clients and students alike. It is my hope that others will also experience my aesthetic practice as transformative in their lives and work.

Notes

1. Kristeva, *This Incredible Need to Believe*, vii, xvi, 11.
2. Ibid., 24–25, my emphasis.
3. Ibid., 25, Kristeva's emphasis.
4. Ibid.
5. Ibid., 4–5.
6. Ibid., 9.
7. Ibid., 24.
8. Ibid., 11.

9. Ibid., 25.
10. Ibid., 12.
11. Ibid., 14.
12. Ibid., 84. Kristeva notes that the proper noun, *Kristev* means "of the cross."
13. Ibid.
14. Ibid., 14–15.
15. Ibid., 18.
16. Ibid., 20.
17. Amy Plantinga Pauw, "Attending to Gaps Between Beliefs and Practices," in *Practicing Theology: Beliefs and Practices in Christian Life* (Grand Rapids: Eerdmans, 2002) 33–50.
18. Ibid., 36.
19. Kristeva, *This Incredible Need to Believe*, x.
.20. Pauw, "Attending to Gaps Between Beliefs and Practices," 36.
21. Kristeva, *This Incredible Need to Believe*, 3.
22. Donald B. Kraybill, Steven M. Nolt, and David L. Weaver-Zercher, *Amish Grace: How Forgiveness Transcended Tragedy* (San Francisco: John Wiley & Sons, 2007), 113.
23. Gregory Jones, *Embodying Forgiveness: A Theological Analysis* (Grand Rapids: Eerdmans, 1995), xii, 35–69.
24. Fraser Watts, "Christian Theology," in *Forgiveness in Context: Theology and Psychology in Creative Dialogue* , eds. Fraser Watts and Liz Gulliford (New York: T. & T. Clark, 2004), 68 and Liz Gulliford, in "Intrapersonal Forgiveness," *Forgiveness in Context: Theology and Psychology in Creative Dialogue,* eds. Fraser Watts and Liz Gulliford (New York: T. & T. Clark, 2004), 84.
25. Fraser Watts, "Relating the Psychology and Theology of Forgiveness," in *Forgiveness in Context: Theology and Psychology in Creative Dialogue,* eds. Fraser Watts and Liz Gulliford (New York: T. & T. Clark, 2004), 5.
26. Craig Dykstra and Dorothy Bass, "A Theological Understanding of Christian Practices," in *Practicing Theology: Beliefs and Practices in Christian Life,* eds. Miraslov Volf and Dorothy Bass (Grand Rapids: Eerdmans, 2002), 18.
27. Ibid., 22.
28. Ibid., 27.
29. Watts, "Christian Theology," 58, my emphasis.
30. Martin Marty, "The Ethos of Christian Forgiveness," in *Dimensions of Forgiveness: Psychological Research and Theological Perspectives* (Philadelphia: Templeton Foundation Press, 1998), 11.
31. Serene Jones, "Graced Practices: Excellence and Freedom in the Christian Life," in *Practicing Theology: Beliefs and Practices in Christian Life,* eds. Miraslov Volf and Dorothy Bass (Grand Rapids: Eerdmans, 2002), 53.
32. Ibid., 60.
33. Ibid., 61.
34. Ibid.
35. Ibid., 76.
36. Ibid.

37. Mary Anne Coate, "The Capacity for Forgiveness," in *Forgiveness in Context: Theology and Psychology in Creative Dialogue,* eds. Fraser Watts and Liz Gulliford (New York: T. & T. Clark, 2004), 136.
38. Ibid., 123–34.
39. Marty, "The Ethos of Christian Forgiveness," 11.
40. Gregory Jones, *Embodying Forgiveness: A Theological Analysis* (Grand Rapids: Eerdmans, 1995), xii, 5.
41. Marty, "The Ethos of Christian Forgiveness," 15.
42. Watts, "Christian Theology," 55.
43. W*ebster's New Universal Unabridged Dictionary,* 2nd ed. 91983), s.v. "forgiveness"; Watts, "Christian Theology," 54.
44. Kraybill, et. al., *Amish Grace,* 134–35.
45. Watts, "Christian Theology," 67.
46. Pauw, "Attending to Gaps Between Beliefs and Practices," 43; Gregory Jones, *Embodying Forgiveness,* 163–204.
47. Anthony Bash and Melanie Bash, "Early Christian Thinking," in *Forgiveness in Context: Theology and Psychology in Creative Dialogue,* eds. Fraser Watts and Liz Gulliford (New York: T. & T. Clark, 2004), 47; Liz Gulliford, "Intrapersonal Forgiveness," 85.
48. Kristeva, *This Incredible Need to Believe,* 92–95.
49. Watts, "Christian Theology," 68.
50. Gregory Jones, *Embodying Forgiveness,* 166–75.
51. Watts, "Christian Theology," 68.
52. William H. Willimon, *Pastor: The Theology and Practice of Ordained Ministry* (Nashville: Abingdon Press, 2002), 175.
53. Carl E. Thoresen, Frederic Luskin, and Alex H.S. Harris, "Science and Forgiveness Interventions: Reflections and Recommendations," in *Dimensions of Forgiveness: Psychological Research & Theological Perspectives* (Philadelphia: Templeton Foundation Press, 1998), 163–92; Everett L. Worthington, "The Pyramid Model of Forgiveness: Some Interdisciplinary Speculations about Unforgiveness and the Promotion of Forgiveness," in *Dimensions of Forgiveness,* 107–37.
54. Gregory Jones, *Embodying Forgiveness,* 47.
55. Marty, "The Ethos of Christian Forgiveness," 25; Fraser Watts, "Relating the Psychology and Theology of Forgiveness," 5.
56. Kenneth I. Pargament and Mark S. Rye, "Forgiveness as a Method of Religious Coping," in *Dimensions of Forgiveness: Psychological Research & Theological Perspectives,* ed. Everett L. Worthington (Philadelphia: Templeton Foundation Press, 1998), 71.
57. Roy F. Baumeister, Julie Juola Exline, and Kristin L. Sommer, "The Victim Role, Grudge Theory, and Two Dimensions of Forgiveness," in *Dimensions of Forgiveness: Psychological Research & Theological Perspectives,* ed. Everett L. Worthington (Philadelphia: Templeton Foundation Press, 1998), 79–80; Worthington, "The Pyramid Model of Forgiveness," 132.
58. Robert D. Enright and Catherine T. Coyle, "Researching the Process Model of Forgiveness Within Psychological Interventions," in *Dimensions of Forgiveness:*

Psychological Research & Theological Perspectives, ed. Everett L. Worthington (Philadelphia: Templeton Foundation Press, 1998), 147.

59. Baumeister, et. al., "The Victim Role, Grudge Theory, and Two Dimensions of Forgiveness," 85.
60. Ibid., 90–91.
61. Enright and Coyle, "Researching the Process Model of Forgiveness Within Psychological Interventions," 154.
62. Kristeva, *This Incredible Need to Believe*, 77.
63. Ibid., 79.
64. Ibid., 78.
65. Ibid., 95.
66. Ibid., 80.
67. Ibid.
68. Ibid., 81.
69. Ibid.
70. Ibid., 83.
71. Ibid., 84.
72. Ibid., 34.
73. Ibid., 35.
74. Ibid., 44.
75. Ibid., 45.
76. Ibid.
77. Ibid., 50.
78. Ibid., 60. See also the discussion of the Eucharist in Chapter Two.
79. Ibid., 37.
80. Ibid., 85.
81. Ibid., 90–91.
82. Ibid., 39, Kristeva's emphasis.
83. Ibid., 96.
84. Ibid., 106.

EPILOGUE

My Own Voice

When I have finished preparing a sermon, I am generally disposed to ask myself: "So what?" Or, "Where do I go from here?" I find myself at the conclusion of a much longer work now asking the same questions—especially since we live in a post-911 world. It is my firm belief that Kristeva's work addresses exactly the sort of religious language and ideology that led to the tragic loss of many lives. When we are each able to recognize the stranger as the one whose image we see in the mirror, perhaps, we will no longer need to classify others as strangers and exact violence upon them. My concern in this project, however, has been a much more limited one.

I have juxtaposed one psychoanalytic theorist with many other theorists of religion and psychology in order to see what new insights I might glean in order to better help a specific category of "stranger"—depressed women. I have argued that language at some level constructs a cultural reality; my primary concern is with Christian religious language which has functioned as one source of women's oppression, thereby contributing to women's depression. It is the manner in which the feminine or the "woman-mother" is described as abject and situated in isolation or exile that concerns me most. The abject mother contributes to the self-alienation and estrangement that depressed women often experience. I have used Kristeva's metaphor of a "subject-in-process/on trial" to describe the developing selves of these women. My study has led me to conclude that, more often than not, their journeys are experienced more as a trial to be endured rather than a process to be enjoyed, precisely because there is not a language which is congruent with their experience. They often come to churches and pastors seeking help with the longing to be included in the message of God's love and grace but experience rejection and abandonment when they attempt to give voice to their stories. How then, can we help them find the ability to say "I" and be understood? They yearn to be heard and have their stories heard as truth; they yearn to be believed.

I was reminded recently of just how difficult this process of finding and maintaining one's voice or a sense of "I" may be in the church. A young woman in early adolescence with whom I am acquainted recently posted a short essay on a church bulletin board arguing that "there is no 'I' in 'team'" when it comes to the work of the church. Tragically, she has already learned at an early age that sacrificing her "I" to the greater good of the church is what is expected from her. This points to what I consider to be an unhealthy environment that exists in many churches in which women are expected to sacrifice and deny themselves at the expense of their sense of "I." This sense of "I" is best described by Erik Erikson as

> the sense of *I* of all human beings...who can join others in a sense of the *We* only by dint of a shared language which, in turn, must fit the way in which the prevailing world view influences not only the general outlook of all individuals in a given region but especially their readiness for a new revelatory voice. The *I*, after all, is the ground for the simple verbal assurance that each person is a center of awareness in a universe of communicable experience, a center so numinous that it amounts to a sense of being alive, and more, of being the vital condition of existence.[1]

What the young woman who posted that essay has already come to believe is that a healthy "we" excludes any sense of "I." Precisely the opposite is true. The shared language of her Christian cultural reality suggests that she may not be ready to accept a "new revelatory voice." What I have described here could be construed as a form of patriarchy which results from a ritualism that Erikson has described as those rituals which "eventually become repetitive and...compulsive–whereupon devotion to revered images can become idolism, adherence to detailed laws can become legalism, and reliance on dogma can become dogmatism."[2]

The corrective to this ritualism is the continuing search for new metaphors that Gerhart and Russell contend are actually "knowledge-in-process" and which facilitate personal growth, healing and transformation of our world view. Kristeva's critiques of religious discourse at least begin to point us in the direction of a discourse that is a "knowledge-in-process" and thus, a partial solution to the experience of abjection and estrangement that depressed women struggle with—an experience which, as I have argued earlier, is often exacerbated in their Christian communities.

Kristeva observes that there is a dearth of language to speak about motherhood. She is not necessarily concerned solely with actual mothers but all women in their uniqueness who are potential mothers and who experienced separation from a mother who is "She is I." Artists portray in images what we very often fail to paint with words and who thus get us closer to that semiotic or precognitive experience of our mothers. The woman-mother is more than an object, she is also a subject; but it is her subjectivity that is endangered when she cannot befriend her maternal tongue or her maternal object representations.

The process of counseling or therapy, during which time a depressed woman struggles to regain a sense of "I," will be enhanced by using more maternal images for God and a language which is sensitive to her unique experience. Why maternal language and images? Because it is this part of herself from which a woman has been alienated. It is also likely to be the case that she experiences some form of estrangement from her actual mother. While reconciliation with her mother may not be a possibility, a reconciliation with the inner experience of her mother will facilitate her finding a voice of her own. I do not contend that maternal God images need to be employed at the expense of paternal ones; I do, however, contend that whatever images are chosen or interpretations offered, they need to be respectful of human experience in a manner which does not continue to contribute to the subordination of women. It is, in fact, the ability to befriend or make peace with these maternal images which will facilitate a depressed woman's reconciliation with a loving father, even if it is only the imaginary father of individual prehistory which serves as a source for all God images. And, if Kristeva is correct, this father is already a substitute for the mother; thus, a Mother-Father God would be most unlike any image we already know, metaphorically speaking.[3] Moreover, if God in the abstract is a loving, protective agency then the notion of agency requires some form of personal pronoun even as McFague argues.[4] God as Word or as Holy Loving Other would at some level render God as an impersonal "It." In this case, God might be beyond male and female but God would likely be understood as distant and remote. This distance and remoteness would not serve to resolve the self-alienation that the depressed woman struggles with because at some level distance and remoteness would diminish the passion of "for-giving" which is central to the therapeutic task.

The counselor, then, I contend, is a functional mother substitute (not an actual mother and not necessarily a woman) who is in the role of a loving and for-giving other in the way that Kristeva has defined it. As I noted in chapter five, the hallmark of the therapeutic task is "an other who does not judge but hears my truth in the availability of love, and for that very reason allows me to be reborn."[5] A restoration of self-love and a voice all her own is the chief aim of the therapeutic task. When the depressed woman has arrived at this place it is a signal that she is ready to be separated from her functional mother. Or as Kristeva has stated more recently: "the 'good enough mother' might be the one who can go away, making a place for the child to have *the pleasure of thinking [of] her*."[6] This time, however, it is a separation that signals healing even if it includes some sadness. At this point the woman struggling with depression has learned to speak confidently with purpose and can answer Kristeva's questions (How am I special? What do I contribute to other women or humanity?) affirmatively. She has sight, insight and a voice—she is recognized.

My own journey as a "subject-in-process/on trial" is incomplete. My use of metaphors is a "knowledge-in-process" that is also incomplete. As St. Paul writes, "I see in a mirror dimly." I do not have, therefore, a complete answer as to how Christian metaphors need to change but expect that as I continue on this journey my questions, as well as my answers, will continue to change. I have learned much from those women who did come to me as "silent strangers" seeking a voice and someone who would listen without judgment but in love. As Kristeva notes, analysis never really ends but the therapeutic contract ceases when "a certain playfulness of spirit returns....There are things that cannot be said, and I am entitled to play around with them so that I can understand them better."[7] In keeping with this thought, I will continue to "play" with the things that still cannot be said, hopeful that my own knowledge will continue to grow even as I attempt to help those who still cannot play.

Notes

1. Erik Erikson, "The Galilean Sayings and the Sense of 'I'," *The Yale Review* (Spring 1981), 323.
2. Ibid., 339.
3. See Kristeva, *In the Beginning Was Love*, 32 and Soskice, "Can a Feminist Call God 'Father'?" 93–94.
4. McFague, *Models of God*, 99.
5. Kristeva, *Black Sun*, 205.
7. Kristeva, *This Incredible Need to Believe*, 46.
8. Kristeva, *In the Beginning Was Love*, 51.

Selected Bibliography

Augsburger, David W. *Helping People Forgive.* Louisville: Westminster John Knox Press, 1996.

Barbour, Ian G. *Myths, Models, and Paradigms: A Comparative Study in Science and Religion.* New York: Harper & Row, 1976.

Bellini, Giovanni. *Madonna with Child* [*Madonna and Child*] 1460–64, *Madonna with Two Trees* [*Madonna degli Alberetti*] 1487, *Madonna and Child* [*Madonna with Child*] 1487, *Naked Young Woman in Front of the Mirror* [*Woman with a Mirror, Venus*] 1515. Web Gallery of Art at http://www.wga.hu; Internet accessed February 2010.

Bons-Storm, Riet. *The Incredible Woman: Listening to Women's Silences in Pastoral Care and Counseling.* Nashville: Abingdon Press, 1996.

Brown, Francis, S. R. Driver, and Charles A. Briggs, eds. *A Hebrew and English Lexicon of the Old Testament.* Oxford: Clarendon Press, 1951.

Capps, Donald. *Agents of Hope: A Pastoral Psychology.* Minneapolis: Fortress Press, 1995.

—— *The Child's Song: The Religious Abuse of Children.* Louisville: Westminster John Knox Press, 1995.

—— "The Lessons of Art Theory for Pastoral Theology." *Pastoral Psychology* 47:5 (1999): 321–46.

—— *The Depleted Self: Sin in a Narcissistic Age.* Minneapolis: Fortress Press, 1993.

Chopp, Rebecca S. *The Power to Speak: Feminism, Language, God.* New York: Crossroad Publishing Company, 1991.

Contemporary Authors, vol. 154, s.v. "Julia Kristeva." New York: Gale, 1997: 247–49.

Crownfield, David, ed. *Body/Text in Julia Kristeva.* Albany: State University of New York Press, 1992.

da Vinci, Leonardo. *The Madonna with the Carnation, Virgin and Child with St. Anne.* Web Gallery of Art at http://www.wga.hu; Internet accessed February 2010.

della Francesca, Piero. *Nativity.* Web Gallery of Art at http://www.wga.hu; Internet accessed February 2010.

Diagnostic and Statistical Manual of Mental Disorders, 4th ed. Washington DC: American Psychiatric Association, 1994.

Doane, Janice and Devon Hodges. *From Klein to Kristeva: Psychoanalytic Feminism and the Search for the "Good Enough" Mother.* Ann Arbor: University of Michigan Press, 1992.

Dunlap, Susan J. *Counseling Depressed Women.* Louisville: Westminster John Knox Press, 1997.

Erikson, Erik. "The Galilean Sayings and the Sense of 'I'." *The Yale Review* (Spring 1981): 321–62.

—— *Toys and Reasons: Stages in the Ritualization of Experience.* New York: W. W. Norton, 1977.

—— *Young Man Luther: A Study in Psychoanalysis and History.* New York: W. W. Norton, 1993.

Fletcher, John and Andrew Benjamin, eds. *Abjection, Melancholia and Love: The Work of Julia Kristeva.* New York: Routledge, 1990.

Freud, Sigmund. "The 'Uncanny'." *The Standard Edition of the Complete Psychological Works of Sigmund Freud.* Translated by James Strachey. Vol. 17. London: Hogarth Press, 1919.

Gerhart, Mary and Allan Russell. *Metaphoric Process: The Creation of Scientific and Religious Understanding.* Fort Worth: Texas Christian University Press, 1984.

Glaz, Maxine and Jeanne Stevenson Moessner, eds. *Women in Travail and Transition.* Minneapolis: Fortress Press, 1991.

Goodwin, Antoinette. "Freud and Erikson: Their Contributions to the Psychology of God-Image Formation." *Pastoral Psychology* 47, no. 2 (1998): 97–117.

Gorsuch, Nancy J. "Gender as Construct and Category in Pastoral Theology: A Review of Recent Literature." *Journal of Pastoral Theology* 10 (2000): 96–111.

Guberman, Ross Mitchell, ed. *Julia Kristeva: Interviews.* New York: Columbia University Press, 1996.

Holladay, William L., ed. *A Concise Hebrew and Aramaic Lexicon of the Old Testament.* Grand Rapids: Eerdmans, 1971.

Jacobs, Janet Liebman and Donald Capps, eds. *Religion, Society, and Psychoanalysis: Readings in Contemporary Theory.* Boulder: Westview Press, 1997.

Jones, L. Gregory. *Embodying Forgiveness: A Theological Analysis.* Grand Rapids: Eerdmans, 1995.

Kim, C. W. Maggie, Susan M. St. Ville, Susan M. Simonaitis, eds. *Transfigurations: Theology and the French Feminists.* Minneapolis: Fortress Press, 1993.

Kimel, Alvin F., ed. *Speaking the Christian God: The Holy Trinity and the Challenge of Feminism.* Grand Rapids: Eerdmans, 1992.

Kraybill, Donald B., Steven M. Nolt, and David L. Weaver-Zercher. *Amish Grace: How Forgiveness Transcended Tragedy.* San Francisco: John Wiley & Sons, 2007.

Kristeva, Julia. *About Chinese Women.* Translated by Anita Barrows. New York: Marion Boyars, 1986. Originally published as *Des Chinoises.* Paris: Edition des Femmes, 1974.

—— *Black Sun: Depression and Melancholia.* Translated by Leon S. Roudiez. New York: Columbia University Press, 1989. Originally published as *Soleil Noir: Dépression et mélancolie.* Paris: Editions Gallimard, 1987.

—— *Desire in Language: A Semiotic Approach to Literature and Art.* Edited by Leon S. Roudiez. New York: Columbia University Press, 1980. Originally published in *Polylogue.* Paris: Editions du Seuil, 1977. And Σημειωτιχη□: *Recherches pour une sémanalyse.* Paris: Editions du Seuil, 1969.

—— *In the Beginning Was Love: Psychoanalysis and Faith.* Translated by Arthur Goldhammer with an Introduction by Otto F. Kernberg. New York: Columbia University Press, 1987. Originally published as *Au commencement etait l'amour: psychanalyse et foi.* Paris: Hachette, 1985.

—— *New Maladies of the Soul.* Translated by Ross Guberman. New York: Columbia University Press, 1995. Originally published as *Les Nouvelles maladies de l'ame.* Paris: Librairie Artheme Fayard, 1993.

—— *Powers of Horror: An Essay on Abjection.* Translated by Leon S. Roudiez. New York: Columbia University Press, 1982. Originally published as *Pouvoirs de l'horreur.* Paris: Editions du Seuil, 1980.

—— *Revolution in Poetic Language.* Translated by Margaret Waller with an Introduction by Leon S. Roudiez. New York: Columbia University Press, 1984. Originally published as *La révolution du langage poétique.* Paris: Editions du Seuil, 1974.

—— *The Sense and Non-sense of Revolt: The Powers and Limits of Psychoanalysis.* Translated by Jeanine Herman. New York: Columbia University Press, 2000. Originally published as *Sens et non-sens de la révolte.* Paris: Arthème Fayard, 1996.

—— *Strangers to Ourselves.* Translated by Leon S. Roudiez. New York: Columbia University Press, 1991. Originally published as *Étrangers à nous mêmes.* Paris: Librairie Artheme Fayard, 1988.

—— *Tales of Love.* Translated by Leon S. Roudiez. New York: Columbia University Press, 1987. Originally published as *Histoires d'amour.* Paris: Editions Denoël, 1983.

—— *This Incredible Need to Believe.* Translated by Beverly Bie Brahic. New York: Columbia University Press, 2009. Originally published as *Bisogno di credere: Un punto di vista laico.* Rome: Donzelli Editore, 2006.

Lampe, G. W. H., ed. *A Patristic Greek Lexicon.* Oxford: Clarendon Press, 1961.

Lechte, John. *Julia Kristeva.* Reprint Edition. New York: Routledge, 1991.

Lobdell, William. *Losing My Religion: How I Lost My Faith Reporting on Religion in America—and Found Unexpected Peace.* New York: Collins, 2009.

Loder, James E. and W. Jim Neidhardt. *The Knight's Move: The Relational Logic of the Spirit in Theology and Science.* Colorado Springs: Helmers and Howard, 1992.

McCullough, Michael E., Kenneth I Pargament and Carl E. Thoresen, eds. *Forgiveness: Theory, Research, and Practice.* New York: Guilford Press, 2000.

McFague, Sallie. *Metaphorical Theology: Models of God in Religious Language.* Philadelphia: Fortress Press, 1982.

—— *Models of God: Theology for an Ecological, Nuclear Age.* Fortress Press, 1987.

—— *Speaking in Parables: A Study in Metaphor and Theology.* Fortress Press, 1975.

Moessner, Jeanne Stevenson, ed. *Through the Eyes of Women: Insights for Pastoral Care.* Minneapolis: Fortress Press, 1996.

Moi, Toril, ed. *The Kristeva Reader.* New York: Columbia University Press, 1986.

Museum of Fine Arts, Boston. *A Guide to the Collection* at http://www.mfa.org; Internet accessed February 2010.

Neuger, Christie Cozad. *Counseling Women.* Minneapolis: Fortress Press, 2001.

The New English Bible with Apocrypha. Oxford Study Edition. New York: Oxford University Press, 1976.

The New Revised Standard Bible. Grand Rapids: Zondervan, 1990.

Oliver, Kelly, ed. *Ethics, Politics, and Difference in Julia Kristeva's Writing.* New York: Routledge, 1993.

—— *Reading Kristeva: Unraveling the Double-Bind.* Bloomington: Indiana University Press, 1993.

Reineke, Martha J. "Life-Sentences: Kristeva and the Limits of Modernity." *Soundings* 71 (Winter 1988): 439–61.

—— *Sacrificed Lives: Kristeva on Women and Violence.* Indianapolis: Indiana University Press, 1997.

Riding, Alan. "Correcting Her Idea of Politically Correct: Feeling Misunderstood, A French Thinker Tries an Individualistic Path." *The New York Times.* 14 July 2001. B9 and B11.

Smith, Anna. *Julia Kristeva: Readings of Exile and Estrangement.* New York: St. Martin's Press, 1996.

Smith, Anne-Marie. *Julia Kristeva: Speaking the Unspeakable.* Sterling, VA: Pluto Press, 1998.

Smith, Joseph H. and William Kerrigan, eds. *Interpreting Lacan.* Psychiatry and the Humanities, vol. 6. New Haven: Yale University Press, 1983.

Taylor, Barbara Brown. *Leaving Church: A Memoir of Faith.* San Francisco: HarperCollins, 2007.

Thistlethwaite, Susan Brooks and Mary Potter Engel, eds. *Lift Every Voice: Constructing Christian Theologies from the Underside.* New York: Harper & Row, 1990.

Tiepolo, Giovanni Battista. *Time Disrobing Truth* [*Time Unveiling Truth*], 1745–50. Museum of Fine Arts, Boston at http://www.mfa.org as accession number 61.1200; Internet accessed February 2010.

Tillich, Paul. *The Meaning of Health.* Edited by Perry LeFevre. Chicago: Exploration Press, 1984.

van Deusen Hunsinger, Deborah. *Theology and Pastoral Counseling: A New Interdisciplinary Approach.* Grand Rapids: Eerdmans, 1995.

Volf, Miroslav and Dorothy C. Bass, *Practicing Theology: Beliefs and Practices in Christian Life.* Grand Rapids: Eerdmans, 2002.

Warner, Marina. *Alone of All Her Sex: The Myth and the Cult of the Virgin Mary.* New York: Alfred A. Knopf, Inc., 1976.

Watts, Fraser and Liz Gulliford, eds. *Forgiveness in Context: Theology and Psychology In Creative Dialogue.* New York: T & T Clark, 2004.

Web Gallery of Art at http://www.wga.hu; Internet accessed February 2010.

Webster's New Universal Unabridged Dictionary, 2nd ed. New York; Simon and Schuster, 1983.

Williams, Robert R., ed. *Theology and the Interhuman: Essays in Honor of Edward Farley.* Valley Forge: Trinity Press International, 1995.

Willimon, William H. *Pastor: The Theology and Practice of Ordained Ministry.* Nashville: Abingdon Press, 2002.

Winnicott, D. W. *Playing and Reality.* London: Tavistock/Routledge, 1971.

Worthington, Everett L. ed. *Dimensions of Forgiveness: Psychological Research and Theological Perspectives.* Philadelphia: Templeton Foundation Press, 1998.

Index